God's Country

*Eagle Bay Area — Fourth Lake
In the heart of the Adirondacks*

by Clara V. O'Brien

1982
North Country Books
Sylvan Beach, N.Y.

Copyright © 1982
by
Clara V. O'Brien
Eagle Bay, New York
ISBN 978-1-4930-7673-4

All rights reserved
No part of this book may be
reproduced without written permission
of the copyright owner

First Printing 1982

DEDICATION

In appreciation of their love for and
Their contribution to this area of God's
Country, I salute in loving memory . . .
Theodore Fuller, Orr Liddle, Alfred Nelson,
John P. Petersen, E. U. Smith, Frank Teich
Howard C. Weller and Seth Burton Youmans.

AND
To my generous and patient husband,
Herbert Sheldon O'Brien,
Who helped me to "Get the Job Done"

Winter Wonderland — First photo taken in Eagle Bay by the author. Winter 1937 — First heavy snowfall in November. The author's footsteps as she walked down Lakeview Avenue. Camps: (1) Sulgers (2) Remington.

Preface

"GOD'S COUNTRY" was the first name by which I knew the Adirondack Mountains. When I came to Eagle Bay in 1937 as John Petersen's wife, I had carried with me since 1917 a mental picture of its beauty. That was when I had first met John, and at that time his description of the country he lived in and loved fitted the name by which he called it. Twenty years later when he brought me to Eagle Bay from Texas, he said we would live in God's Country. Two days after arriving in Eagle Bay I walked down to the beach. Looking over the blue waters of Fourth Lake to the triple rim of mountains surrounding it with Dollar and Cedar Islands lying in the middle of the lake, and the lush evergreens and majestic trees covering the mountains and the islands, it was not difficult for me to see God's handiwork in it all. Truly I had come to God's Country. To me the majestic sunrises and sunsets over the lake became His paint brushes, and later the snows became winter-wonderland for it all. From the southern plains of Texas where space and horizon challenge the eyesight, and where clear blue water is ever at a premium, I was overwhelmed by the fresh new beauty around me. I yearned to capture it and put it into words, but I had other work to do at that time. However, the yearning persisted.

Once I was asked, "What does Eagle Bay have, anyway?" Well, that was a challenge! I wanted to tell people of some of the wonderful things the little hamlet did have. So I began to list things I knew about, and lived with. Then I looked into the past. I wrote it all down and found even more than I anticipated. I found that Eagle Bay was an enviable location on the Fulton Chain of Lakes. Few places in the Adirondacks can boast of a more beautiful natural sand beach. It has a favored, wide, deep, protected natural harbor. Captain Jonathan Meeker sought it out for his steamboat, *The Hunter*. The early steamers also sought out the harbor. The men who flew the seaplanes sought it out. There is a glorious triple rim of mountains standing sentinel over Eagle Bay's expansive view of Fourth Lake. It has some of the most beautiful trees in the Adirondacks. Aside from many new and loyal residents, it is home to many people who bought from the developer, Howard Weller, and some summer homes now are harboring fourth generations. Eagle Bay is a natural crossroad to other villages that are closely interwoven into its life fabric. It has a spirit that never says die.

So it came to pass a few years ago I felt that truly the Eagle Bay area had a great deal to write about. The problem is with this history, as it is with so many, the tale is being told too late, and by one who had not the privilege to live and experience the total story. Yes, so much has been missed. The old timers knew a different Eagle Bay. It has been difficult to catch and record the spirit of the past, but some of it is told, and much of it is left to the imagination. Be kind to the author and to all those dear people who have helped. Please enjoy what has been told. Try to imagine how it was one billion years ago; then ten million; then when the Eagles nested in the tall pines on Eagle Cliff. Imagine back as recently as 75 or 80 years ago when the trains came through; when the steamers plied their course and all stopped at Eagle Bay Harbor for passenger connection with Raquette Lake Railroad. Try to imagine prestigious hotels using tents for guest rooms and building prestige for themselves while doing it. Look realistically at the changes that have been wrought in those hotels over the last thirty years. There is history and change all around us. Inadequately as it might be done, I wanted to capture some of the story before it was all lost.

Many of the people who built this area have populated it with their offspring who are carrying on. I have tried to point up some of the differences in approach and in accomplishment. Times change, people change, the profile of a community changes, but under all the change there often surfaces the underlying foundation that is the basis of it all. We need to go back and look at the foundation in order to build better for the future. We need to look at the total beautiful Adirondack picture from the Mohawk Valley to the neighboring Canadian border. We need a solution to the creeping menace of acid rain and other environmental hazards that the founders never heard of.

Contents

Chapter I
   Introduction to Eagle Bay   1

Chapter II
   Foot Trails to Rails   11
      A Colorful History of Transportation

Chapter III
   Evolution of Eagle Bay Park   33

Chapter IV
   Hotel Boom in Eagle Bay Area   47

Chapter V
   Rental Housekeeping Camps and Cottages
      in Eagle Bay Area   87

Chapter VI
   Growth of Eagle Bay Business   103

Chapter VII
   Eagle Bay Area Private Estates   137

Chapter VIII
Longstaff Camps
Summer Mecca for Girls and Boys
173

Chapter IX
People — Life Blood of a Community
187

Chapter X
Aviators in Adirondack Skies
219

Chapter XI
Organizations, Churches and Schools
Integrate Communities
254

Addendum   263

Index   274

Foreword

This book has been carefully researched from abstracts, maps, collections of papers, and personal interviews with the best available authorities on a particular subject. Prejudices have not been recorded. It is the hope of the author that any question of authenticity will be verified through the same type of research.

It was the author's hope that an extensive collection of documents which were used could be reproduced in the appendices but that reproduction was limited. Some are there, however, for the reader's information.

All New York State cities appear without the state label. A city outside New York appears with the name of its state.

The author is not conversant with technicalities of railroading, steamship building, nor with aviation. The stories of these important parts of history have been gathered from people who were close to them, and from what has been written about them. Perhaps if the technical aspect is missing the reader can supply that part in his own way. The author is especially regretful if any such omission detracts from the skills of these people. It was the author's purpose to try to reflect the warm, human, daring element that these men brought to God's Country, along with the information on their accomplishments.

People who gave so much information regarding their housekeeping, and rental cottages are not always named personally in credits, but some of the best information which is contained in this book is from some of those people.

County line is not a boundary in the information gathered from this book. The Eagle Bay area was limited by an old map (about 1905) and by people or places who had used Eagle Bay Post Office, or in some instances by owners within the above limits saying, "Yes, Eagle Bay was also our village." In this limitation we sought the best advice from people with a grasp of "how it was." The histories of Big Moose, Inlet, and Old Forge are books within themselves, and have been, or are being written.

There are so many wonderful people who have done their part in the area's development, both old and new residents. The author wanted to name them all, and did begin the list. It outgrew the book, reading very like a telephone directory. So limitations had to be made. Names are left out which should have been in the book. The oldtimers whose information was available, those persons who very early did help with the original development of the area, the hotel and cottage owners are named if possible. This research has revealed too much to be included between the binding. Especially some of the most wonderful neighbors and friends in the world were not included.

CHAPTER I

Introduction to Eagle Bay

Eagle Bay, New York, lies in the heart of the Adirondack Mountains, on the Fulton Chain of Lakes. In a favored location in God's Country near the head of Fourth Lake on the chain, it is surrounded by mountain ranges, with some well known peaks. About six miles to the south is famous Bald Mountain, nearby are Black Bear and Rocky Mountain, while in the village of Eagle Bay there is Eagle Cliff.

Since Eagle Bay is an integral part of the Adirondacks, its history relates to the total evolution and evidence of continued doming of these mountains. Scientific studies indicate that the mountains' bedrock is more than a billion years old, but the landscape was produced by glacial ice less than ten thousand years ago.

In Eagle Bay Park there is a large area of rock-free land surrounded in half moon shape by a ridge, back of which the land does contain bedrock. Standing on the top of Eagle Cliff, one can view this semicircle of rock-free land which may well be one of the sand terraces geologists say resulted from the glacial lakes. This part of Eagle Bay Park partially surrounds a bay of clear blue water extending out to merge with the waters of Fourth Lake, which many historians have called the queen of the Fulton Chain.

Looking over the waters of Fourth Lake to the triple rim of mountains beyond, one sees an ever changing kaleidoscope of colors ranging from grays to often intense shades of blue. Mixed with the total scene are the varied shades of summer green or the beautiful tree foliage which with autumn becomes almost every hue of vibrant color known to the forest. Then in winter, the bare trees are sprinkled with snow, while the evergeens stand out as decorated Christmas trees with their glistening white dresses of frozen snow. A billion years in time and change have created a beautiful geological work of art.

Named for Eagles

After many years, legend always becomes a part of history, and so it is with Eagle Bay. The dominant legend is that once two very tall pine trees grew on top of Eagle Cliff. In these pine trees bald eagles nested year after year. Perhaps early hunters came by and saw the eagles and named the little mountain Eagle Cliff. The name easily transferred to Eagle Bay. One fall a heavy windstorm blew down the tall pines and the eagles then found a safer nesting place. There can be little doubt that the names, Eagle Cliff, Eagle Bay and Eagle Bay Park, were derived from the eagles that once nested on top of Eagle Cliff.

The first inhabitants of this area of the Adirondacks were the transient Indians. The Adirondacks formed a sort of buffer ground between the Iroquois and the Algonquins. The Iroquois annexed the entire Adirondack wilderness and called it the "Couchsachrage," which means "The Beaver Hunting Grounds of the Iroquois." This was the first proper name applied to all the region. Not only was it Iroquois hunting ground; the Moose River and Fulton Chain region offered to the Indians a partial water route to Canada. This was especially true of the Algonquins, whose northern division claimed Canada as home. The more favored way to the north led through Lakes George and Champlain, but at times the weather could lash those waters with such fury that even the hardy Mohawk, a skilled waterman, avoided them.

The Fulton Chain was much more friendly to the birch bark canoe and other forms of Indian navigation. As the Indians entered the Moose River Valley they followed its tree-cloistered waterways to the Fulton Chain of Lakes. Not only did they find safe passageway, but encountered on the way an abundance of game which let them combine the pleasures of travel with the profits of hunting. Leaving the Fulton Chain, they traveled through Raquette Lake, and then by a choice of routes to the St. Lawrence.

At intervals parties of the nomadic and improvident Montagnais, tribesmen of the Algonquins, met with Iroquois expeditions. When they did, gruesome and bloody episodes of Adirondack history were enacted. Joseph Grady, area historian, says it was a feud between the Iroquois and the Montagnais that resulted in the name "Adirondacks." Unlike their longhouse foes, the Montagnais were not agriculturists. They subsisted on the spoils of their chase, and at times when their hunt proved unproductive, the hungry Montagnais turned to munching roots and twigs to avoid starvation.

The Iroquois became aware of their enemies' habit of eating wood and, in derision referred to them as "Ho-de-ron-dah," which means "eater of trees." In Iroquois guttural enunciation the term sounded like "Adirondack" and thus these mountains became known to early white traders. In 1837, Professor Ebenezer Emmons applied this name to the range of which Mt. Marcy is the highest peak. It gradually replaced the terms "The Brown's Tract," "The Northwoods," and "The Wilderness." "Couchsachrage" was historically the more appropriate name, but certainly not as well fitted to the white man's tongue. So the Adirondacks became the geographical name.

The Indians left trails which the hunters followed and later made into rough roads only a little wider than foot trails.

FROM WELLER'S ADIRONDACK EAGLE —
SUMMER, 1925
INDIANS IN THE ADIRONDACKS

A gentleman from New Rochelle has called our attention to the fact that the Adirondack Mountains were never the home of the Aborigines. They were the hunting grounds of those residing in the lowlands to the South and through them ran trails to the North.

As a consequence, evidences of the one time presence of the Indian are rare in the Adirondack wilderness. It is recalled that the New Arrowhead Hotel took its name from the discovery of an arrowhead at that spot. There also reposes in the museum of the Oneida Historical Society at Utica a stone spearhead found at Eagle Bay some dozen or more years ago.

The discovery of Celts in the Adirondacks, however, is of rare occurrence. Unfortunately there are no recognized local authorities on Indian lore — no local Catlin or Schoolcraft who from a vast store of lore and learning can throw intelligent light upon our early Indians.

The most interesting features of the wilderness region is its lakes as Professor Lardner Vanuxem observed in his volume *The Geology of New York State.*

> The chain of lakes is placed so nearly upon a level that but little labor from man is required to connect those of several counties together. The Lakes of Herkimer and Hamilton (counties) are arranged upon a line that parallels the St. Lawrence River and Ontario Lake and Ohio, not appearing to be accident merely, but the result of a law whose operations were in their directions in several parallels. These lakes, if a communication were opened from East to West, would be much resorted to. The beauty of their waters, their elevation, and the wild scenery which surrounds them would not fail to attract visitors.

This Adirondack area has a long history of trial and failure at colonization, beginning with John Brown of Rhode Island, his accidental ownership and his attempts at settlement, then later attempts by Brown's son-in-law, Charles Herreshoff. His attempt to recoup the family fortune by mining and by colonization of the area which is now Old Forge ended in tragic failure.

a) An air view of Eagle Bay Park showing some of its more than 250 camps. Some of the lakefront camp docks can be seen.

b) Airview of Eagle Bay shoreline showing Cedar Isle in center and Dollar Isle to the left.

c) Eagle Bay, its beautiful sand beach in foreground. Postcards by Fynmore Studio.

Brown traveled in about 1802 from Rhode Island to his wilderness kingdom in a low-slung buckboard. He came to the area over the 25-mile wagon road which he had sliced through the wilderness from Remsen to Old Forge along an old Indian trail, called the Remsen Road.

It was John Brown's son-in-law, John Francis, who was responsible for the Brown ownership of the vast Adirondack "Brown's Tract." John Brown had entrusted to the young man a partnership in the Brown shipping business. When in about 1798 one of the Brown cargo ships was expected to come into New York harbor from the Far East with $210,000 worth of Oriental freight, Brown sent young Francis to the city to receive and dispense the shipment. Francis received cash for the settlement, but he had fallen in with a group of cunning land traders who had cultivated his friendship. Among these shrewd men were Aaron Burr, James Greenleaf, Phillip Livingston, and a man named Morris. In the end John Francis found he had given these men his $210,000 cash received for the ship's cargo for about 210,000 acres of Adirondack wilderness. Francis' unplanned purchase followed nearly a decade of land transactions by speculators.

Alexander Macomb, an Irish immigrant, fur trader and shrewd soldier of fortune, was the first hopeful purchaser to look at the more promising than factual maps of the great Adirondack wilderness. He persuaded two wealthy acquaintances to join him in acquiring for the purpose of speculation a huge portion of what was known as "New York Waste Land." The two men, who with Macomb formed a syndicate, were William Constable and Daniel McCormick. The territory involved in the transaction was a contiguous tract of land lying in seven counties (Herkimer and Hamilton included). Jospeh Grady gives this account of the deal:

> The first of a series of patents, conveying title to a portion of the foregoing area, was issued by New York State to Alexander Macomb in 1792, and the final patent was issued in 1798. An approximate payment of $600,000 was made as a first installment. The deferred payment provision enabled the syndicate to resell part of the tract as a means of financing the whole transaction. With the Macomb syndicate transaction and the issuance of the 1792 patent, public interest in the Adirondacks quickened. Although Macomb's interest terminated soon after the first grant was issued, the more than five thousand square miles conveyed by the patent during the six years became known, and is still known, as "Macomb's Purchase." Most of the transactions were map sales and the purchaser's profit depended on his ingenuity in unloading his sale on some gullible

prospect before his own small equity should perish in the ever-present foreclosure proceedings.

In June 1792, Constable acquired title to Macomb's holdings which Macomb had obtained from the state only six months before. The Constable title included an area of 1,900,000 acres in Jefferson, Lewis, Herkimer and Hamilton Counties. It lay in the western and southwestern section of the Macomb purchase and was designated as Great Tracts IV, V, and VI. The abstract of title records the consideration of fifty thousand pounds. In December 1792 Constable sold to Samuel Ward of New York 1,280,000 acres of this tract for 100,000 pounds, which gave Constable a gain of 50,000 pounds, and he still held title to 620,000 acres. He was one of the few speculators who profited extensively through ventures in the public waste lands of New York.

The last exchange in this great tract before John Francis' purchase occurred came in November 1794, when Samuel Ward and his wife, Phoebe, conveyed by warranty deed 210,000 acres of their tract to James Greenleaf for 24,000 pounds. This acreage lay in the Moose and Beaver River Valleys and included First, Second, Third and Fourth Lakes of the Fulton Chain, and sites of a number of future settlements extending from McKeever to Big Moose. Soon after the purchase of this tract, it appears that Greenleaf became pressed for money, for the abstract reveals a mortgage dated July 25, 1795, recorded in favor of Phillip Livingston. Greenleaf was probably unable to meet his obligations, and both his and Livingston's affairs became involved in litigations.

Unplanned Purchase

How natural for these speculators to make advances to John Francis as they were socializing in New York City, especially since they no doubt had heard of the cargo he was due to exchange for $210,000 cash. How Aaron Burr came into the picture is not clear, but no doubt the involvement was to Burr's profit. Anyway, instead of returning with $210,000, John Francis went home with a doubtful title to 210,000 acres of Adirondack wilderness. The title search reveals that John Brown received December 29, 1798, by virtue of a suit in Chancery, a master's deed to the entire 210,000 acres. Within the boundaries of that 210,00 acres of wilderness land lay the tiny beauty spot now called Eagle Bay.

The John Brown story is not finished with the end of the Chancery suit. Brown made the one visit to the wilderness holdings and after Brown's death in 1803, one of his sons-in-law, Charles Herreshoff, failed in his efforts to colonize the area around Old Forge, and to open an iron mine. His resulting suicide left the few people who had helped him distraught and after Herreshoff's burial most of them soon disappeared.

For several years after Brown's death, Old Forge was the setting for the continued story of wilderness settlement. However, the Eagle Bay story is a part of the land transactions that followed Brown's death. For many landowners in the Eagle Bay area, abstract of title cleared back to William Seward Webb is guarantee that the abstract gives clear title. Occasionally, the question does arise as to who owned the land in the Eagle Bay area after Brown and up to Webb. Research has revealed much of the answer to this question. Starting with the death of John Brown and his will, the heirs of the Brown family were for many years the principal owners. Frances A. Nichols of the Central New York Abstract Company in Herkimer County Courthouse gave some answers to this question. But the work is voluminous, and anyone who really desires all the answers can find them by using the names of owners listed below and tracing back through the deed records in Herkimer County Courthouse.

SOME OWNERS OF TOWNSHIP EIGHT FROM BROWN TO WILLIAM SEWARD WEBB

John Brown, before his death, divided his Adirondack holdings into eight townships: 1. Industry; 2. Enterprise; 3. Perseverance; 4. Unanimity; 5. Frugality; 6. Sobriety; 7. Economy; 8. Regularity. These names are taken from eight important business principles which formed part of John Brown's day-to-day code of living. In John Brown's will, dated September 13, 1802, he designated certain of the above eight tracts to his heirs. Eagle Bay is concerned only with Regularity or Township 8, from which it was carved. Here are listed names of principal owners: James Brown, John Brown Francis (son of James Francis and said to be John Brown's favorite grandson); John Brown Herreshoff; Sarah Herreshoff; Lyman R. Lyon; parts were sold to Hollister, Ballou; and mineral rights to Judson; Frederick Hollister; Ballou, Mary Austin; Storm, Hamilton, Stanton, Railroad, and Theodore Ballou; then there are Hollister, William P. Ballou, Lyon, George Tracy and Theodore Ballou. Owning some of the land were Isaac and Charles Storm; a fractional part by Edwin C. Hamilton and Thomas E. Hastings, William B. Ballou, Henry Stanton. Much land was sold to the railroad. Harvey R. Wilcox; Mary Austin and Isaac Townsend, trustee. David Thurston, trustee; Rebecca and Austin G. Fox and Ballou were involved again. The Sacketts Harbor & Saratoga Railroad Co. and the Lake Ontario & Hudson River Railroad Co. (Sacketts Harbor Railroad name was changed to Saratoga Railroad Co. to the Lake Ontario & Hudson River Railroad). Alrich Hubbell, Jezron A. Johnson and The Adirondack Estate and Railroad Co., Andrew Dexter; N. Edson Sheldon; Albert N. Cheney; Enoch Rosecrans. Then there were several partitions and divisions. William West Durant and William Suthpen and The Adirondack Railroad Co.; Robert W. Cromley; Chauncey S. Traux, as trustee; Ravand K. Hawley, president of Adirondack Timber and Lumber Co., from September 3, 1889 to May 28, 1891. Several names enter during this ownership. May 1891 Hawley sold most of Township 8 to William Seward Webb.

Eagle Bay was mentioned by name as early as 1875, when E. R. Wallace in his *Guide to the Adirondack Mountains* says, "One may follow the trail (not cut out) from Eagle Point, Fourth Lake, three miles to Cascade Lake. This lake (Cascade) is seldom visited except by the hardy hunter."

Transportation to and from the Adirondacks gradually grew from Brown's 25-mile wagon road, which he had sliced through the wilderness from Remsen to Old Forge area along an old Indian trail. Jonathan Meeker, pioneer in transportation on the Fulton Chain of Lakes, was instrumental in at least an indirect way in the development of Eagle Bay as was Fred Hess, the founder of Inlet and among the very first hotel builders in the Fulton Chain area. About 1890 Hess put up a sawmill in Inlet and he, as Meeker had done, cleared timber from land around Eagle Bay. When builders came, the Eagle Bay Hotel and the stores along the highway were built on land these two men had cleared. In the 1870's Hess built a shanty on Cedar Island in Fourth Lake just in front of Eagle Point. At first he took care of a sick friend, but soon others came, and he found himself the owner and operator of Cedar Island House.

Fuel for Steamboat

Jonathan Meeker cut timber, on what is now the business area of Eagle Bay, for fuel for his steamboat, *The Hunter*. He squatted on land just a short distance east of Eagle Bay. This land was later purchased by Frank Anderson of Brooklyn, and later owned by Harry Clark. Here in 1883 Meeker, "Capt. Jack," tied up *The Hunter* at night. He used various material to fuel it, but largely his fuel came from timber he cut from the area where the Eagle Bay Hotel was built in 1896 and from the land where Eagle Bay business vicinity was later built.

The following dates are important to the history of Eagle Bay:

1838 — In May the town of Wilmurt was formed from part of Russia and Ohio townships.

1883 — Steam navigation started on the Fulton Chain of Lakes.

1892 — The Fulton Chain Telephone Company was formed.

1892 — The census for the town of Wilmurt District 3A by J. A. Harvery enumerator listed Franklin Sperry, born in U.S., guide; Ida Sperry, born in U.S.; Louie Sperry, born in U.S.; Benjamin Sperry, born in U.S. This was repeated in the 1905 census.

1892 — Rocky Point Inn was built.

1896 — The town of Wilmurt was divided, creating the town of Webb and giving the rest of the land to Ohio (Township).

1896 — William Durant built a private carriage road from Eagle Bay near the head of Fourth Lake to South Inlet to the head of steamboat navigation on the inlet of Raquette Lake.

1896 — Durant's wagon road extended as a winter road to Big Moose Station to connect Camp Uncas with the railroad.

1897–98 — Monyehans cut a wagon road from Eagle Bay to Sucker Brook Bay on Raquette Lake.

1900 — The Raquette Lake Railroad was opened to the public with one of its principal stations at Eagle Bay.

1900 — Dr. R. G. Wallace was residing at Eagle Bay.

1900 — The main highway around north shore of Fourth Lake was being built from Eagle Bay to Sixth Lake.

1901 — According to Frederick Aber, Jr. and Stella King's *History of Hamilton County*, Dr. Wallace of Eagle Bay was in attendance at the birth of the first child born in Inlet, Elizabeth Burr, born to Peter Burr, guide, and his wife Libbie Kelley Burr.

1901 — Boundary fixed between Herkimer and Hamilton Counties. It split the northern portion of Eagle Bay.

1902 — On March 26, Dr. R. G. Wallace of Eagle Bay was appointed health officer of Inlet.

1905 — Mr. William Pulling became railroad station agent at Eagle Bay.

1906 — By 1906 Dr. R. G. Wallace had moved away from Eagle Bay.

1911 — The rails of Raquette Lake Railroad were replaced by heavier rails.

CHAPTER II

Foot Trails to Rails
A Colorful History of Transportation

With the failure of Charles Frederick Herreshoff to successfully settle the Brown's Tract and his resulting suicide, the land mostly went back to nature. While an agent for the Brown family did make further attempts at colonization, the efforts dwindled, the cabins rotted away, brush took over, and by 1830 there was little left of the Brown-Herreshoff attempt at colonization except the almost impassable Brown's Tract Road, which had replaced Brown's original Remsen Road. Even with the newer road, it was noted after the Arnolds had taken over Herreshoff Manor and made it into a hotel of crude sorts, that people came this way at their own risks, which were great in this wild unsettled country.

One of the important early Indian trails went up the Fulton Chain of Lakes, then through Raquette Lake and River. There was a short carry which is still called Indian Carry just west of Saranac Lake. It came out on Saranac Lake and then overland to Lake Champlain. In his Book, *Adirondack Country*, William Chapman White says, "Except for the remembrance in Indian Pass and Indian Carry and small relics found at the latter place, no trace of this trail remains today." This author believes this to be the trail celebrated in *The Last of the Mohicans*.

The Traveler on Foot

Much of the early transportation in the Eagle Bay area of this unbroken wilderness was by foot from railway stations at Remsen, Boonville and other points. They walked, often with a guide, via the Brown's Tract road to Old Forge. At such point a guide was usually waiting with a boat paddled by hand. So the forbidding wilderness was broken by men of endurance and purpose. Also at times, in the summer, women would dare such a journey equipped with (according to E. R. Wallace's *Descriptive Guide to the Adirondacks*, 1875):

> Short walking dress or Turkish costume, closely fitting at the ankle, flannel underclothing; light, soft fur hat — gentleman's, leather balmoral boots — roomy; rubbers and thick camp slippers; rubber coat and cap waterproof.

The head net, for black fly and punkie protection, is described as "a Swiss muslin bag, which may be placed over the head and then gathered around the neck with an elastic band." The armlets of the gauntlet, made of firm cotton cloth or sheep or chamois cloth should be long enough to button at the elbow, Wallace advises.

Travelers usually walked from one lake to the other, crossed the lake in a row boat and then walked again. In between, camps were set up for night resting. This mode of transportation is still used on canoe trips through the Fulton Chain of Lakes on into Raquette, Blue Mountain and Long Lakes, a favorite summer route for Boy Scouts and seasoned hikers.

In the more remote parts of the wilderness the only safe mode of transportation in winter was either by foot or by sled. In summer the buckboard was used. It was only a spring board with a seat in the middle supported by two axles. This was the only reasonable means of light transportation over roads through the wilderness. Such roads had been cut mostly by loggers, sportsmen, hermits and adventurous people of both sexes who came to the wilderness in larger and larger numbers as transportation began to improve.

Transportation by Sleigh and Guide Boat

Celebrated by poetry and song the horse-drawn sleigh, often with bells on the elaborate harness, was a common mode of winter transportation in the early years of the Adirondacks. As late as 1925, or until the pavement of Route 28 was completed through Eagle Bay, the local school children were carried during the winter months to Minnowbrook school on horse-drawn sleigh. The school was a one room building located near the Burnap entrance to Route 28.

The Charles Snyder family of Cascade Lake owned a place in Eagle Bay where they kept horses during the winter. The family often spent winter weekends at Cascade. When they disembarked at the Eagle Bay train station, they hitched the horses to a sleigh and drove on to Cascade. Charles Snyder was attorney for William Seward Webb, and the Adirondack Railway Company. He had a home in Herkimer, but loved his Cascade retreat and was a landowner not only in the village, but in the Eagle Bay Park as well.

In 1890 guide boat building became an established industry in Old Forge. There was a large demand for this type of craft and Riley Parsons and Theodore Seeber equipped a small shop on the third floor of the Garmon and Crosby mill, which stood on the South Shore of the Moose River beside the State Dam. Both men were artisans of exceptional skill. Seeber and Parsons conducted their business in the mill loft until 1892, when they built a two-story shop on the opposite side of the river adjoining the dam.

In 1895 Parsons purchased Seeber's interest in the business and continued the building of Parsons' model guide boats and the heavier St. Lawrence boats. In 1902 he moved the shop to a location between the Eagle Bay Road and the North Shore of Old Forge Lake. After their father's death Riley's two sons, Ben and Ira, carried on the construction of Parsons' model boats in a shop adjoining the Eagle Bay highway on the outskirts of Old Forge. Some of these boats are still in use. One of the St. Lawrence boats was used by John Petersen until his death in 1950.

In the Eagle Bay area, as in all of the Fulton Chain area, the first more rapid mode of transportation was the steamboat.

Joseph Grady says boat builder Seeber gives this information about the lake steamers and boats in the latter part of the 19th Century:

> In 1885 (Other historians have given this date as 1883) I brought to the Fulton Chain a small steamer, *The Hunter*, capacity 40 persons, cost $900. It was for Captain Jonathan Meeker who in 1887 sold it to Jack Sheppard who had bought the larger cabin job, *The Fulton*.
>
> In 1887 the *Eddie S.*, capacity 15 persons, cost $600, which was built by me at Boonville, was brought in. It was run for two years, then I sold her to outside parties.
>
> About 1888 I built *The Fulton*, 80 persons capacity, a cabin boat, cost $2,100 for the well known Jack Sheppard, which boat had been run ever since.
>
> About 1890 two small steamers were added, the *Buella*, capacity 20 persons, cost about $700, and the *Old Forge*, capacity 40 persons, cost about $900. Both were second hand and now out of commission and useless.
>
> About two years ago (1894) the steamer *ZYP*, capacity about 50 persons, cost $1,000 was built in Rome, N.Y. and brought here.
>
> In 1894 the *Stowell* was built by Captain Sweet with my assistance. It is a fine substantial boat of 150 persons capacity and cost about $7,000.
>
> On Seventh Lake there is the steamer *Gazelle*, capacity 30 persons and cost $600.
>
> On Eighth Lake a small steamer of 20 persons capacity operates. This steamer cost about $500.

In *The Story of a Wilderness* by Joseph Grady this information on Jonathan Meeker can be found.

> The first steam-driven vessel to ply the lower four lakes of the Fulton Chain became known to the travelling public

Captain Jonathan Meeker. First Steamboat, *Hunter*, on Fourth Lake 1883. Credit Joseph Grady.

The Steam Yacht Hunter. Captain Jonathan rests in the bow as Peter Giroux scans the horizon for storm signals and belated patrons.

Alonzo Wood

H. Dwight Grant

The *Clearwater*, circa 1900, built and launched from Alonzo Wood hotel clearing. Credit T. R. Fallis.

through printed advertisements as the *Steam Yacht Hunter*. It was owned and operated by Jonathan Meeker, a veteran Adirondack woodsman. Jonathan had spent thirty-five years in the Central Adirondacks and was widely known as a guide of marked ability and integrity. After launching his pioneer enterprise in 1883, he became known as Captain Jack, an appellation of distinction which he bore with his usual solemnity and unassuming dignity.

The Hunter was screw-propelled, thirty-five feet in length, with an eight foot beam. Its upright, six horse power, wood-burning boiler generated a driving power of from seven to eight miles an hour. From its canopied top waterproof curtains could be lowered in protection against rain and wind. The cost of construction, delivery and launching slightly exceeded eight hundred dollars but the undertaking returned a profit that fully justified the investment.

The vessel was designed and built by Dwight Grant in his Boonville boat shop in the winter of '82 and '83. In the spring of '83 it was skidded on horse-drawn sleds along the Moose River and Brown's Tract Road into the deep woods, and then along a narrower bark road to Minnehaha on the Moose River, five miles below Thendara. There it took to the water, unacclaimed and unchristened, and under its own power navigated the freshet-swollen river to Old Forge, where it was skidded around the dam and launched again in Old Forge Lake. The latter launching was almost as sensational a procedure locally as Robert Fulton's launching of the *Clermont* in the Hudson River seventy-six years before.

Meeker bought land on the north shore of Fourth Lake, south of Eagle Bay in 1895, and built a tidy public camp which for years was called Camp Meeker. After Mrs. Meeker's death it was owned and operated by the daughter, Mrs. Ida Peterson.

Five years after *The Hunter* was launched on the Fulton Chain, Captain Jack Sheppard had built the larger, cabin-job called *S.S. Fulton*. This larger boat was Meeker's first real competition and was mostly responsible for putting him out of business.

The Fulton Navigation Company managed by Maurice Callahan and said to be financed by William Seward Webb was responsible for the full development of Fulton Chain Navigation.

The best known of the boats on the Fulton Chain, especially Fourth Lake area, were *The Fulton, The Clearwater*, launched from Alonzo Wood's Hotel, and *The Uncas*. There were also *The Mohegan, The Nehasne* and others.

1981 version of *The Clearwater* and *The Uncas*. Traveling through the Fulton Chain loaded with sightseeing vacationers. Now owned by Don Lawson. Credit Clara O'Brien.

Steamer *Uncas* at Eagle Bay, Fourth Lake. Old Eagle Bay Hotel and boathouse in background. Credit Henry Harter collection.

18   God's Country

Steamers Important

The steamers played an important part in Eagle Bay village because they brought excursionists from all around the lakes to connect with the Raquette Lake Railroad for the trip to Blue Mountain usually twice each week during the summer months. Bert Gardner of Raquette Lake, who was conductor on this short railway from 1923 to 1933, when it was disbanded, says in summer he had as many as 150 passengers at a time from Eagle Bay to Raquette. There they were transferred from the railway to another steamer across Raquette Lake to the Marion River railroad (shortest in the world), from which the excursionists again boarded steamers to cross Eagle Lake, Utowana and Blue Mountain Lake to the Blue Mountain boat landing. From there they began their climb up the mountain.

The Fulton Navigation Company made the steamboats a big-time business on the Fulton Lakes. Eagle Bay, with the commodious Eagle Bay Hotel, as one of the focal points of this business. *The Clearwater* was the pride of the steamers, with a capacity for 300 passengers, or 250 hotel guests with luggage.

For several years these steamers plied their courses through the lakes, making as many as six trips a day each way. Fogs were dreaded but the skilled pilots "simply felt their way along the channels," according to Don Burnap.

There were steamboat wrecks on the lake. It is believed *The Hunter* was sunk after its sixth season since it was not deemed worthy of repair. The most serious wreck in the Eagle Bay area was years ago when the small freighter *Caprice* carrying a too large load of lumber sank in choppy waters of Fourth Lake off Cedar Island. One passenger was trapped in the cabin and went down with the boat. His body was never found. David Beetle tells this story in *Up Old Forge Way* and says Arch and Eri Delmarsh were then building an ice house on Cedar Island. They heard the shouts and rowed to the rescue. The four remaining occupants of the steamer were holding onto floating planks. By making two trips the Delmarshes rescued the four occupants.

The Clearwater stopped its regular trips when the Eagle Bay highway was completed in 1926. About 1938 *The Clearwater* burned to the water's edge where it was beached on First Lake.

Clearwater II and Uncas the 2nd

Don Lawson is the owner and designer of the "Clearwater II" and the "Uncas, the 2nd." The "Clearwater II" was constructed at the Baldwinsville Boat Yard, Baldwinsville. Construction began the fall of 1975, and it was completed in 1976. It is a Bicentennial boat and has been cruising as a tour boat on the Fulton Chain of Lakes (First through Fourth) each summer since 1976.

Construction of the "Uncas, the 2nd" was begun at the Baldwinsville Boat Yard, but completed near the pond in Old Forge in 1979. It has been cruising each summer since 1979.

Road Building

In 1896 William West Durant built a private carriage road from Eagle Bay, near the head of Fourth Lake to South Inlet, the head of steamboat navigation on the Inlet of Raquette Lake. This made it possible to drive buckboards from the steamboat landings at Eagle Bay and South Inlet without making changes. After his wagon road had reached Eagle Bay, Durant extended it as a winter wagon road to Big Moose Station on the New York Central to connect Camp Uncas with the railroad, because during the winter steamships could not run on the lakes. The road was cut by Durant's brother, and J. P. Morgan helped him finance it. Some years later the township took it over and graded it as a wagon road. In 1897 Monyehans cut a wagon road from Eagle Bay to Sucker Brook Pond.

The road from Eagle Bay to North River (Route 28) and the only artery through the Central Adirondacks was in rough, almost dangerous condition until as late as 1952. It was narrow, bumpy and slippery. About Labor Day of 1952 or 1953 the section from Eagle Bay to Inlet was resurfaced.

Frederick G. Aber, Jr. and Stella King in their *History of Hamilton County* note that in January 1904 repairs were authorized for the Eagle Bay-Sixth Lake Dam road. The early transportation to Cedar Island from Eagle Bay and points around the Fulton Chain was by steamboat. From Eagle Bay in winter it was by snowshoe or sled.

The Raquette Lake Railroad

The Raquette Railroad branched from Clearwater (later called Carter) to Eagle Bay to Raquette Lake. In 1893 Dr. William Seward Webb's railroad from Herkimer to Malone, completed in 1892, was taken over by the New York Central. This development in railroading led to the building of two independent standard gauge short line roads. The Raquette Lake railway, which branched off from Clearwater, used the Marion River Carry which was far from any other railway line. There was also a third short line from the New York Central station, now called Thendara, to the village of Old Forge to the Forge Pond, where it connected with the steamers.

Some historians say Durant was the originator of the idea for extended railway facilities; others have given at least three other origins. First, Governor Dix wanted a way to get his lumber from a point near Clearwater to the main line. Secondly, Mrs. Collis Huntington did not like the boat changes and buckboard rides necessary for her to get from the train at Old Forge to her summer home, Camp Pine Knot, at Raquette Lake. She informed her husband at the end of one particularly tiresome trip that if he could build a railroad from New Orleans to San Francisco, he could certainly build a little short road for her, or never again would she accompany him to Pine Knot. Thirdly, Huntington, it is said, had just undergone a particularly trying trip through the lakes sitting on a keg of nails. This gave him the needed impetus to listen to Durant's idea that such a project of building a railroad was entirely feasible.

Incorporators of the short railroad were Morgan, Huntington, Webb, Whitney, Dix, Robert Bacon, Harry P. Whitney and J. Harvey Ladew, all of New York City; Samuel Calloway, president of New York Central; Chauncey M. Depew, Charles E. Snyder, Huntington's lawyer in Herkimer; Edward M. Burns, who managed Webb's Adirondack interest; W. W. Durant and Dr. Gersner, who joined to please Durant. The $250,000 capital of the Raquette Lake Railroad was mainly subscribed by the first four men. The others subscribed only nominal sums, except Dr. Webb who also received shares for granting right-of-way over his property. Some extra shares were given Dix because he had turned over to the Adirondack Railway Company the private line which he had built to Clearwater for his lumber business.

The officers of the new line were Huntington, first president; Burns, Huntington's assistant, vice-president; I. E. Gates, secretary; Charles Burnett, Webb's assistant, treasurer. Webb took over as president after Huntington's death in 1900. The directors were Morgan, Bacon, Durant, Calloway, Dix, Huntington, Snyder, Burns, Webb, Depew and two Whitneys. Historians note that in the beginning this was the wealthiest board of directors in the country for such a small project.

Political Stratagem

In February 1899, the Raquette Railway charter provided that it was to be a street surface railroad, standard gauge, and that it was to be constructed "upon the highway leading from Clearwater, Town of Webb, Herkimer County, to Raquette Lake." Pehaps these intentions were never founded on fact. There was a "highway" over only part of the route (not really a highway but a dirt road from Eagle Bay to Raquette Lake which was far too narrow and uneven to support an electric railway). It seems the organization had no intention of building such a road. However, in this guise the Raquette Railway Company's charter was filed with the New York State Board of Commissioners.

The only objection was the proposed high passenger and freight rates. This objection was overcome and the charter was approved on April 11, 1899. In its certification the board said its electrical expert had inspected the route and plans and had reported favorably. However, on June 9, 1900, the Raquette Lake Railway applied for permission to use oil-burning locomotives and on June 20 the application was granted. It was feared that coal burning locomotives would not be approved because of the severe Adirondack forest fires of 1896, many of which had been started from New York Central's locomotives. Collis P. Huntington was the author of this rather devious but successful legal and political stratagem. There was only one minor fire caused by the train during its years of service.

The construction of the road was begun in April 1899 and Dr. Gersner went to New York on the new railroad on October 6, 1899. About the same time Huntington and a party of friends made a special trip over the new road in two private cars. With him were his Japanese servants from California who had been with him for many years. The Japanese created as much excitement as did the private cars.

On July 1, 1900, the Raquette Lake Railway was opened for public traffic. During its thirty-three years of service, the summer service between Raquette Lake and New York consisted of two trains each day each way — one a day train and the other a sleeping car train. During the winter there was only one day train three times a week. The road's two locomotives were lighter than the standard locomotive. They burned oil from about April 1 until December 1, when they switched over to coal for the winter months. Mr. Hochschild in his *Life and Leisure in the Backwoods*, Adirondack Museum, Blue Mountain Lake, is the source of much of the above information.

The Marion River Carry Railroad was built by W. W. Durant in the summer of 1899 and was ready for traffic by early spring of 1900. This tiny railroad, only about three-quarters of a mile long, was about six miles from the end of the Raquette Lake Railroad tracks. All local historians seem to agree that it was the shortest standard gauge railroad in the world. Durant equipped it with three horse-drawn carriages, one for baggage and two for passengers. He paid $25 apiece for them.

Durant had bought a small coal-burning engine, and while it was being converted to oil by the Schenectady Locomotive Works, service over the small road was in one of the street cars drawn by a

Eagle Bay Hotel where steamers landed to make connection with Raquette Lake Railway trains. Credit Marion Holmes — Town of Webb Historical Society.

An original picture of the Eagle Bay Railway Station, Circa 1906. Mr. Pulling standing on porch. Credit Mr. & Mrs. Wm. Pulling, Jr.

Mr. and Mrs. William Pulling. They met in the Eagle Bay Railroad Station when Mr. Pulling was station agent. Credit Mrs. Wm. Pulling, Jr.

Fairview-Flag Station on Raquette Lake Railway between the Old Onondaga Hotel and Becker's. Credit Alonzo J. Snyder.

Rondaxe Flag Station. Credit Gene Rando — nephew of Albert G. Lashaway.

Road and Railway between Eagle Bay and Raquette Lake. Copied from postcard.

Circa 1920 — Train leaving Eagle Bay just south of Eagle Bay. Credit Henry A. Harter collection.

Apparently a morning train coming into Raquette Lake from New York. It is being helped with a N.Y. Central engine. Credit Edward Baumgardner collection and Henry Harter.

Raquette R.R. Locomotive ran out of water, and being pulled in by Dillon's horse. Credit Gene Rando, Herkimer.

Raquette Lake R.R. train wreck of 1913. Killed in wreck one-half mile south of Fairview Station: Ben Hall, engineer, John Case, fireman; Albert G. Lashaway, brakeman. Credit Gene Rando, Herkimer.

Crane brought from Utica for 1913 Raquette Lake R.R. train wreck. Credit Gene Rando, nephew of brakeman, Albert G. Lashaway.

The Marion River Carry taking passengers from Raquette Lake R.R. station to Utowana. Circa 1911. Credit Gene Rando, Herkimer.

*"The derailment at Eagle Bay occurred in the winter of 1925 after a heavy snowfall. The train was headed south toward Carter. Wet snow under pressure forms ice. The engine went off the icy rails on the Big Moose crossing. A crane was sent to Eagle Bay from Utica by locomotive. Slim Manning took the pictures. Guzzardo's new store in second picture." No fatalities.

Train derailment at Eagle Bay, circa Winter 1925. Credit Doris Lamphear from Gardner collection.*

Left to right on the train: Slim Manning, Bert Gardner, center Darius Waldron. Credit Doris Lamphear from Gardner collection.*

A crane was brought by locomotive from Utica to Eagle Bay. Credit Doris Lamphear from Gardner collection.*

Laurine and Bert Gardner. Credit Doris Lamphear.

horse. However, when the engine arrived it was found to lack the power to draw loaded freight cars and by mid-summer was replaced by a larger locomotive rented from New York Central for $5 per day.

Eagle Bay railway station was the connecting link with the Raquette Lake Railroad and passengers from the Fulton Navigation Company's boats that brought them from around the first four of the Fulton Chain of Lakes. The Eagle Bay Hotel Company charged some sort of bounty for the passengers to walk from the steamers across the hotel property to the train station.

Henry A. Harter in *The Fairy Tale Railroad* gives the following information:

> The March 23, 1899, *New York Times* carried this story:
>
> THE RAQUETTE LAKE RAILWAY — Believed to be for the benefit of a Few Rich Men — Albany, March 22 — The application of the Raquette Lake Railway Company, recently incorporated, for permission to construct a nineteen-mile railroad in the Adirondacks will be heard by the State Railroad Commission on Wednesday next. The company must convince the Railroad Commission that public necessity and convenience requires the construction of the road. The company prefers to operate the road by air power, but if this is not feasible electricity will be utilized. The reason for this preference is to lessen the liability of fire in the woods. There is always liable to be leakage from feed wires, which it is hoped to obviate by air power.
>
> The *Morning Herald* reported on September 12, 1899:
>
> CLEARWATER — RAQUETTE LAKE — The New Railroad Between These Two Points Practically Open — Raquette Lake, Sept. 11 — (Special) — C. P. Huntington left New York City in his private car Saturday morning (September 9) for Raquette Lake, arriving here that evening over the new railroad from Clearwater. This is the first time anyone has made this through trip by rail from New York.

The railroad passed through an almost unbroken forest of principally spruce and hardwood timber. A strip about 50 feet in width had been cleared for its path. In January, 1900, the construction company was using a small, soft coal-burning locomotive for transporting its laborers and materials, and at the same time, carried any freight offered for transportation, along with passengers who paid for the ride in a caboose.

No regular trains were run at this time, though connections were to be made with the afternoon passenger trains on the Mohawk and Malone Railway. The New York Central and Hudson River Railroad Company operated a log train over the road from Clearwater Junction to near Eagle Bay, a distance of about six miles. G. C. Ward, engineer for the Railway Construction Company with an office at Eagle Bay Station, was in charge of the property.

The Raquette Lake Railway was officially opened to the public on July 1, 1900, with summer service of two trains daily in each direction. One was a day train and the other carried sleeper cars. During the rest of the year service varied from one train a day to a three-days-a-week schedule in later years. (Bert Gardner gave this same schedule for his years as conductor.) The operating department of the Raquette Lake Railway after January 1, 1901, was conducted by the New York Central and Hudson River Railroad Company.

Stations Along Way

By 1901 the railroad inspector listed stations along the way:

> At Clearwater there is a combination passenger and freight station of good design, new and properly equipped. At Eagle Bay, which is near the head of Fourth Lake on the Fulton Chain, there is also a new and convenient freight and passenger station. At Raquette Lake there is a commodious freight and passenger station with restaurant included, all new and of modern design, neatly and properly finished. The other stations are small, about 12 × 12, with covered shed about the same dimensions and at these no agents are employed.

The first two decades of the 20th Century were the best years of the Raquette Lake Railway, Harter observed. The well-to-do arrived at Raquette Lake in their private railroad cars which were left on a siding or under a shed which covered a spur track just beyond the station. Pullman service was available from New York City.

One of the most unusual incidents in railroading occurred in August 1908. Heavy traffic had developed from a large excursion and the little 4-6-0 bringing the train into Raquette Lake ran short of water. It had to leave the train near Uncas and try to make the water tank at Raquette Lake. Apparently the engineer realized that he was taking too great a chance and so he drew the fire. He secured a horse to pull the head engine to the water tank at the terminal. But it all turned out well. The engine was fired up and went back towards Uncas for the train. An enterprising photographer took a picture of the engine being towed, thus recording the incident.

World War I brought changes in the opulent society. The cost of maintaining and using such luxury items as private railroad cars and cost of staffing large estates became prohibitive to many. Highways were being built that made the great outdoors more readily accessible so many people could enjoy it.

The railroads were beginning to feel the pinch in their short line operational expense ratios. This was to become an increasing bugaboo to them, especially during the depression years of the 1930's.

Boat-Train Connections

The Official Guide of the Railways in 1905 shows the Fulton Navigation Company maintaining a regular schedule of boats departing from the Old Forge Station of the Fulton Chain Railway. Boats made regular connections with four trains a day each way. The boats also made connections with the Raquette Lake Railway at Eagle Bay.

In 1906 the railway reported it carried nearly 20,000 passengers and over 2,700 tons of freight, with a slight profit resulting.

Beginning about 1906 and continuing every winter until 1922 one of the great freight-producing items was ice. It was understood that most or all of this ice was stored by the New York Central in its own icehouses and was used to refrigerate milk cars and other such units requiring cooling. The Fulton Chain Railway was authorized by the Public Service Commission in 1908 to establish a special rate of fifteen cents per net ton on ice in carloads between Old Forge and Fulton Chain Station.

Hochschild in his *Life and Leisure in the Adirondacks* says that ice was cut the first part of the winter at Old Forge. When the ice within one half mile of the railroad had been cut, the equipment was moved to Raquette Lake. This ice was also used by the New York Central Railroad. In 1908 the Public Service Commission authorized the Raquette Lake Railway to establish a special rate of twenty cents per ton on carloads of ice, minimum weight twenty-five tons, from Rondaxe and Raquette Lake to Clearwater.

A Note from Bert Gardner

According to Bert Gardner, a conductor on the Raquette Railroad from 1923 to 1933, Summit was not a station, but a passing track. This was where the road turned from Carter north to Eagle Bay. Gardner says:

"When three or four sleepers were carried on the train, there was no way we could get up over the hill. We would drop off the sleepers and take the main train over the hill and then come back for the sleepers. So Summit was a passing track, not a station."

CHAPTER III

Evolution of Eagle Bay Park

Early Settlers Around Eagle Bay

The development of Eagle Bay and Eagle Bay Park began with William Seward Webb's purchase of most of Township 8 from Ravand K. Hawley, and his subsequent sale of a portion of that land to William J. Thistlethwaite. It was the Thistlethwaite land in the Eagle Bay area which later became Eagle Bay Park.

It seems pertinent to note some land owners in the surrounding area who, before Howard Weller's time, gave impetus to the development of the Eagle Bay vicinity. The boundary of the Eagle Bay area was partially determined by an old map of Fourth Lake land owners made in 1905.

Beginning with the location of the original Fairview Hotel on the north shore of the lake and south of Eagle Bay the following owners are listed: Milo Bull, Becker (an uncle of Freda Westfall), Nichols, Franklin, Christman, Fawcett, Lawrence (presumably Lawrence Point), Bull (again), some illegible names, Foulds, A. Wood, Sheppard, J. R. Freeman, Mrs. H. H. Longstaff, T. A. Barry, W. J. Thistlethwaite, Eagle Bay Post Office, the Raquette Lake Railway and Eagle Bay Station.

North of Eagle Bay on the north shore of Fourth Lake the following are named: F. P. Anderson, Becker and Bellinger, J. E. Frankie, Dr. R. G. Wallace, Grace D. Walker, G. L. Mooney, Mrs. J. O. C. Reddington, H. Hart, E. L. Paddock, M. Howe, Mrs. Holliday and Rocky Point Inn.

Dr. Edward Gaylord owned Dollar Island, and Cedar Island was owned by Joseph Porter.

It is difficult to say with accuracy which of the structures around the Eagle Bay area was built first. According to Joseph Grady, The Alonzo Wood Camp, located two miles below Eagle Bay near the present Kenmore Hotel on the North Shore Road of Fourth Lake, was built in 1880. Grady says it was the first full-fledged hostelry on Fourth Lake. This hotel was formally opened to the public in 1881. When built it had seven guest rooms, boat house facilities, guides' quarters, and kennels. Several guest rooms were added in 1881. It became immediately well known and attracted a high class clientele of sportsmen and their ladies.

Fred Hess had built a small place on Cedar Island in the late 1870's. He later converted this into a hotel that burned in 1934. It is known from a note on a picture of Fred Hess which was left in Dollar Island House that he was also the builder of that structure. The Eagle Bay Hotel was probably completed during the winter of 1896–1897.

The primary developer of Eagle Bay Park was Howard C. Weller, who came to the area in the early 1900's. Records show that in 1907 he revised a map of the subdivision of lots of Eagle Point, Fourth Lake, for J. Thistlethwaite. The first drawing had been made in 1906 by David Wood, who had earlier surveyed the Eagle Bay Thistlethwaite allotment.

In Mr. Weller's 1929 report of Eagle Bay Park Association meeting, he tells of a dream he had.

> A few years later (meaning after Webb had sold to Thistlethwaite) a young engineer who was surveying in the area, which was later to become known as Eagle Bay Park on Fourth Lake, said to his helpers,'This is the best location for a residential community or summer resort development in the entire Adirondack Mountains. Here I will build a town — a place for summer homes where the maximum of convenience and comfort may be had at a minimum cost through cooperative community improvements.'

Weller's Story

Mr. Weller's story spans the period from World War I through the depression years of the 30's. What Weller, with the cooperation of interested people, accomplished is something of a miracle.

His account continues:

> This was not to happen immediately, however, as there was not a heavy demand for summer homes at that time and it was still possible to buy large holdings of land on these lakes, but the young engineer began purchasing tracts and making plans. Several years later, in 1915, he laid out and improved the first section of Eagle Bay Park.
>
> The development met with the approval of persons who had long wanted summer homes but had not been disposed to invest large sums in undeveloped tracts and then have all the trouble and expense of building roads, beaches, docks and water systems, so necessary for thorough enjoyment of Adirondack homes.
>
> Notwithstanding the fact that the highways leading to Eagle Bay were very poor in those days — and remained so until the

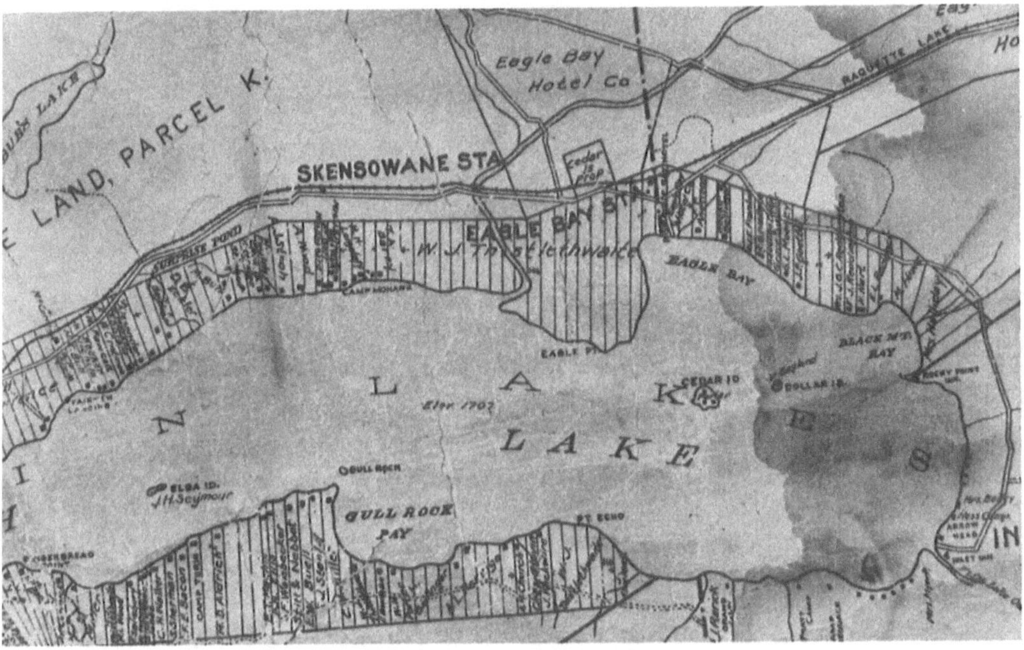

Circa 1900 — Residents and land owners along the Old Forge-Inlet highway. Credit Map of Eagle Bay Area 1899 — about 1904 — Historical Society — Town of Webb.

Circa 1925 paved roadway being put through Eagle Bay. Smith's store on right; beyond is the little corner building — first Weller's office. Beyond that the Tea Pot Dome. On left are buildings on Burt Youman's land. Credit Helen Liddle.

Aerial view of Eagle Bay Hotel and Cedar Island with undeveloped Lone Pine Park to right. Credit Freda Westfall.

1918 — Cutting the road through to the Fallis' Camp Dorla from what became East Avenue. Credit T. Fallis.

Camp Dorla in Eagle Bay Park Deep Woods. Credit T. Fallis.

One of Eagle Bay Parks' first log cabins — Circa 1919. Credit Weller papers.

Theodore R. Fallis Camp. Note tree through roof. Was this Eagle Bay Park first camp? Credit T. M. Fallis.

Mrs. T. R. Fallis sitting; Theodora left; Theodore P. right. Credit T. M. Fallis.

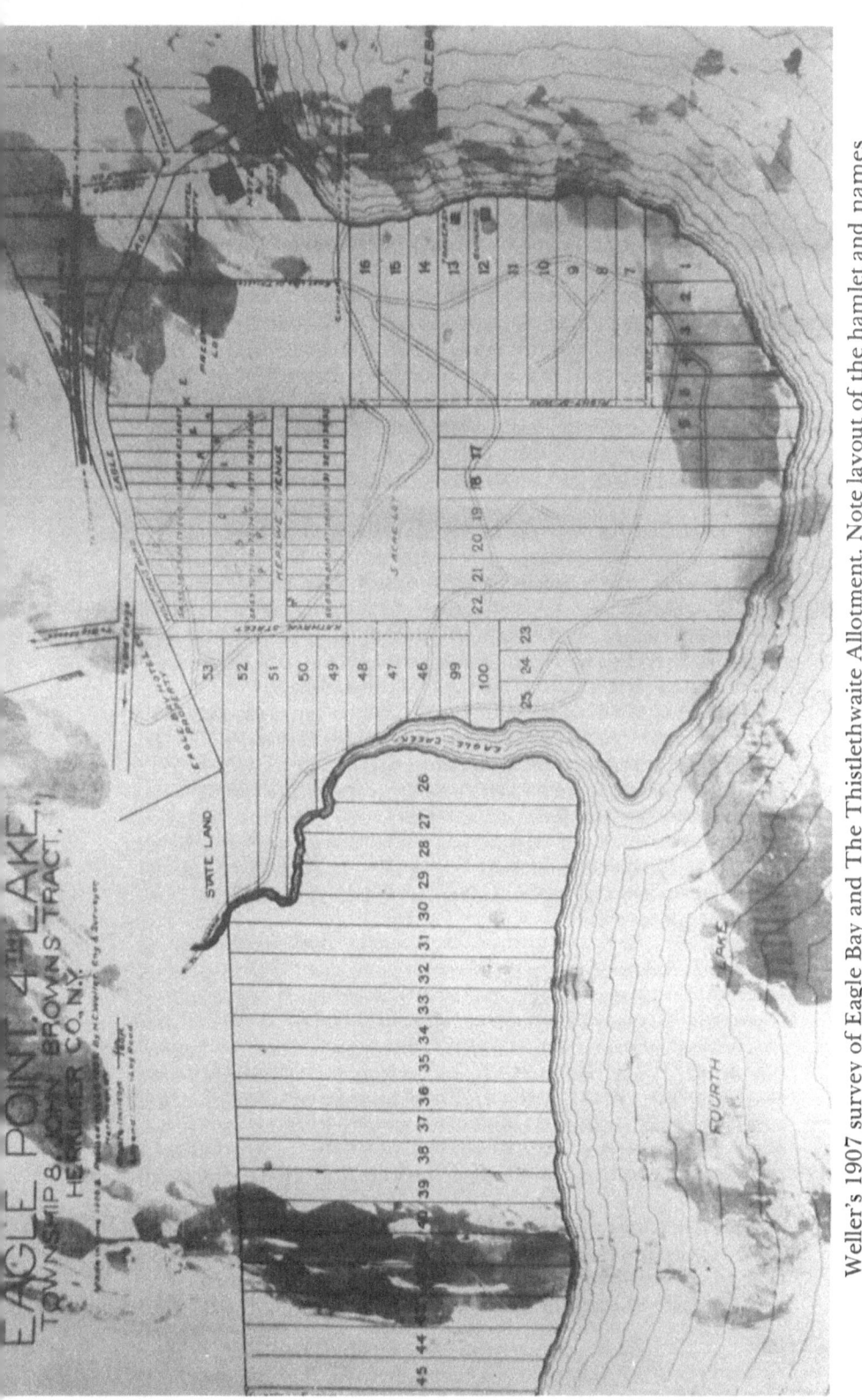

Weller's 1907 survey of Eagle Bay and The Thistlethwaite Allotment. Note layout of the hamlet and names of streets. Credit O'Brien collection of mapes. (Kathryn, Williams; Kepewe)

completion of the concrete road ten years later — many persons visited Eagle Bay Park and several summer homes were erected. Then the United States entered World War I and Eagle Bay Park remained practically stationary until conditions again became normal.

In 1920 the improvement of the first section was completed and the engineer-developer proceeded to consolidate and develop the adjoining tracts. Construction of summer camps, cottages, dwellings and business places was resumed, and there are now — on Jaunary 1st, 1929 — seventy-eight summer homes and dwellings, and twelve business places. The latter are all confined to the state highway, as the avenues and roads of Eagle Bay Park are restricted to camps, cottages and dwellings.

Various useful restrictions as to sanitation, use of property and location of buildings, are enforced by the community-government which consists of a lot owner's association, owning and maintaining the avenues, roads, park, bathing-beach, dock and water system. At the annual meeting in July, officers and directors are chosen from among the owners of camps and dwellings, to direct the affairs of the community.

There exists in Eagle Bay Park the highest type of community spirit, and cordial relations among the residents. Social gatherings and entertainments are enjoyable features of every season. At a beach party, last summer, one of the oldest residents, who has traveled and lived in many parts of this and other countries, stated that he has never known a place where all of the inhabitants measure up to the high standard which exists here, without any snobbish or 'high hat' attitude to spoil anyone's pleasure.

Eagle Bay Park is within a few minutes' walk from lands of the great Adirondack Forest Preserve, maintained by the State of New York as a huge park and playground, aggregating upwards of two million acres. Although in the heart of the mountains and situated on one of the most beautiful lakes in the world, Eagle Bay Park is accessible over paved highways and the New York Central railroad lines from all of the big cities in the East, and has telephone and telegraph communication, two mails per day in season, electricity, water supply, plumbing, good stores, motion pictures and other entertainment.

The engineer and developer is Howard C. Weller, in 1929 residing at Eagle Bay, who has spent the greater part of his time for twenty-five years in this part of the Adirondacks. Now that his labors in connection with the development are completed, he is offering the remaining lots for sale at lower prices than would be possible for property developed under present day conditions. While it is certain that values will greatly increase, he must close out his holdings to reduce overhead costs and enable him to give his attention to other business interests.

In consideration of the loyal support of his customers, Mr. Weller offers to give a certain percentage of his receipts from lot sales in 1929 to the lot owners' association for improvements by which all members of the association are benefited.

Officers of the Eagle Bay Park Association, Inc. in 1929 were Thomas E. Howlan, Utica, president; Ernest U. Smith, Eagle Bay, vice-president; Harvey T. Remington, Rochester and John P. Petersen, Eagle Bay, directors. Weller was secretary-treasurer and general manager. (From H. C. Weller's 1929 Report)

Weller's Land Transactions

Weller's abstract goes back to Ravand K. Hawley as president of Adirondack Timber and Mineral Company and his sale of most of Township 8 to William Seward Webb in 1891.

In December of 1909 a right-of-way deed from William G. Barrett and his wife, Maude W., and William A. Guinand and his wife, Dora J., was given to Howard C. Weller. This deed gave him the right to use the land as a right-of-way for a road or street from Eagle Point.

January 5, 1909, William J. Thistlethwaite of Ilion sold Weller a parcel containing 12.45 acres of land. On a map revised by Weller in 1907 this 12.45 acres appears to be in the area now bound by Lakeview, East and West Avenues and the Old Forge highway. This tract was under mortgage to William Thistlethwaite from January 5, 1909 until June 28, 1915. In 1910 Thistlethwaite released lot 66 from the mortgage and deeded it to Weller's wife, Kathryn. By November 18, 1910, she had sold lot 66 to Orr M. Liddle. On July 6, 1915 the Citizen's Trust Company of Utica, gave to Weller a quit claim deed to the original purchase which he made in January of 1909.

An interesting succession of ownership from Thistlethwaite to Howard Weller is listed below:

June 1, 1907, William Thistlethwaite sold to William Preston seven and three-tenths acres of land which appeared to front on the Eagle Bay-Old Forge Highway and northerly, adjoining the Eagle Bay Hotel property on the west. This purchase covered one lot later purchased by Orr Liddle. Preston mortgaged this tract to Thistlethwaite the same day it was purchased, June 1, 1907.

By 1911 Preston had died and his widow and son, Alfred, had

transferred the land to the Citizen Trust Co. of Utica, March 6, 1912. On July 6, 1915, Weller received from the Citizen Trust Company of Utica, a quit claim deed to some of the original Preston tract of land. The lots which were deeded to Weller were numbers 288, 289, 312, 313, 314, 315, 316, 317, so designated on a map of Eagle Bay Park made by Weller April 19, 1920.

Among the earliest residents of Eagle Bay was an Indian family named Traversy June 27, 1906. James Thistlewaite and his wife, Anna, sold lot number 13 to Mary Anne Traversy of Eagle Bay. On April 12, 1913, William Traversy and Mary Anne, his wife, gave a warranty deed to Franklin W. Christman of Herkimer for $100. The deed was subject to a mortgage for $500, given to Emma J. Greene. Howard Weller later bought this lot from Christman.

William G. Barrett and wife, Maude W., of White Plains, deeded to Weller, October 18, 1921, lots 7, 8, 9, 10 and the south one-half of lot 11 of the Thistlethwaite allotment in Eagle Bay. A right-of-way was granted in 1918 across the north half of lot 11 and over and across lot 12. A road put over this right-of-way was to be located at least three hundred feet from the shore of Fourth Lake. William Thistlethwaite and wife, Gwendolyn, sold to Adirondack Development Corp. of Old Forge all of their right, title and interest in Township 8 of John Brown's tract, in the Town of Webb, excepting lots 215 and 216 and Thistle Island.

The Adirondack Development Corp. of Old Forge gave a quit claim deed to Howard Weller, November 16, 1921, in Township 8, more particularly in Eagle Bay, lots 137 consecutively to and including lot 153 and the east one-half of lot 154.

Weller made several other purchases, including the land formerly owned by the Yacht Club, and the Lone Pine Park land, but the above seems most important to the development of Eagle Bay Park.

On October 1, 1925, Weller and his wife, Florence, gave a quit claim deed to Eagle Bay Park Association, Inc. of Eagle Bay for Eagle Point Road.

A certificate of incorporation of Eagle Bay Park was recorded at latest by July 31, 1920, by H. C. Weller in the Herkimer County Clerk's office. The objectives of the corporation are given in the first two paragraphs of the Association's Constitution:

Eagle Bay Park Association, Inc.
Constitution

    I. NAME

This Corporation shall be known as the Eagle Bay Park Association, Inc.

II. OBJECTIVES

The objectives of this Corporation are:

(1) The regulation, management and supervision of the Community affairs in a summer camp colony at Eagle Bay, Fourth Lake, Herkimer County, New York, and the control of restrictions, reservations and rights applying to the use of camp sites, roads, docks, water front and utilities to any extent made possible by the titles held by this corporation and the members thereof.

(2) The establishment, construction and maintenance of roads, walks, playgrounds, docks, water system, sewerage system, lighting systems, and other utilities for the use of lot owners and the collection of assessments, dues and other charges covering the cost of installation and maintenance thereof from the Lot Owners benefited thereby.

The review of the meetings of Eagle Bay Park Association reveals much of the management and development of Eagle Bay Park and is relevant to the history of Eagle Bay. The minutes of Eagle Bay Park Association meetings between 1929 and 1959 were not available. This thirty-year span covered the depression and the World War II years. It is known, however, that the Association did serve, and function during those years.

The Park minutes from 1959 until 1975 were made available for this research. After more than 60 years, has Weller's dream come true? Were his ambitions realized?

> Here I will build a town — a place for summer homes where the maximum of convenience and comfort may be had at a minimum cost through cooperative community improvements.

That he said was his dream, and he worked at it. When he died he left a $1,000 bequest to the Eagle Bay Park Assocation. Some have said Howard Weller was a wheeler-dealer. Others have said he was an opportunist. Some thought of him as a benefactor. None will deny that he was a driving force in the establishment of Eagle Bay Park as a place for summer homes that has survived and is continuing to grow through cooperative community improvement.

"Cooperative community improvement" has not always been easily attained. The Park Association minutes which were available reveal much of hard work and sacrifice on the part of the men and women who have conducted the affairs of the association during the years from 1920 to the 1980's. Their accomplishments are worthy of mention.

The Eagle Bay Park Beach, one of the most beautiful on Fourth

Lake, has from the beginning been a source of pride to the Park owners and has remained as it was intended, a private beach for the use of camp owners and their guests. Docks have been built and rebuilt, repaired and constantly maintained. Boat slips have been added according to the need. A rental charge for the slips has added to the treasury.

A pavilion was erected on the beach and was rebuilt several years later. A flower bed surrounded by stone was built in memory of Mrs. Howard Weller. Each summer the association employs a patrolman to maintain privacy and order on the beach.

The Park Association water system was a major problem year after year. One of the first water systems seems to have been a simple village pump to which all residents went for water. Some residents along the highway and on Cedar Island were supplied with water from the Eagle Bay Hotel which in early years had at least three springs available.

Old-timers have told of the first pressure system in the Park, a water tank placed high up on Eagle Cliff. The source of the water for this tank was supplied by the village pressure pump which Bill Cusack says was operated by a gasoline engine. The tank was there for several years and water from the tank was used by Eagle Bay Park residents. According to Yock Youmans, his father, Burt, brought the tank from Boonville to Eagle Bay tied on the back of his Model T Ford.

In the early 1940's Charles Parker supervised the Park water system. Burt Youmans and his son, Yock, laid a new water system in the park in the 40's. In 1964, new water lines were installed on the Ledge, the Big Moose Road, Forest Lane, and Eagle Point Road, and a new water main was laid along Central Avenue. Many camp owners have always had their own water wells. Since his father's death, Yock Youmans has serviced the Park water system.

The Park Association made a study of water pollution from septic tanks along the Park shore and corrections were made. Further steps toward antipollution of the Fourth Lake waters were taken when the Association officers decided to have a representative on the Fulton Chain of Lakes Antipollution Organization.

For several years Eagle Bay had no fire protection and Inlet's fire department was called in case of fire. Since the organization of the Volunteer Hose Company in the 1940's, the Eagle Bay Park Association has annually contributed $100 and upward to that department. William Lennon and Ralph Corts were instrumental in obtaining a fire truck and tank of 2,000 gallon capacity for the fire department. The Park Association paid $200 required for painting and lettering the truck which was then given to the Hose Company.

The Association also gave the Volunteer Hose Company $250 to help install a water hydrant in the Park.

A step forward in giving the officers of the Park Assocaition the power to act in money matter emergencies was taken in 1964. The president and secretary were empowered by action of the Association membership to effect loans, advances and other forms of credit needed for the operation of the Association from Oneida National Bank and Trust Company of Utica.

Again alerted to the pollution problems, the Eagle Bay Park officers were concerned with a water chlorination system relative to a New York State ruling. The chlorination program for Eagle Bay Park was installed at a cost of about $2,000.

Since the beginning of the 18th century adventures into the Adirondacks, black flies and punkies have been the irritating enemies of the adventurers. These pests continue to be an annual problem. Eagle Bay has attacked them in many ways. From complete body covering to all kinds of bottle sprays, to automotive sprays from the back of trucks, to the now more popular use of the airplane spraying system, nothing has relieved the vacationists and the natives of the black fly-punkie problem. The Park Association management continues to try to defeat these little enemies. DDT was a disaster, because of its effect on bird life. The summer battle continues all through June each year.

Perhaps it was the closeness of Cedar and Dollar Islands and the water routes to the Islands that prompted the increased interest in navigational aids placed in Fourth Lake. Such aids were finally installed.

During the Indian occupation of Moss Lake from 1973 to 1978, the authorities of the Eagle Bay Park Association were concerned with the problems presented by the Indian encampment. Eagle Bay Park Association was in complete agreement with COPCA (a Big Moose based organization working as a go-between with the Indians and the State of New York). Members of the Association were urged to individually support the fine objectives of COPCA. Letters were sent to COPCA, and other assurances of Eagle Bay support were extended.

With Park Association minutes not available before 1929, and from 1929 through 1958, then again from 1975 to the present writing, it is not possible to give all the names of persons involved in the management of the Park Assocaition. The persons named below were involved either as officers and directors, or as Park police, or simply as persons who spoke up at the meetings. Some were committee members.

The men who have served as Eagle Bay Park police or night

watchmen whose names can be verified are: Johnny Gorman, Daniel Sheehy, Mr. Rutledge, Larry Fee, Mr. Adams, Dick Retting, William T. Wallace and Frank Schumacher.

Persons who were elected as members of the Park board of directors served mostly three to six years. Since minutes from 1929–1959 were not available some names will be missed. The persons listed below did serve. Their office and years of service are not given: William Cusack, Alvina Searing, Mr. Vicks from Whitesboro, Jim Kirkland, Herb Kolb, Stan Stever, Frieda Nelson, Ike Chapell, Al Perry, Ralph Corts, William Sullivan, Richard Howden, William Lennon, Allen Smith, Gerald Finke, John Dillon, Barbara Pope, John Vaccaro, Leo Peglow, Dave DePrez.

Many people were influential as members of the Park Association simply by voicing their opinions or suggestions in the annual meetings. In the minutes the following names were mentioned: Carl Griebno [sic], F. Bonville, L. Beauchamp, A. Cook, John Gundmunson, Clark McKee, Joseph Feeny, Bob Searing, Sidney Parker, Ted Fuller, Mr. Aeillo, Gertrude Wikander, Mr. Reittinger, Jack Nolan, Mr. Feol, Ben Whittaker, and Roger Dean.

The Association board members have carried on the business of Eagle Bay Park over a period of almost sixty years. The organization has survived and is functioning. There are always those who feel improvements are needed and improvements are continually being made.

CHAPTER IV

Hotel Boom in Eagle Bay Area

The Alonzo Wood Hotel, Cedar Island House, Rocky Point Inn, The Eagle Bay Hotel and perhaps Hart's Inn were in the Eagle Bay area before the Raquette Lake Railroad was built. Later to the south there were Freeman's Kenmore and Carrie Longstaff's Mohawk Hotel. Eagle Bay Hotel was perhaps one of the most important factors in having the Railroad Company build one of its main stations at Eagle Bay between 1900 and 1901. Eagle Bay station was ready for passengers by 1901, which is the date given the the Railroad superintendent who was stationed at Eagle Bay.

Another plus in the hotel development around Eagle Bay was the natural harbor facilities for steam boat landings. As early as 1883 the harbor was used by Jonathan Meeker for his *Hunter*. By 1900 the *Clearwater* and other steamers were using the harbor. These transportation conveniences attracted may vacationers.

Eagle Bay Hotel

On October 10, 1895 William Seward Webb and his wife, Eliza Osgood of New York City, sold the land on which the Eagle Bay Hotel was later built to Dwight Sperry of Old Forge. One of the express conditions of the transaction was that Sperry:

> within two years from the date hereof, erect, finish and have ready for use and occupancy, a hotel having a capacity to accommodate fifty guests, board and lodging.

If Mr. Sperry did not erect the hotel, then he would forfeit and lose all moneys advanced and paid on the purchase price of the lots. The Eagle Bay Hotel Company was incorporated December 31, 1896 and the directors were David C. Wood, Herkimer; Patrick Moynehan, Glens Falls; Dwight B. Sperry, Old Forge; Dennis Moynehan, Newcomb, and J. George Thompson, Blue Mountain.

July 1, 1897, Dwight Sperry conveyed to the Eagle Bay Hotel Company all of the land described in the deed from Webb to Sperry, subject to the same conditions. Historians have said that Eagle Bay Hotel was built by the hotel company. The above facts seem to indicate that the Eagle Bay Hotel was built between 1895 and 1897 by the company. Also other transactions indicate that Dwight Sperry never relinquished his right to be involved with this hotel company.

Ben Sperry — Owner of Eagle Bay Hotel. Picking up the mail at E. U. Smith's store. Credit Town of Webb Historical Society.

Eagle Bay Hotel built 1896 — burned 1945. Credit Mary Evans.

Eagle Bay boathouse and Casino. Steamers docked near here. Credit Mary Evans.

Eagle Bay Hotel band. Gardner Hinman sitting at piano. Hinman's band. Joseph Pepper holding violin. Others not known. 1924. Credit Sandra Hinman Nilo.

The land boundary of the hotel was well up the Big Moose Road to Eagle Creek and the highway to Old Forge, and also included the clearing on the Uncas Road just above the corner (junction with Route 28), which was where the hotel management grew their potatoes.

Without doubt William Preston was at one time manager or leasee of Eagle Bay Hotel, but the records given below seem to indicate he was never owner.

In 1907 William Thistlethwaite sold land to William Preston of Eagle Bay. The deed described the purchase as being bound by Eagle Bay Hotel property thus:

> Beginning at a stake set at the southwesterly corner of the Eagle Bay Hotel property and running thence northerly along the westerly line of said Eagle Bay Hotel property and the easterly line of the Thistlewaite property, crossing the Eagle Bay highway, about eight hundred and sixty-five (865) feet to the right-of-way of the Raquette Lake Railway — etc.

This description makes it evident that this purchase was not the Eagle Bay Hotel property. Over this parcel of land the Hinckley Fibre Company had laid out a road which was being used by this company and others for hauling logs out in the winter, and for the use of camp owners on Eagle Point. This deed was also given subject to the lease of the Inlet Lumber Company of the small strip of land fifty feet wide lying between the Raquette Lake Railway and the Eagle Bay highway.

The records show that the Prestons owned their tract of land from October 22, 1907, until March 27, 1912. Howard Weller eventually became owner of most of this Preston land, and Orr Liddle became owner of one of the Preston lots.

Roy Higby, owner of Higby Club, Big Moose Lake, whose mother was a sister to Dwight Sperry, adds this information:

> My uncle, Dwight Sperry, was one of the builders of Eagle Bay Hotel, I was told. After he sold the Glenmore at Big Moose about 1915, he purchased Eagle Bay Hotel with more than 300 acres of land. At his death in 1918, he left the hotel to Benjamin Sperry. Ben was to pay $20,000 to the estate on easy terms. Sometime in the early 20's, Warren Harding stayed at the hotel, as did Nan Britton, who later wrote *The President's Daughter*. She came to the Higby Club in the mid-thirties with her daughter, Elizabeth Ann Harding.
>
> The Hamilton County Line ran through the hotel. When local option was voted (ie: Liquor), one county was dry, the other sold liquor. My uncle, Dwight Sperry, simply moved his bar to the other end of the room and was in the county in

which he could sell liquor. The bar was at the east end of the hotel.

Roy Higby offers this interesting clipping taken from the Four Tract Series — Publication of the New York Central Railway. Title — *The Adirondack Mountains* — About 1900, published yearly. quote re: Eagle Bay Hotel.

> This new hotel is elegantly furnished and heated by steam making it comfortable on rainy days and cool evenings. Water is from one of the finest springs in the Adirondacks. Hot and cold baths are on each floor. Sanitary plumbing. Good hunting and fishing nearby. Boat and carriage livery. Fine dandy beach for swimming. Rates $3 to $4 per day and $12 to $25 per week according to location of rooms. N.A. Briggs, Old Forge, N.Y.

The spring mentioned above was close to the Big Moose Road, toward Big Moose from where the Cascade Road turns off, on the east side of the highway.

In Herkimer County Court House is recorded a deed dated Dec. 10, 1902, from Ne-ha-sa-ne Park Association to William J. Thistlethwaite, over 400 acres of land. The deed incorporated all the usual Webb restrictions regarding fire, timber, etc. Thistlethwaite, fourteen days later, Dec. 24, 1902, deeded:

> Same premises conveyed by Abstract No. Two except reserving the right-of-way of the Raquette Railway Co. as now located and surveyed over said land and also reserving the right-of-way heretofore deeded to W. W. Durant for a highway across and over said lands (reference no doubt to the Big Moose-Raquette Lake roads) to Eagle Bay Hotel Company (a corporation).

Just before his death Dwight Sperry once again became sole owner of Eagle Bay Hotel property.

Provisions of Will

Dwight Sperry's will was made December 6, 1917, and admitted to probate June 6, 1918, before the Surrogate of Herkimer County. The hotel property contained 350 acres of land, all of which with furniture, tools, automobiles and equipment was to be sold by his executor to his nephew, Benjamin Sperry, for $20,000 payable in annual installments of $800 of principal and interest until the purchase price was fully paid. These were the terms, provided Benjamin Sperry wished to purchase the property. Proceeds were to be converted into cash and distributed equally by his executor, Clarence R. Sperry, among Dwight Sperry's brother and two sisters. Three acres of this land, triangular in shape and lying with frontage on the Old Forge-Eagle Bay highway, were sold to John Petersen September 9, 1926.

Eagle Bay Hotel Burns

In 1944 a deed was given to Elizabeth O'Leary from Dwight Sperry's administrator for the Eagle Bay Hotel property. Mrs. O'Leary owned the hotel at the time of the fire. Yock Youmans said his father, Burt, told him only a few days before the fire that there was going to be a fire at Eagle Bay Hotel if the management continued loading the electric fuses.

On the night of August 7, 1945, the night watchman smelled smoke. He at once alerted others to the danger. Chefs James Coswell and Clarence Moore ran through the hotel corridors awakening the guests, who escaped clad only in their night clothes, many with blankets wrapped around them. In less than one hour the loss was total. The chefs who had warned the guests escaped by jumping from upper floor windows. One of them was seriously injured and had to be hospitalized. The escaped guests were taken into other buildings on the grounds and into homes of Eagle Bay residents for the night.

The next year after the fire Leon E. Schopfer of Syracuse bought the hotel property from Elizabeth O'Leary.

John Schopfer has given Mary Evans, present owner of the Eagle Bay Villas, a written history of the transformation of the Old Eagle Bay Hotel into Eagle Bay Villas, a type of cottage-motel combination of sleeping and housekeeping units. He explains how this was carried out. In the summer of 1946 after they purchased the hotel, the Schopfers rented rooms in the original buildings, outside the main hotel that had burned. In the fall of 1946 work began on a rather massive scale. The fire debris had to be cleared away and the cellar filled. The bulldozers worked for months. Several of the original hotel buildings were demolished and the lumber salvaged and stored on the tennis court for use in the new buildings to be erected.

The most intensive building project began in 1949–1950. The Dick Paynes, Sr. and Jr. of Inlet were in charge of the construction crew. Work began while snow was still on the ground. The whole project was rather large in scale and the last cottage was barely finished for the July, 1950 rental season. This project left the beach strewn with debris until it could be cleared. Two cottages built in 1950 really began what is the present Eagle Bay Villas operation.

In 1954 the building on the lake was converted into what became the motel. In 1963 kitchenette bars were installed in the motel units.

An attractive new cottage was built in 1959-60 by Bud Kopp. Other building changes were made in 1960.

Father John Schopfer has this to add to the history of Eagle Bay Hotel:

> The large mound in the center play area near the walk to the cottage in the woods is the site of the fireplace of Eagle Bay Hotel. The bulldozer worked a long time and when it came to digging a hole to bury the remains of the fireplace the driver misjudged it just a bit. Thus, we just piled dirt around it and that was that. The fireplace must be very close to the top of the ground.
>
> Much of the furniture contained throughout the cottages was a part of the Eagle Bay Hotel operation. There were a lot of wicker items. We threw them out, painted them, cut off legs, etc. These items would be worth a lot today.
>
> *The Boat Harbor.* This area was changed somewhat with the beginning of the Windhausen seaplane operation. A small creek was redirected to the inlet side of the Windhausen property line. With increase in boating popularity, we decided it could be used to make full use of the natural harbor facilities we had. It had been used for quite some time by sightseeing and other craft.
>
> There was an extremely large tree on the point where Bud Windhausen eventually built his airplane dock. When this was chopped down to make room for the seaplane dock and the Gray cottage, the tree was saved. Alfred Nelson engineered its use as the mainstay of the boat harbor. You can still see the extent of it by examining the logs in the harbor dock. Considerable bulldozing was also required, and Alfred cleaned away the area of the beach where rowboats are now kept. This project was done in the spring of 1955 or 1956.

Eagle Bay Villas Sold

Leon Schopfer sold the Eagle Bay Villas property (formerly Eagle Bay Hotel) to E. Cunningham December 30, 1968. The Cunninghams owned the property only four years. Very little change was made in the physical aspect of the property during this brief ownership. Then in the spring of 1972 E. Cunningham sold the entire old Eagle Bay Hotel property to James and Mary Evans of Eagle Bay. James Evans had taken over the Burkhard-Evans Realty and Insurance Agency in Inlet and he and his wife had built a lovely year-round home on the Big Moose Road in Eagle Bay.

Eagle Bay Villas

All-Season Accommodations

Mary and James Evans completed the transformation of the old Eagle Bay Hotel into a modern, winterized colony of cottages which are called Eagle Bay Villas. There was time for only basic changes in 1972 after the Evans' purchase from Cunningham. However, in the fall of 1972 heavy equipment was brought in to pick up the two-bedroom cottages known as the "Teen-Agers," and set them over on the lawn. Concrete cellar walls were then poured. The cottages were again picked up and set onto the walls. All six of the cottages were done in this manner. Floor furnaces were installed in each of them as well in Cottage Number 25. A new water line to the cottages was put in at a depth of six feet so the water would not freeze from the heavy winter frosts.

Business allowed further improvements for three four-bedroom cottages. These were also winterized and furnaces installed in each. The office building, which had served as the Schopfer home, was remodeled with a new kitchen and the entire cottage was paneled. In 1975, Evans purchased the Windhausens' home. The land had been purchased by the Windhausen brothers from Eagle Bay Villas when they established their seaplane base at Eagle Bay.

Progress continued in 1976–77. During these years a new sewer system was installed for all the cottages and for the motel. The cottages called the "Teen-Agers" were all paneled, carpeted and new kitchens installed. In 1976 the Evanses applied for and received permission to put the breakwater in where it had been at the time the steamers docked at the Eagle Bay Hotel. The land over all these years had eroded back about 35 feet.

In October of 1978, while empty, the office building burned. The fire caused no further serious damage. The motel was carpeted, and the breakwater was completed across the entire lake frontage at the Villas except for the beach area. Other improvements included a macadam entrance drive and a new sign enhancing the total appearance. All the cottages were repainted, changing in most cases from white with red trim to red with white trim. Many new roofs were installed. Interiors were improved with all new beds, drapes, hide-a-beds in the living rooms, and other furniture for the comfort of guests.

The site of the Old Eagle Bay Hotel, later the Villas, is an historic spot. Never a year since 1896, even with a disastrous fire, has it failed to open its doors to enthusiastic vactioners. In so doing it has brought to the village of Eagle Bay a rewarding amount of business and goodwill.

From Weller's *Adirondack Eagle* — Summer 1925:

Special Appeal of the Hotel

For real, genuine comfort you can go a deal farther and find nothing that comes up to the Eagle Bay Hotel. Here's where you want to get out of the stiff clothing of the cities, because you are going to live in the open all the time you are here.

The Hotel is putting in a new water supply from its famous mountain spring. It is said this is about the purest water in the world. The immense kitchens of this Hotel have been rebuilt and among the new equipment is an electric diswasher with a capacity of 4,000 dishes an hour.

Its cozy dining room now comfortably seats 136 guests. This well known hotel is so popular that the entire month of August has been booked — not a room left for August, unless some reservations are cancelled in the meantime.

The garden of this hotel is one of the largest and best on the lake. Mr. Sperry, the proprietor, is having a hard time with it just now, because the deer, with the help-yourself-to-other-people's-goods of the most advanced socialistic school, insist upon browsing on the toothsome vegetables, lettuce, etc.

This account in the August 8, 1925, *Adirondack Eagle* gives an indication of the social life and activities program in the heyday of the hotel:

Friday last the first winter carnival by Bob Croasdell was held. The winners of the races were: Boat race for ladies — Mrs. W. C. Mulsein, Canoe Double for ladies — Mrs. Hendricks. Single Canoe race — Miss E. Bente. Fighting and tilting contest won by Wm. L. Lebleaur who defeated W. Mulsein by two falls out of three with a left swing to the body which disappeared under the water. One Hundred dash obstacle race won by Mr. W. C. Mulsein. There was an attempt to suicide but when he appeared at the surface again we found a rube — another prank of Bob Croasdell's.

Thursday night the prize baby contest took place. All guests were dressed as babies so if any mother lost her child, she is requested to call for it at Eagle Bay Hotel. Wednesday evening a masquerade ball was held and Friday night a hay ride and song supper in the woods near Raquette.

Guests registered at Eagle Bay Hotel in the summer of 1925: Fred R. Krebs, F. W. Perkins, Skaneateles, N.Y.; H. C. Woods, E. L. Carey, Benton Klein and wife, F. A. Meehan and wife, Miss J. L. Gofarty, Miss E. Hoffman, C. F. Meeten, N. W. Forest and wife, W. J. Campbell, A. T. Maclean, N.Y.C.; I. Cole, Cedarhurst, L.I.; Mrs. Lizzie S. Vincent, Mrs. Florence A. Skellinger, R. G. Baker and family, Mr. & Mrs. J. Steingenwald, Mr. & Mrs. LL. J. Steingenwald, Miss Betty Baynton, Mr. J. Schaner, Irene Dalgiel, Carl Mayer, Anna M. O'Heiber, Syracuse, N.Y.; J. A. Mobley, S. Reichler, Golden R. Smith and son, Mrs. R. Smith, Alice R. Smith, F. Brennan and wife, Mr. & Mrs. C. J. Ulrich, Clarence A. Mizer, Miss Helen Burke, M. H. Palmer, J. E. Hart, C. R. Casler, Utica, N.Y.; Mrs. Jas. Murnane, John Richardson, Herkimer, N.Y.; W. Earl Loomis, Bethlehem, Pa.; Mrs. John Desmond, S. D. Bennett and wife, Rochester, N.Y.; Anna Stark, Henry Barmore, Edna C. Winslow, Anna Schwaner, F. S. Schwaner, Brooklyn, N.Y.; John P. Livingston, Rahway, N.J.; Misses Elizabeth H. and Vera Cudahy, Jackson Heights, N.Y.; Margaret W. McCann, Dorothy M. Smith, Glen Morris, N.Y.C.; Albert Haight, R. M. McCue, L. M. Gillogly, W. F. Corbett, J. S. O'Brien, M. A. McGee, R. M. DeVaney, Loretta Pfister, Mildred Knoer, Eileen McTigue, Marie McPhee, Lilliam M. Goss, Ruth H. Moran, Chas. C. Ernst and family, F. Bowen and wife, C. H. Van Brocklin and wife, A. J. Peer, H. H. Holmberg, Mr. & Mrs. Federlein, Eugene Hackford, Albert B. Trankley, Buffalo, N.Y.; William Ely, Mr. & Mrs. John F. Hott, Hackensack, N.Y.; Eleanor Putnam, Ithaca, N.Y.; W. E. Tubbs and wife, Harriet E. Baker, Mrs. S. E. Smith, Croton-on-Hudson, N.Y.; L. A. Creighton, Ossining, N.Y.; M. L. Webber, B. J. Gager, Hartford, Conn.; Charlotte Fairchild, Cleveland, Ohio; Katherine E. Edwards, Dansville, N.Y.; Josie Murnin, Hugh Murnin, Harmon, N.Y.

Rocky Point Inn

The location of Rocky Point, jutting out into the waters at the head of Fourth Lake, cried out for development. An Oneida furniture firm, the Niles Company, built a hotel there in 1892. Naturally, it was called Rocky Point. The main building, standing straight and high, was constructed of native pine, hemlock and spruce sawed at the mill operated at Inlet by Fred Hess. Hess had built the Cedar Island House and then had gone to Inlet to build the structure that is now the Wood Hotel, then known as the Hess Camp.

In Rocky Point Inn in 1892 there were forty sleeping rooms, but no baths. According to a brief history of the hotel by Arch Delmarsh II, the operation of the hotel between 1892 and 1908 was not "conspicuously successful." Other than the rooms in the hotel at this time and perhaps for some years after, there were tents pitched for guests. The cottages were built later. Delmarsh records this information:

> The small cottages along the tennis court were built by A. A.

Rarrick for $300 each, lumber furnished, but no plumbing . . . there were no roads — only a trail around the lake kept open by law. (This was the requirement put into all early Webb deeds.) Guests who were here then have said that woods came right to the back of the Inn. The lights were kerosene, and red and green lanterns were hung around the shore line at night.

An early advertisement on Rocky Point Inn has this information:

> We have built four new rustic cabins containing two rooms each 14 by 16 feet sided up with bark, with large rustic porches, making them very attractive in every sense. Each room is brilliantly illuminated with acetylene gas. The playgrounds around the cabins have been graded and filled in to a depth of two feet with coarse gravel, making the grounds high and dry and making it impossible for any dampness to gather around or underneath the cabins or tents.

The first page of the advertisement carries in a block form this information:

> Compliments of —
> ROCKY POINT INN COMPANY
> JAMES H. NILES, PRESIDENT
> JOHN CRAWFORD, TREASURER
> ELMER BLAIR, SECRETARY

The advertisement further states that about two hundred feet of new sea wall or breakwater had been built around the south bay "seeded down and beautifying that part of the grounds." Also a new sewerage system had been put in making it "as clean and sanitary as city homes." A new gravity water system had been installed that will give an abundant supply of water throughout the house and grounds. The above gives a rather clear picture of services given by Rock Point in the early days.

In 1908 the Niles Company sold or leased the hotel to Mark Wallace. In 1909 Dr. H. H. Longstaff, whose wife was running the Mohawk, took over until 1910. The hotel must have changed hands again for a short time, because it was in 1910 that Arch Delmarsh, Sr., who had been running Cedar Island House for ten years previously, bought Rocky Point Inn and property from D. H. Burrell of Little Falls. He paid Burrell $23,000 for the property.

Delmarsh adds:

> From 1910 until 1929 most of the present cottages and pleasant additions to the Inn were constructed by Arch Delmarsh,

Theodore R. Fallis and Mary Dussalt married 1898, spent honeymoon at Eagle Bay Hotel. Credit T. M. Fallis.

Mary Dussalt.

Aerial view of Rocky Point Inn. Credit Standard Supply.

Mr. and Mrs. Arch Delmarsh Sr. and Arch Delmarsh II in his father's arms. Arch Sr., manager of Dollar Island House, and owner of Rocky Point Inn. Credit Arch Delmarsh III collection.

Rocky Point Inn has hosted people many years, including three generations under the reins of the Delmarsh family with a fourth generation knocking at the management door. Credit Town of Webb Historical Society.

Sr., including the two tennis courts, docks and boathouses, garages, employee quarters and roadways.

Then the article, which Arch II published in honor of his mother's 80th birthday, continues below as he told it:

As the railroad displaced the boats during the early 1900's, so the roads and automobiles later displaced the railroad. The Eagle Bay station and Raquette Lake Line expired in 1933. A relic of the days when the guests arrived by double deck steamer with trunks that filled the wide halls of the Inn is the iron wheeled cart used as a service cart at the cookouts. Of the same vintage or earlier is the guide boat with carrying yoke. Before the roads, the fastest way to journey from upper Saranac Lake to Old Forge was by guide boat and carry. Power was by the oar pull.

Arrow Fastest Launch

The center of life in those days was the area off the glassed-in sun porch. The check-in office was off the lobby and once in, a guest seldom came down to where the autos come out as that was then the back of the house. Hikes and mountain climbing were the daily fare and boating and fishing sports were the main attraction of the area. The fastest launch on the Lakes was the *Arrow* of Rocky Point, which made 15 to 16 miles per hour.

Rocky Point belongs to a generation of Adirondack hotels that began with Paul Smith's at Lake Clear and flowered into such grandiose structures as the Prospect House of Blue Mountain Lake. It was when William West Durant was copying Swiss and Chinese architecture in his fabulous camps at Raquette Lake. It is one of the last of the generation and remains today in relatively good shape due to the many years of hard work, construction and reconstruction, and many dollars of upkeep and new construction money poured into it during the years 1948–1972 by Arch Delmarsh, Jr.

In our office and around the Inn we have placed a few mementos of early life here. It was over seventy years ago (1892) that Delmarsh Sr. rowed Niles to this point to ascertain if a resort could be constructed here. They might be pleasantly surprised to discover the rooms of the old Inn still finding use each summer and at this writing all occupied. — Arch Delmarsh.

But the story of Rocky Point does not end with Arch II. There is now, and has been for several years past, Arch III, who is the power behind the Rocky Point Inn administration. Improvements are still being made. The dining room is more scenic and colorful than ever. The food and service continue to improve. Guests still come in large numbers, some now are of the third and fourth generation. Improvements made to the cocktail lounge have attracted the attention of many guests. Other members of the Delmarsh family are actively involved in the upkeep of the high standards and services offered by the Inn for years.

Arch Delmarsh III and his wife Shirley have three sons: Arch IV, 18; Terry, 17, and Chris, 11. All are actively engaged in the operation of Rocky Point Inn. Even though the peak days of the Adirondack summer resort hotel seems to be over, the family operation at Rocky Point Inn continues and all evidence points toward a fourth generation of owners and administrators for this one-of-a-kind hotel. A fourth generation of operators is something of a record for this Eagle Bay-Inlet resort area.

These instructions for reaching the Inn appeared in an advertisement preserved in the Rocky Point collection of memorabilia, with no date given:

> From the South, East and West, connection is made at Utica with the New York Central; the West Shore; the Delaware, Lackawanna & Western, and the New York, Ontario & Western railroads.
>
> From Utica, and also from the North, the route is via the Adirondack Division of the New York Central System to either Clearwater or Fulton Chain station, and thence by one of the following routes:
>
> (a) From Clearwater station, via Raquette Lake R'y., to Eagle Bay station (On Fourth Lake, near the head), and thence by steamer or drive to Rocky Point Inn, distance of about one mile.
>
> (b) From Fulton Chain station, via Old Forge R.R. to Old Forge; thence by steamer (through the Fulton Chain of Lakes) to Rocky Point Inn — a distance of about twelve miles. Steamers, by either route, land guests at Rock Point Inn dock.
>
> Also through train and parlor and sleeping car service to and from both Eagle Bay and Old Forge stations.
>
> Attentive representatives meet incoming trains to assist guests.
>
> For further details, please address inquiries as follows:

Until July 1st,
   ELMER BLAIR, Secretary,
   445 Western Ave., Albany, N.Y.
After July 1st,
   ROCKY POINT INN CO., Eagle Bay, P.O., N.Y.

Documents pertaining to the sale of the Rocky Point Inn property to Delmarsh also are included in the collection:

Little Falls, N.Y., Jan. 17, 1911

MEMORANDUM OF SALE, made this day to Mr. Archie Delmarsh, Manager of Cedar Island Property in Fourth Lake.

D. H. Burrell sells to Mr. Archie Delmarch, all of Rocky Point Inn Property up to and including all of Lot No. 114, at and for the price of $23,000. Payments to be made as follows:

Cash or its equivalent..................... $ 5,000
Balance to run on Mortgage or on contract,
as Mr. Delmarsh may desire, at
4½% interest 18,000

SALE to include all personal property now at Rocky Point Inn.

One Thousand ($1,000) minimum to be paid annually providing improvements are made on the property by purchaser, so as to keep up its value.

The Purchaser, Mr. Archie Delmarsh to have the right to pay as much faster as he pleases, and interest only to be charged after, for the amount remaining unpaid.

D. H. Burrell also to give Mr. Archie Delmarsh option for Three Years to purchase Lot No. 115 for One Thousand Dollars ($1,000).

The above terms and conditions are hereby agreed to.

D.H. Burrell
Archie G. Delmarsh

D. H. BURRELL & CO.

Little Falls, N.Y., U.S.A.   Feb. 13, 1911

Mr. Archie G. Delmarsh,
   Inlet, N.Y.
Dear Sir:

We hand you herewith letter to Arthur A. Rarick, instructing him to deliver to you the keys to the Rocky Point Inn property.

We are also handing you herewith enclosed, by registered mail, key to the store room of Rocky Point Inn, in which you will find quite a number of supplies, canned goods, etc. Also, another key to the property. You will find the other keys in Rocky Point Inn.

      Yours truly,
      Loomis Burrell
      for D. H. Burrell

L/s We have just had the ice house filled at an expense of $46.00, and this you are welcome to.

David Burrell Successful in Business

David H. Burrell, who sold Rocky Point to Arch Delmarsh Sr., was a talented businessman. Early exposure to the milk business allowed David Burrell to learn the business from the farm to the market. When he was only 14 his father, Harry, started him contracting for dairy cheese on which his father by 1896 had gained somewhat of a monopoly. In 1927, farmers commissioned David Burrell to distribute their entire season's make of cheese. When David was 17, he was hired by the New York offices of his father's firm and at 22 he alone purchased 33,000 boxes of cheese in two months and had them shipped to New York, where he sold the whole lot for a profit of two dollars a box. He went to Scandinavia, learning how Sandinavia's superior cheese was manufactured. From David Burrell's creative salesmanship the business spread and prospered.

New machinery, new techniques, new products were added to the business. The Burrells began the manufacture of equipment and machinery to supply the dairy industry. This then became their principal business, rather than the previous profitable dairy products. Eventually, they consolidated their Little Falls industry with that of the J. G. Cherry Company of Troy Mills, Iowa. The incorporation of Cherry-Burrell in 1928 involved the merger of seven separate companies, a feat never accomplished before or since, according to the history of the two parent companies. (The above story taken from a pamphlet furnished by Burrell's nephew, William H. Wing.)

Delmarsh, Sr. Popular Guide

When Arch Delmarsh, Sr. took over Rocky Point in 1914 he was widely known as a guide and hotelman, having been in the woods since 1891. At the age of 12 he had already become a veteran hunter and fisherman. When he came to Cedar Island at 21 years of age, he was skilled in all arts of the woodsman.

Roger B. Spaulding, writing in the Nov. 18, 1935, *Syracuse Post-Standard*, says of him:

It's as a husky, fun-loving woodsman at old Cedar Island before the turn of the century that Del is best remembered by sportsmen of this city. Good roads and automobiles have killed the guiding business of that period when to hunt or fish in the Adirondacks meant 'roughing it' in earnest.

Spaulding noted that hunters in the years when Delmarsh was a guide traveled on the old Adirondack line to Thendara (then called Fulton Chain Station), from there by stage to Old Forge and up the lake by steamer or rowboat.

When they went after deer in those days the guides packed their own provisions on their backs and trudged into the woods for miles to stay for weeks. The deer they shot were often brought out by pack-horses — if a hungry she-bear and her cubs didn't get there first.

The guides were adept at building shacks or open face lean-tos for shelter, and the grub they cooked was irresistible. Delmarsh was for years the envy of housewives whose husbands never ceased extolling the magic of his frying pan and kettle.

Caroline M. Longstaff's Camp Mohawk

On the 19th day of June 1896 William Seward Webb and his wife, Eliza Osgood Webb, sold to Caroline M. Longstaff lot 160 in Township Eight in the Town of Webb of the David C. Wood survey dated August 30, 1893. There was a large cottage on this lot on the shore of Fourth Lake. During one winter while workmen were laying in ice and wood, fire destroyed this large cottage.

Dr. H. H. Longstaff, at that time a dentist in Herkimer, and his wife had, during the different summers, entertained friends from the Valley. When the fire took the cottage, several friends suggested the Longstaffs build a small hotel and let even more friends come. After much figuring, the decision was made to build back from the lake at the foot of the hill. Dr. Longstaff had considerable interest in architecture and construction; therefore they soon had a small hotel built which they christened "Camp Mohawk."

The hotel guests created more demand for rooms as the years went by. In 1902 the Longstaffs had purchased an adjoining lot, number 161, from Robert Ash and wife, Ella. They also purchased some adjoining cottages. In the fall of 1909, Dr. Longstaff supervised the construction of the much larger building, The Mohawk, which was completed and opened for guests, July 4, 1910. A remarkable feat.

For many years this construction made Camp Mohawk one of the most modern area hotels. It had some private baths, hot and cold running water in each room, and a complete electrical system which not only furnished lights, but powered a modern laundry. Most of the workmen were brought in from Herkimer, and it is interesting to note the construction wages in those days were $2 and $3 per day. The huge fireplace in the lobby cost only $300. The hotel prospered and became one of the most prestigious on Fourth Lake.

Transportation was by train to Skensowane, or train to Fulton Chain, then transfer to steamers up the lakes. Hotel bellboys met boats or trains and brought trunks and bags by wheelbarrow from the dock or from Skensowane, to the hotel while guests walked with them. In later years there were automobiles and trucks for this chore, but the flavor of the early years was special.

The departures of guests were unique. No matter if one or a dozen persons were leaving on the "sleeper" a crowd went to say goodbye. The send-off was singing around a bonfire until the whistle blew as the train left Eagle Bay. Then with a lantern a bellboy would signal for the train to stop at Skensowane. The engineer would acknowledge the signal with two "toots" indicating "will stop."

Varied Activities

In the earlier days most guests came to the hotel for the entire season; so there was time for gracious living. Daylight hours were occupied by swimming, boating, tennis (Camp Mohawk had two courts, one of which was clay, and very fast), horses to ride or use for buckboard rides over the old lumber roads, campfires, cookouts, hikes to such places as Eagle Creek at dusk to quietly watch the beaver at nocturnal works of magnificent engineering. There were regattas, tennis matches between the hotels, boat trips on either the big steamers or Brushes' *U-GO-I-GO*. Their second boat was christened the *U-GO-I-GO II* which was later purchased by Allen Wilcox and rechristened *The Nat Foster*. It was dry-docked and is now a cottage on the property.

Evenings brought excursions. Some of these were all day to and from Blue Mountain via boat to Eagle Bay, train to Raquette Lake, boat to Marion River, then over the Carry by short railroad to Utowanna, where boats were used for the rest of the trip through Eagle and Blue Mountain Lakes. Some of the hotels of the early days had dance halls either over their boat houses or in separate buildings. It was believed the Mohawk was the very first to have a ballroom. Because of the special atmosphere at the Mohawk, there was chamber music after lunch, and evening dance music. There were Sunday concerts and occasional masquerades and other special events.

Good taste rather than formality was the order of the day. At no time did a man enter the dining room without jacket and tie. Saturday dinner was formal. Friendships were easily formed. As each new guest arrived, Mrs. Longstaff made certain he or she was introduced to other guests and made to feel part of the family. The bellboys and waitresses were carefully chosen and had part in making the lovely atmosphere which prevailed. Most of the help were either college graduates or working their way through college.

Big Ed Bolton and Others

In the early days the Mohawk had a fine garden. Big Ed Bolton was the gardener. One time he had set dynamite under a boulder to make more room in the garden. He set the fuse, turned to run and stumbled over four-year-old Caroline Longstaff. He literally picked her up by "the seat of her britches" and ran to safety. Caroline says she adored Big Ed, and one time followed him up a ladder when he was tarring a roof to show him her baby kitten. She tipped the bucket of tar on her kitten, and Dr. Longstaff had to use his trusty razor to trim the tarred fur off the poor kitten.

Henry Froelick, Mohawk chef, married Marion, the housekeeper from Boston who had a trained and beautiful singing voice. Henry and Marion bought a small place on Sixth Lake and Henry guided hunting and fishing groups into the Plains during season. It was there he had a fatal heart attack. Many wonderful people worked at the Mohawk. There were sad and happy times. Fortunately the latter were many. People came to the woods because they loved them and were happy returning year after year to this bit of God's Country to smell the burning birch of campfires, to find the beautiful wildflowers and to watch the birds and animals — even catch them in their cameras.

Then there were Lustig, Fred Hodges, the Indians, the organ grinder, and the man with the bear. Lustig came by boat to display his lovely embroidered linens. Fred Hodges also came by boat to display and sell his lovely watercolor photos of the Adirondacks. Caroline is not sure how the organ grinder or the man with the bear came, but the Indians came by boat with their assortment of sweet grass baskets. How good they smelled!

George S. Snyder — Adored Grandfather

Caroline said among her and her brother's fondest memories of their growing up years at the Mohawk were of their grandfather, George S. Snyder, Mrs. Herbert Longstaff's father. He was one of their most wonderful influences, and Mrs. Longstaff's devoted helper. Mr. Snyder was a quiet, private person, very gentle — a true gentleman, loved by all who knew him.

The hotel was extremely fortunate through the years in its clientele. In 1933 Mrs. Longstaff retired and turned the management of the hotel over to the capable hands of Allen and Margaret Wilcox.

The Mohawk Inn

In 1933 Margaret and Allen Wilcox leased The Mohawk from Carrie Longstaff and in 1944 purchased the property from Dr. George Longstaff.

Margaret and Allen Wilcox soon began their program of renovation and expansion. During the 40s and 50s a private bath was added to each bedroom in the main building; new furniture for the bedrooms, lobby, dining room, game room, and music room was purchased. The cocktail lounge and the additional dining room, plus a children's dining room, were added to the present building. The old lobby fireplace was replaced by a beautiful rose granite fireplace and complete new chimney. The original wooden porch and steps of the hotel were removed, and new stone terrace and steps built. Three old annex cottages were razed, and the remaining guest cottages refurbished and rebuilt. Six additional lots on the Eagle Bay side of the hotel grounds were purchased; twelve new guest cottages of varying sizes from one to three bedrooms and bathrooms were built. All of these cottages had fireplaces and heat, and most of the rooms were paneled in native pine. Also, four new staff cottages were built. The native pine was sawed by Allen Wilcox at his private estate, Beaver Lake. This timber was the result of a fall in the big windstorm of 1950, Thanksgiving Day. Most of the cottages had full kitchens or kitchenettes added to them. A large pier and a 1,400 foot beach were constructed. A road was built adjoining the highway from the Eagle Bay side of the grounds toward the lake to the farthest point of the property on the Old Forge side of the grounds, making all guest cottages accessible by automobile.

From 1933 to 1975 under the Wilcox management The Mohawk grew and developed many firsts in the Adirondacks in sports and recreation (horseback riding, water skiing, children's program, putting green), as well as outstanding food and service. The cornerstone of this most successful operation was based on the certainty that each meal would be excellent. The food service was developed and operated by Margaret Wilcox. It was recognized by a number of colleges and universities as one of the best training grounds for students. The consistently outstanding, good food was the chief reason the guests continued to return each year. The lovely pine paneled dining rooms decorated with Adirondack ferns, and with picture windows overlooking the lake and a rock

Main building Mohawk Hotel built in 1910. Left wing added 1947–48. Dining room addition (upper left) cocktail lounge (lower). Credit Mohawk collection.

Dr. George H. Longstaff with his first grandson. Credit Caroline Longstaff Nelson.

Adolph and Caroline Longstaff Nelson. Caroline born and reared on the Mohawk property. Credit Caroline Nelson.

Allen Wilcox at Thendara Station with Mohawk guests departing by train. Credit Mohawk collection.

Allen Wilcox (owner-manager of the Mohawk) on his beautiful Sultana. Credit Allen Wilcox.

Edwin and Marietta Schultz Kelley in front of their Cherokee Lodge; formerly Mohawk property. Credit C. O'Brien.

Summer outdoor fun — Mohawk Hotel ski team. Credit Mohawk collection.

Indian Room Cocktail Lounge at the Mohawk Hotel, Circa 1947. Credit Mohawk collection.

The *U-Go-I-Go II* rechristened *Nat Foster*. Now a cottage on Fourth Lake Mohawk Grounds. Owned 1980 by Mr. & Mrs. Chester Gacioch. Credit Mr. & Mrs. Gacioch.

Becker's 1907 showing the old Meurer Camp and saloon. Credit Freda Westfall collection.

garden, were a delightful setting and atmosphere for the delicious food.

There was a fine wine cellar with a large stock of European as well as domestic wines. The "Indian Room" cocktail lounge was graced by a huge rose granite fireplace, and the room decorated with a large selection of McKinney and Hall original Indian lithographs.

Marietta Schultz began her career at The Mohawk in 1940. In 1944 she was in charge of the offices and reservations, and influential in plans for expansion and renovation. In 1959 she became a part of management, an officer and part owner of The Mohawk when it incorporated as The Mohawk Inn, Country and Boat Club.

Allen Wilcox, in addition to managing The Mohawk, was active in the New York State Hotel Association, having been a director and officer for many years, and president from 1956 to 1958. He was also associated with the American Hotel Association and a founding member of this organization's Resorts Division. For many years Wilcox was involved in the Eagle Bay Volunteer Fire Hose Company, Inc. As a director of the company, he was generous with his time and gave to the company one small and one large pump engine. He served in a number of local endeavors, such as getting a law passed for black fly control and acting as a member of the local Planning Board for many years. He was instrumental in having the Inlet and the Thendara golf clubs converted from 9 to 18-hole courses, having been a director of both clubs for years.

The love of horses was one of Allen Wilcox's primary motives in establishing a fine riding school at The Mohawk in the thirties and forties. The school was developed and headed by Col. Koritsky, who had instructed the children of the Czar of Russia. Mr. Wilcox chose his horses from the crossing of the American saddle horse with the Morgan horse. His favorite saddle horse was the beautiful Sultana, bred, raised and trained on the Fox Ranch in Canada.

Aside from the owners of The Mohawk, the people who were responsible for the prestige of this resort were the capable department heads and other key employees, some of whom were with The Mohawk more than 20 years. Their faithful work, warm personalities, and expertise — and the continuity of staff, management and clientele — insured The Mohawk's success through the years. To mention the names of all these fine people from 1933 to 1975, and give credit where credit is due, would take several chapters.

There were a number of local contractors who helped build The Mohawk and who kept it going. It was the management, the "crew," the local contractors, and above all the loyal guests who returned each summer that made The Mohawk such an outstanding resort recognized not only in the Adirondacks and New York State but throughout the United States.

An atmosphere of friendliness, good management and high standards brought many families together year after year, and lifetime friendships, and many weddings resulted from associations at The Mohawk. It was a happy place loved by all its clientele. Many families visited The Mohawk over the second, third and fourth generations, and one family over the fifth generation.

In the early and mid 1960s the cottages and land of The Mohawk's extensive holdings were resurveyed into new lots and sold to Mohawk guests and Mohawk management. Allen and Margaret Wilcox were ready for retirement. Marietta Schultz had married and wished to withdraw from the hotel business. They dissolved The Mohawk Inn, Country and Boat Club in 1975. Allen Wilcox leased the hotel for a few years, but continued as owner of the hotel and its lot through most of 1981.

In September 1981 The Mohawk Inn was purchased by "Mark Seven at The Mohawk," a Catholic foundation for the deaf, The Rev. Thomas Coughlin, O.SS.T. Executive Director. The Mohawk will now have a happy and constructive use for many years to come.

Becker's Hotel

Mr. and Mrs. Fred Becker came to Fourth Lake in 1902 from Albany County, New York, because of Mr. Becker's failing health. They rented Camp Onondaga, later called Northwoods Inn, and operated it as a summer boarding house, as such places were then known. Mr. Becker was a farmer who loved the outdoors. Living in the Adirondacks did help his precarious health; so they decided to remain.

The Beckers operated the Onondaga for two years. Then in 1904 they purchased the Emil Meurer Camp, the present site of Becker's on Fourth Lake. The Meurer Camp, built in early 1890 by Emil Meurer from Alsace-Lorraine, France, consisted of one small main camp and a saloon near the lake. They catered mostly to hunting and fishing parties and built up a fine clientele. When Mr. and Mrs. Becker bought the place from Meurer, they cleared more land and built a larger main house. As the years went by they added several cottages and annexes. Mr. Becker loved the wilderness and was well acquainted with its lore. Guests took pleasure in his stories of the area.

Becker's is an historic spot because in the early days the location was known as *Big Moose Landing on Fourth Lake.* This landing was an access to Big Moose by the use of trails via Bubb's Lake, Moss and Dart's Lake. At the time Dart's Camp was built, the founder, Bill

Tents at Becker's 1907. In the early years of hotel days tents were common accommodations for summer guests. Credit Freda Westfall.

A charming hostess — Mrs. Becker. Credit Freda Westfall collection.

Becker's in 1915. Credit Freda Westfall collection.

Mr. Becker. He was devoted to God's Country. Credit Freda Westfall.

Becker's 1965 Hotel at top, area of dining room at bottom. Credit Freda Westfall.

Becker Resort — New Look. Circa 1970's. Credit Simm's collection.

Becker's Resort — New Look. Circa 1970's. Credit Simm's collection.

Dart, was known to transport some 750 pounds of materials from the landing by back-packing over trails to Bubb's Lake, rowing across Bubb's Lake, moving on to Moss Lake by trail, rowing across Moss Lake, then again by trail to Dart's.

It has been said that genial Mrs. Becker was the driving force behind Becker's hotel growth. At its peak the hotel could accommodate 150 people. It was operated on the American plan with three meals a day and became well known as a typical family resort. Many guests returned year after year. In Howard Weller's *Adirondack Eagle* dated July 4, 1925, he had this to say about Becker's: "So many people come to Becker's year after year, that a guest once said they might as well publish last year's register for this year."

The Beckers operated the hotel from 1904 until 1934 when their daughter, Freda, and her husband, Leo Westfall, purchased the property. Freda Becker Westfall was born at Becker's Hotel; so she is a true Adirondack native. Leo Westfall became one of the Town of Webb's leading citizens, and one of the Adirondack's best hotel men. He was secretary of the Old Forge Winter Sports Association and president of the Central Adirondack Association for fifteen years. The Westfalls have twin daughters, Ann Dunn of Big Moose and Old Forge, and Connie of White Plains.

Mrs. Westfall and her husband operated Becker's Hotel from 1934 until they sold it in 1971. Freda Becker Westfall, a very modest, forthright person, says her husband was the driving force behind the hotel during the years of their ownership and that she ran the kitchen and the house. One way or the other, the Westfalls continued the fine standards set by Mrs. Westfall's parents so many years before. For almost 70 years Becker's held its place among the very best of Adirondack hotels under the ownership of two generations.

Resort Changed Hands

Becker's resort was purchased from Leo and Freda Westfall on June 1, 1971 by Joseph and Hilda Guzzardo, and James and Margaret Pearse. During the five years the Guzzardos were involved in the Becker Resort there were few changes or innovations. Joe Guzzardo's health was failing. In April 1976 the Pearses and Guzzardos sold the property to Richard and Joanne Sims.

The Sims family came from Fayetteville. Mr. Sims was formerly a vice-president and member of the Board of Directors of J.G.A. Construction Corporation in Syracuse. He is a registered civil engineer and a graduate of Syracuse University. Mrs. Sims is the former Joanne Nagy of Ithaca. They have five children. Both Mr. and Mrs. Sims and the older children were active in the management and operation of Becker's Resort.

The Sims family made many changes and some innovations in the format and the operation of the hotel-cottage plan.

The Kenmore

On Fourth Lake of the Fulton Chain is the Kenmore, now a housekeeping cottage colony owned and operated by Richard and Winifred McCarley, who came from Kenmore, in 1953. The main building, the annex and the boat house were built as a hotel by the Freemans in 1901. It was advertised as having gas lights and a bathroom on each floor. In that era of the Adirondack hotels such conveniences as gas lights and a bathroom on each floor were considered modern. The hotel was operated by Mrs. Freeman about 20 years.

In 1920 The Kenmore was sold to George Becker (no relation to Beckers of Becker's Hotel nearby). The George Becker ownership was of short duration. In 1930 Oswald and Sylvia Schoelz left a hotel which they owned in New Jersey to purchase The Kenmore and renamed it The New Kenmore. Mr. Schoelz was a chef of some skill, having been trained in Europe, and the New Kenmore became known for excellent meals. In the side yard he had a vegetable garden from which fresh vegetables were served to his guests. Also during World War II Mr. Schoelz served beef from cattle raised on the hotel property.

Mr. Schoelz accomplished the impressive feat of moving the annex from its original lakeshore location to the top of the steep hill overlooking the lake. One of the five cottages which Schoelz built during his ownership of the New Kenmore is named for his daughter, Mrs. William (Louise) Weiss, with whom he went to live after retiring. Mr. Schoelz died at age 93 May 16, 1981, in Carlstadt, New Jersey.

In the spring of 1953 Richard and Winifred McCarley, who had a six-week-old baby, bought the Kenmore from Schoelz and began operation on the American plan. In 1966 the main building of the Kenmore burned and the boat house, which had been turned into six motel units, was gutted. Since the summer season was about to begin, the McCarleys hastily remodeled the annex building into a dining room and kitchen to accommodate the American plan guests for the summer. About four years later they changed their operation to a housekeeping colony.

During the American plan years, as is true with most such hotels in the Adirondacks, the owners did most of the cooking and remodeling work. At present The Kenmore is operated by family members. The McCarley children are an integral part of the operation. The McCarleys are now owners of the most attractive Country

The Kenmore — Circa 1924. Credit Town of Webb Historical Society.

Cliff House and grounds facing north end of Fourth Lake. Credit Freda Westfall.

Eagle Bay first postoffice (date not known). Old timers place this summer postoffice at the Cliff House. Mail was distributed from Eagle Bay Hotel also during the winter months. Credit Adirondack Museum.

Ledgedale Hotel circa 1905. Date not verified. Ledge no longer is a hotel. Private property 1981. Credit Charles Kiefer Postcards.

Fred and Violet Schmidt Dittl. Owners of Idlewood Lodge from 1945 to 1969. Their son Alfred and his wife, Beverly, from 1969. Credit Alfred Dittl.

Alfred Dittl estimates this old camp's age between 130 and 150 years old. Idlewood property. Credit Alfred Dittl.

Lane Gift Shop next to Becker Hotel property on Route 28. They also lend their many talents to community life and projects.

Idlewood Lodge

Idlewood is an American-Plan cottage-hotel operation. Many forms of recreation, including swimming, tennis, boating, hiking and just resting under a shade tree are provided the guests. This beautiful shoreline of God's Country has 500 feet of waterfront looking over Fourth Lake to the South Shore mountains.

Milo Bull, according to the old map of Fourth Lake landowners, first owned this land. Then Burke was owner for a while. He sold to Arthur E. Lee, who in 1945 sold this beauty spot to Fred and Violet Dittl.

Fred Dittl was born in Austria, and during World War I became the second youngest major in the Austro-Hungarian Army. He served in the Emperor's personal regiment and commanded the honor guard at the funeral of Emperor Franz Josef of Austria. Dittl came to the United States in 1923. In New York City he married Violet Schmidt, who had come from Austria in 1922.

In 1969 this beautiful lodge was taken over by Fred and Violet's son, Alfred, and his wife, Beverly, who were married in St. Anthony's Church in Inlet. They, with their four sons, the two youngest being twins, operate Idlewood today.

Alfred Dittl believes an old house on their property may be up to 150 years old. With the original bark on the log siding, beautiful very narrow wainscot ceiling and large windows which appear to be modern picture windows but are not, it is unique. According to Dittl, "About 30 years ago an old man came to our place and asked my mother if he could look inside the old house. My mother took him inside, and with tears in his eyes he said to her, 'I am now 84 years old and I was born in this house which was an old house then.'" If old houses in this area could talk, what stories they would be able to tell!

The Cliff House

Briefly told, the land transactions of The Cliff House are thus recorded: September 16, 1905, James Bellinger of Little Falls, sold to Alice E. Lee of Buffalo, for $250 all of lot 131 of the David Wood survey on Fourth Lake of the Fulton Chain of Lakes in Township 8. Then on January 20, 1906 Alice E. Lee sold one-fourth of the above described lot 131 to Delia M. Lee.

Here enters an interesting historical land transaction. March 21, 1906 J. Pierpont Morgan and his wife, Frances J. Morgan of New York City sold to Delia M. Lee of Buffalo, lot 132 of Brown Tract,

Township 8 in the Town of Inlet. This lot joined on the east the lot 131 purchased earlier from Bellinger by Alice E. Lee. Research has not revealed why J. P. Morgan owned this lot, or whether he had a building on it. But J. P. Morgan did once own land in the Eagle Bay area, and that land became a part of The Cliff House.

There were other transactions between Alice Lee and her brother Frank and his wife Delia. They deeded land to the State of New York for Highway 28. On December 20, 1915, Alice Lee acquired both lots 131 and 132 from Delia Lee.

Hoagland Purchases The Cliff House

Claude Hoagland had his own dance band in the Hotel Pennsylvania of New York City. He came to Inlet in the late 1930's to present an outdoor concert and fell in love with Fourth Lake. He returned shortly thereafter and bought The Cliff House from Alice Lee, who sometime after 1915 had married a Mr. Wagner. There were some parts of the original lots withheld from the total, since these parts had been previously conveyed to George D. Owens and to the Eagle Bay-Sixth Lake highway.

Alice Lee Wagner had run The Cliff House on the same high standards of food and entertainment as had all of the larger hotels in the area. Claude Hoagland added a bit of New York City zest to his operation. An advertising pamphlet issued by Hoagland gives a description of the hotel:

> The Cliff House is located in the heart of the Adirondacks, the story of which is an alluring saga of mystic waterways, and intriguing tales of forests and mountains. The Cliff House and Cottages are set in a grove of pines on the north shore of Fourth Lake, the magnificent expanse of shimmering blue water of the largest of the Fulton Chain. From The Cliff House windows, verandas and grounds — east, south or west — Fourth Lake forms an enticing foreground forever changing, ever alluring views. There are sunrises, sunsets, clouds, and moonlight with the majestic Adirondacks as a background.

The Cliff House accommodated 100 guests and was operated on the American Plan. In the late 1950's Claude Hoagland sold The Cliff House in parcels to several different buyers.

The last issue of the *Adirondack Eagle* was published September 5, 1925: (The *Eagle* was revived for the summer of 1930.)

> This is the last issue of *The Adirondack Eagle*. As the publishers move to Florida and our sales season draws to a close on September 21st we discontinue its publication.
> To the hotels on Fourth Lake which have so courteously furnished us with news we extend our thanks. We trust that in

some measure we have helped in the prosperity which they have enjoyed and which prosperity by their service and comprehension of the needs of guests they have so highly deserved.

As a slight token of our appreciation we list below the Hotels which have made the publication of *The Adirondack Eagle* possible. It is our hope that they may long continue to enjoy their present popularity.

The Araho	Camp Mohawk
The Arrowhead	Iroquois Lodge
Becker's Camp	The Kenmore
Brush's Camps	The Ledgedale
Burnap's Camp	Mingo Lodge
Camp Fulton	Minnowbrook Lodge
Camp Le Bon Air	Mountain View Camps
Camp Monroe	The New Neodak
The Cliff House	The Pontiac
The Cohassett	The Ramona
Eagle Bay Hotel	Rocky Point Inn
Hart's Inn	The Wood

Ledgedale and Hart's Inn

Ledgedale and Hart's Inn were both smaller, but nevertheless popular hotels situated between Rocky Point and Eagle Bay. Detailed research has not been made on these two hotels, which are now privately owned estates.

Hart's Inn was sold partially to Paownyc and partially to Albedor at the time Colonel Simmons purchased and built his palatial summer home.

Ledgedale has been in private ownership for some time, although it operated for some years after Hart's Inn.

The Ledgedale
Weller's Adirondack Eagle
July 18, 1925

Justly considered one of the most beautiful Hotels on Fourth Lake, The Ledgedale makes an appeal that is unique.

The Hotel is built upon an immense ledge overlooking Fourth Lake and before the guest is spread a view that once seen will never be forgotten. The lower portion of this superb Hotel is built of massive stone — the immense living room is of stone — the ceiling of rafters made from forest giants. This room is furnished with the most inviting wicker and reed chairs. On one porch are chairs hollowed from solid logs. Adjoining the Hotel is a large dance hall where guests nightly enjoy themselves.

The trees surrounding this Hotel are forest giants. Noteworthy is a mammoth birch tree 300 years old.

Hart's Inn Information Bureau
From the Weller's Adirondack Eagle
July 18, 1925

The Information Bureau on State Road near the entrance to Hart's Inn is proving more popular than last season. At this early date dozens of tourists driving thru the Adirondacks or to their destination somewhere in the Adirondack Park, stop and ask "Julius" — He Knows — directions for travel, road conditions, time of ferry departures, and many other questions that worry travelers.

The name "Hart's Inn" was especially appropriate during June. Several happy honeymooning couples spent their first week of married life here during the past few weeks. Principal among these were Mr. and Mrs. L. G. Hart of Brooklyn, N.Y.

The last few days of warm weather have made tennis, canoeing and swimming especially popular, and the number of boats and canoes on the water in front of Hart's Inn is increasing daily.

CHAPTER V

Rental Housekeeping Camps and Cottages in Eagle Bay Area

After World War II there was a decided change in the summer vacationers. Many of them stayed only over night and then went on their way to see more of the mountains. Some came wanting to stay a week or more, do their own cooking and vacation without the regimentation of a hotel program. In order to meet the demands of this new breed of vacationer, many hotels converted to housekeeping cottages, or some owners built housekeeping cottages on unbroken sites. This proved a profitable innovation, especially since the beginning of snowmobiling and other recreational sports.

Alexander's Lakeside Cottages

Alexander's Lakeside Cottages afford an impressive view of Fourth Lake. Special features of this view are the ever changing shades and colors of water, the trees and the beautiful rim of Adirondack Mountains.

The Alexander property joins The Kenmore property on the south. As in all of this area of Fourth Lake, their property has an historical background. Christ and Jo Alexander know that the oldest house was built in 1900 and is the one in which Kurt and Anna Dickow resided in summers during their ownership of the land from 1939 until the late 1960's or perhaps later. The Dickows' winter home was in Auburn.

The property was inherited by the Dickows' son Fred, who sold the land and buildings to Ray and Sally Edwards in the mid-seventies. In November 1979 Edwards sold the property to the Alexanders who have since done extensive remodeling on the cottage property.

Lakeside cottage, the original home built in 1900, perhaps by Sheppard, contains a beautiful, typical Adirondack stone fireplace and has been completely winterized. The porch has been replaced. The former ice house was converted into a delightful small cottage, as was the pump house which is named Cozy Cabin. An enclosed sun porch was added to each of these cottages.

This house on the Alexander property is about 100 years old. Perhaps built by Sheppard who according to an old map once owned the land. It was the Dickow home. Credit The Alexanders.

Formerly an icehouse this old building has been converted into a charming cottage. Credit The Alexanders.

The above pictures have hung on walls of the Kane home for years. Though not labeled, authorities believe the top picture is that of the Alonzo Wood hotel, and the lower one his boathouse. Note canoe and men with pack baskets — a typical scene of the way things were at Alonzo Wood's. Credit The Kanes.

The Alexanders maintain a winter home in Whitesboro, where Christ is principal of Whitesboro Junior High School and Jo, an instructor at Mohawk Valley Community College.

As with most cottage colonies of the 70's and 80's the Alexanders run a family operation. With their son and daughter, John and Kiki, they have their cottages open all year 'round, thus taking advantage of the snowmobile tourism.

Alonzo Wood Hotel Property Becomes Torokan

When Tom and Rose Kane bought their historical bit of God's Country, in 1961 they were not fully aware of the history of the old place. Area historians Joseph Grady and David Beetle, both said that Alonzo Wood, of the early Raquette Lake Woods, and his wife, a daughter of famous Otis Arnold, built the first hotel on Fourth Lake "that you could get taken care of in any sort of 'style.'" Theirs was "a full-fledged hotel," and the Woods introduced the long popular fishing and hunting sort of camp. It might be said that the Alonzo Woods were the innovators of the competitive hotel entertainment that took over from the 1890's until the 1980's.

According to the Kanes' records, the Alonzo Wood residence was sold in 1911, to Harney and Sperry for taxes due of $15.95. The sale was described as "E ½, Lot 164, John Brown's Tract, Town of Webb, Herkimer County." The land was "redeemed December 18, 1916 by Fred Powers." Powers sold lot 164 to Tarbells and built the home in which the Kanes now live. In turn some years later Tarbells sold lot 164 to Frank Robak who in 1971 sold it to Tom and Rose Kane.

This purchase of the Kanes was added to one made ten years before in 1961 of lot 165 from Ferdinand and Helen Huber, who had acquired it from Fred Powers in about 1944. Powers, it should be noted, was a residential builder, his mark being fine workmanship.

Another historic note added to the Kane property is told by Mrs. Kane: "We were told that the large building on the back of the property was used as a carriage house in the early years for South Shore residents." It seems, before the South Shore road was built, South Shore people would leave their horses and conveyances at Wood's place and row across the lake or go by steamer. Over the years, the old carriage house has been converted into two cottages which are now used as rental property.

The Alonzo Wood property was the site of the building and the launching of the *Clearwater* in 1900. This steamer was built on the Wood property because in all the area there was not another clearing so large as the one which Lon Wood owned.

Tom and Rose Kane love their spot in the Adirondacks and come each summer from their winter home in Katonah to their rental holdings here. They have seven children who join them from time to time. Torokan is a five cottage colony with a clientele that comes regularly to enjoy the magnificent view and the pleasures afforded by the location where once stood the Alonzo Wood Hotel.

Grandma Alonzo Wood
By Freda Westfall

My mother, Mrs. Fred Becker, was a close friend of Mrs. Alonzo Wood or Grandma Wood as she was called and when I was a small child my mother used to put on her snowshoes and take me in a pack basket and visit first Grandma Wood at Wood's Camp near the Mohawk and then down to her daughter's home, Mrs. Milo Bull (Millie Wood) at Fairview Lodge. My clearest recollection of them is the great big molasses and sugar cookies with three big raisins in the center that they used to give me.

Grandma Wood was a very tanned, short haired, rugged, outdoors woman. In winter she wore a man's long black overcoat and heavy work boots.

The Woods were great hunters and fishermen and Bubb's Lake was named by them for Mrs. Wood's brother.

The Turner Camps 1914–1981

Alexander Adams and Ina Brush Turner bought eight acres of land from Isaac Turner (no relation) in 1914. Isaac Turner had previously purchased this property from Leo Alexander. This eight-acre tract extends from the shores of Fourth Lake to the State of New York Conservation property line across Route 28. In the beginning the plot was called "Camp Woodland." There was a ten-room house on the waterfront called "Tumble Inn." The Turners ran the large house as a boarding house for several years.

In 1923 fifty feet of waterfront, two hundred-seven feet in depth, was sold to Dr. F. Carr, whose family still owns the land on which is their cottage called "Sha-wan-da-see." In the early 1920's the Al Turners began building cottages, and by 1950 there was a cottage colony of eight houses. The original house was destroyed by fire in December 1941.

Because of advancing age and failing health, Al and Ina Turner transferred the property to Al's younger brother, Edwin W. Turner and his wife, Thekla A. in October of 1958. The Edwin

Turners still own the property. Edwin Turner began coming to the Turner Camps when he was 13 and in 1922 he began running a passenger launch, *The Labelle,* on the Fulton Chain. From this venture he earned enough money for his college education.

During the years modern conveniences have been added. Each housekeeping cottage now has gas heat and electric refrigeration. In 1961 a mobile home was added to the colony, and in 1964 an A-frame house was built for the Turner's son, Carroll. Although the Al Turners no longer owned Turner Camps, they continued to live on the place until January 1973, when their house burned. At this time they retired to the Masonic Home in Utica. Al Turner had been a member of the Masonic Northwoods Lodge in Old Forge for fifty years. He passed away in 1974 at the age of 89. His wife continued living in the Masonic Home.

A new home for the Edwin Turners was built on the Turner Camp property in 1976 making ten separate housekeeping units at Turner Camps. A section of the property on the northwest corner of Route 28 was sold in the 1920's to Arthur Southard. Here Southard built a restaurant which he and Emma, his wife, ran for several years. Then it passed through the hands of various owners and is presently known as The Lanterns Restaurant.

The entrance to the Turner Camps is between The Lanterns Restaurant and the Country Lane Gift Shop. A black top driveway runs from Route 28 to the Fourth Lake shoreline of the Camps. Families enjoy the fine beach and the docking privileges for their boats. A campfire once each week is enjoyed by the campers, especially by the children who roast marshmallows around the fire.

For 68 years this business has been owned and operated by the Turner family. The Edwin Turners say they hope it continues as a family business for many more years.

Palmer Point

The property known as Palmer Point was purchased in 1898 by Milo E. Bull from William Seward Webb and Elizabeth Osgood Webb, his wife. The price for one thousand feet of frontage on Fourth Lake reaching back to the state lands (or approximately Route 28) was $400.

In 1901 Milo Bull sold four hundred feet (lots 173 and 174) to David B. Eckler at $1.50 per front foot. Mr. Eckler sold the same in 1915 to Elizabeth M. Brush and her husband, Melvin A. Brush.

Mr. Brush filled the lower land toward the lake, using a pair of tracks from the higher ground to the lower. He raised the banks of the outlet stream from Surprise Pond near the present Route 28 (between Becker's and the Brush property). At the mouth of the stream, entering Fourth Lake, he built a substantial pair of docks extending to a depth sufficient for larger boats. In the boat-canal and boathouse he berthed his *U-Go-I-Go* twenty-five passenger boat, which had the first internal combustion motor on the Fulton Chain. He met the stagecoach and, later, the train from Thendara at the Old Forge dock, then carried the passengers to Eagle Bay. There they boarded the Raquette Lake Railroad train with connections on the Raquette River, the Marion River Carry Railway enroute to Blue Mountain Lake. Thus people left New York City on an evening pullman, arrived at Thendara the next morning, lunched at the Prospect House at Blue Mountain Lake, returned to their pullman at Thendara, and were back in New York next morning — just one day away from the city.

Meanwhile the Brushes built their main camp, and seven cottages, which Mrs. Brush and her faithful maid, Louise, operated for twenty-five years. Among the many unusual tools left by Mr. Brush was a "level" sixteen feet long for leveling the "other side" of a foundation. (It was a small hose fastened to a pole with an upright glass tube, showing the water level, at both ends.)

When Mr. Brush passed away in the late 1930's, he left word that he wanted his ashes scattered over the waters of his beloved Fourth Lake. The following week, the Town of Webb Board ordered that no more ashes were to be scattered on the Fulton Chain.

In 1941, the Rev. Stephen and Katherine Palmer purchased the Brush property, with its ideal sand beach, for their summer holidays, with their sons, Stephen Jr., 17, Robert, 15 and David, 11. They had not planned to go into the "cottage" business, but former tenants kept coming back, bringing their friends, filling the camps each year. One day, following the purchase, the Rev. and Mrs. Palmer returned from the store to find a large paper sign *Palmer Point* at the roadside. The boys had chosen the name and so it was to be!

In the winter the ice house was filled with ice from the lake for the refrigerators in the cottages. The boys' first task each morning was to "ice" the refrigerators, bring wood for each Ben Franklin Stove, and kerosene for the water heaters. The ice house became the "study" and with its picture window toward the lake became a favorite "camp." Refrigeration is electric. Heating and water heaters are now automatic L.P. gas.

One day David asked his mother if he could rent her rowboat. With the two dollars he earned, he bought a decrepit boat, rebuilt it, painted and fitted it, and rented it out to begin his fleet and marina which grew to eighty boats, from ski boats and large sail boats to fishing boats, Sun-fish sail boats and canoes. As the years passed, he interested other sailors in a weekly sail boat race. This led to the formation of the Central Adirondack Sailing Association which, in summer, holds an exciting regatta each Saturday.

With the boys away and in their chosen professions, Stephen Jr. in the U.S. Department of State, Robert in the Christian ministry, and David teaching, Dr. and Mrs. Palmer considered selling the camp. Immediately word came from their sons in three parts of the world: "Don't sell the camp; it's our real home base." So the deed now carries David's name and he comes from teaching each year to his beloved boats and cottages.

Dr. and Mrs. Palmer traveled widely on each of the world's continents. Mrs. Palmer died of a heart attack on a freighter in the Indian Ocean in 1976 and was buried at sea.

Dr. Palmer has since married Helen Whiley, whose husband had died of a heart attack after they had spent 28 years in mission service in Cameroun, Africa.

McKees Evergreen Lodges

The McKees Evergreen Lodges are unique in Eagle Bay Park in that it has developed from one residence into a cottage colony. In 1936 Clark McKee purchased from Howard Weller two and one-half lots with a house which is now known as Log Lodge. This house, built by Alfred Nelson, is located on the corner of West and Lakeview Avenue.

Weller and his wife, Florence, had intended using this house for their home, but decided to sell it to McKee. No electrical work had been installed, and the house was unfurnished, since it had never been occupied. Weller gave McKee the option of buying the Eagle Bay Park tennis courts adjoining the property if the courts ever proved a nuisance to the family. About 1938 after some disagreement with the Park Association, Mr. Weller insisted that McKee buy the tennis court, and made such an attractive offer that McKee purchased the property.

After Clark McKee married the present Mrs. McKee in 1945, many of their friends wanted to rent Log Lodge. Since the McKees were spending the entire summers in Eagle Bay at this time, they decided to build another house, for rental purposes, on the sizeable land which they now had, and, in 1950, Charles Parker built the cottage now known as "The Chip." In 1951 the McKees purchased two lots opposite Log Lodge from Francis K. Remington, a Rochester attorney and son of Judge Remington, an owner of one of the first summer homes in Eagle Bay Park. They later sold these lots to Stanley Stever of Honeoye Falls. On the back of the lots Stever built a beautiful lodge which, after his death, became the property of Marion Ruby of Rochester.

In 1956 the McKees bought about three acres of land adjoining their property from Mrs. Grace Hudson, on which they added three other lodges. The entire estate was called "McKees Evergreen Lodges." Four of the five houses were winterized for year-round business. Also, their own complete water system was installed. This was primarily a project to provide Clark McKee with an interest for leisure time after retirement.

Following his death in 1979, the property was subdivided by Mrs. McKee. The Log Lodge is now owned by D. C. McLoughlin, Rome; The Chip by M. K. Birnie, also of Rome, and The Hemlock by G. Wright, Spencerport.

Sylvanshor — The Harold Hudson's Cottage Colony at Eagle Bay

A charming, secluded development at Eagle Bay is the Sylvanshor cottage colony developed over several years by Mr. Harold Hudson, an executive of Eastman Kodak Company of Rochester.

Betty Nelson Spencer obtained the following information from Mrs. Harold Hudson. Mrs. Hudson says Harold Hudson, her husband, and her father, John Rathke, bought the first lot at Sylvanshor in 1924 from Mr. McDougal. She didn't know Mr. McDougal's first name, but apparently he was from Florida and bought up land in Eagle Bay Park for speculation. She said the actual sale of the land was handled through H. C. Weller. In 1944, Hudson bought thirty more acres and subsequently built the other five cottages. Alfred Nelson did most of the work on cottage number 2, but the rest of the building was done by Mr. Hudson, co-workers at Kodak, and the youth group from North Presbyterian Church in Rochester. In addition to hard work, they always had a lot of fun, and there was always a lot of horseplay. The six cottages in the cottage colony have now been deeded to Hudson's two sons, Donald and Robert, who live in Rochester. Mrs. Hudson has life use of the cottage in which she and the family spend their summers.

In the late 30's and early 40's the Hudson boys were popular members of the young summer crowd in Eagle Bay. When World War II came along, Donald and Robert went off to war and made outstanding records for themselves and their country. Mr. and Mrs. Hudson were for years leading citizens of the summer population at Eagle Bay. After Mr. Hudson's death, Mrs. Hudson returned each summer to her beloved colony at Sylvanshor. She continues to come, but has turned the business over to Don and Bob.

Main house (original) Turner camps, Fourth Lake. Credit The Turners.

Edwin W. and Thelka A. Turner, owners and managers — Turner Camps 1980. Credit The Turners.

The open camp popular with hotel guests for open fires and outdoor picnics. This camp was moved from Becker's to Turner Camps. Credit The Turners.

Kathy McKee and her horse Jamie, a crossbreed and 30 years old. Buggy of 1890 vintage. Picture by Michelle Kopp de Camp.

McKee's home "Log Lodge" in their cottage colony "Evergreen Lodges" 1933. Credit Kathy McKee.

Camp Meeker built by Jonathan Meeker about 1894. Credit Ledgers.

Camp Meeker boat landing. Credit Ledgers.

Mingo Lodge — side view showing addition to left half of building in about 1921 when it became The Mingo. Credit Lois Burke.

Howard Cottages and Eagle Point Camps

Two of the oldest cottage colonies in the Eagle Bay area were The Howard Cottages in Lone Pine built by Remington Howard and later owned by his wife. Mrs. Howard sold the cottages to Neal Ottaway in 1949. They were demolished and new cottages for private homes built on the grounds.

The second group were the cottages long known as Eagle Point Camps. The land on Eagle Point was first purchased by Thistlethwaite from William S. Webb. After Thistlethwaite the Eagle Point land was owned by Guinand and Barrett until Weller bought it and subdivided the lots. In 1923 Weller sold lots 338 and 339 to Frank W. Huntley, who built the Eagle Point Camps on these lots. For some years Huntley owned and operated these Camps.

After Huntley there was a series of ownership until James Lawrence Turner of Central Square bought the Eagle Point Camps and dismantled some of them. On October 29, 1974, Turner sold the large two-story red camp, which is built right on the water's edge, to Warren V. Blasland of Liverpool and his son, Warren V. Blasland, Jr. of Clay.

This red camp was sold as two separate houses, upstairs-downstairs sort of condominiums which are shared by the Blaslands, father and son. The Blaslands brought life to the large old red house with new paint and other work needed to make it attractive and liveable.

Shortly after this in the fall of 1979, Howard Hart from New Jersey bought the two cottages on the lake front from James Lawrence Turner. They were remodeled, repainted and made into attractive two-story cottages. These two cottages are used as rental places except when the owner is in residence.

The Albert Evans property, formerly the Rosamond and Edward Lindsey home, was bought first by Edward J. McDonald, August 30, 1923. McDonald probably built the small camp which is incorporated in the Evans remodeled home. McDonald owned the place until July 12, 1927. After that there was a succession of ownership and mortgage holders until January 1947, when it came into the ownership of the Edward J. Lindsey family.

Albert Evans bought the property in 1977 and did extensive improvement and remodeling. This completes the tracing of the lots subdivided by Howard Weller (lots 337, 338 and 339) in 1922.

Meeker and Grant Property Become Ledger's Housekeeping Cottages

Harriet Meeker bought Fourth Lake lake front property from William S. Webb on August 10, 1894. According to historians, Jonathan Meeker built the hotel about this time. The name, *Camp Meeker,* survived for many years.

Housekeeping Camps and Cottages 101

Harriet Meeker owned and ran Camp Meeker until April 24, 1918, when she was joined in ownership by the Meeker's daughter, Ida Pfendler. Mrs. Pfender, who became Ida Peterson in January 1927, is listed as co-owner of Camp Meeker with her mother until December 1946.

May 1, 1947 Ida Peterson sold Camp Meeker to Victor and Gerda Carlson. April 27, 1961 the Carlsons sold the Meeker property to Gordon and Ruth Deagman, who in turn sold to Daniel and Eileen Zymoski, December 5, 1972.

Also in 1894 in November, Dwight Grant, of the famed team of Dwight and Louis Grant (father and son), guide boat builders from Boonville, acquired lake front property south of the Meeker land. Louis built a house in 1895, and took over the property from 1905 until 1921. In the succeeding years the property was obtained by Arthur and Emma Southard, who added some cottages to the land.

In 1967 the Southards sold to Terry and Eleanor Ledger, and they added to their property by acquiring Camp Meeker from Zymoski in October of 1980. This combination of two historic properties became Ledger's Housekeeping Cottages.

The Ledgers have changed the main house extensively. To each side of the main building, large wings were added, and a large central fireplace was built. On April 4, 1979 while removing the wall between the living room and the porch, Ledger found an old block of wood on which is written: "House built in 1895 — Two verandas added to the living room in 1926." There exists on this property an old concrete ramp and iron rails used in the Grant boat industry. Some of the Grant's guide boats were built in the Ledger's boathouse.

The Ledgers built a new and larger dock and the boathouse was enlarged for the benefit of their summer guests. The cottages are rented in the summer only, but they and their five children live year 'round in the main building.

Terry Ledger is a contractor, builder in the area, and Eleanor works in real estate sales for a local real estate company. Their Cottage Colony is a family business. Their five children help with the cottages and with the maintenance of the property.

Arthur Southard, a lover of trees, was careful to teach the Ledgers the art of trimming, pruning and caring for their trees. They follow Art's instructions to the letter.

Since the old Meeker Hotel had burned before the Ledgers bought the property the grounds were groomed into a large lawn. Walking over the grounds one can sense the spirit of old Jonathan Meeker of *Hunter* fame, and of the enterprising Dwight Grant and his son who gave so much of their ingenuity to Adirondack Boat building.

Mingo Lodge

Among the historic spots on Fourth Lake of the Eagle Bay area the Mingo Lodge enjoys a commanding view. In the beginning this lodge was not a hotel, but a private residence passed on by a number of owners, according to an old map of the Eagle Bay area of Fourth Lake.

The tax research shows the land being acquired by a series of owners and evidently used as private residences until part of the land was purchased by Ceceilia O. Wilcox in 1921. In the early twenties Mrs. Wilcox and her nephew, Raymond Spring, built an addition on the side of the original building.

Mrs. Wilcox deeded the property to Spring in early 1942 and Raymond and Sophie Spring operated the Mingo as a hotel and cottages on the American plan until October 1971, when they sold it to Norman Hannah. During the Hannah ownership most of the cottages were sold off.

In 1976 F. Kenneth and Lois W. Burke bought the property of the original Mingo Lodge and two of the cottages which they operated as rental cottages with no meals. The Burkes are doing some remodeling and winterizing of the original house in which they live. Mr. Burke bought the property as a retirement investment. He continues to work in Rochester and returns to Mingo on weekends to join Lois, who in her husband's absence during the week is a secretary for a real estate company in Old Forge.

The Original Fairview

Milo Bull married Millie Wood, a daughter of the Alonzo Wood. They bought lake frontage on which they built the original Fairview Lodge. Millie became the third generation of the Otis Arnold family to entertain visitors as a hotel owner, since her mother was a daughter of the well known Otis Arnolds.

The Bull property was just south of what became The Mingo, which at the time was owned by several private owners, including a Mr. Becker, an uncle of Freda Becker Westfall. Becker had at that time at least two large lake front tracts. The original Fairview property has in later years been conveyed to several different owners. Richard and Beverly Speach own some of the highway 28 frontage which in 1981 was known as Mountain Side Lodge. The Speaches operate a restaurant-motel business. In years past this restaurant business has housed many types of tourist accommodations.

Pehaps the most interesting historical note other than the original ownership is that Fairview was from 1900 until 1933 a flag station on the Raquette Lake Railroad.

CHAPTER VI

Growth of Eagle Bay Business

E. U. Smith

In the 1920's Jessie Liddle, the young woman who worked in the general store, sometimes sat on the seat at the plate glass window facing East Avenue and watched the "Eagle Bay world" go by. Though this was one of her favorite pleasures, she didn't have much time for people-watching through the window, as she and the proprietor, E. U. Smith, spent long hours serving their customers — residents of the thriving little community and the many visitors.

E. U. Smith in later years was considered a local institution, a reliable merchant. Those were the days when storekeepers really served their customers, using "one of those gizmos for taking things off high shelves," a reminiscing village resident recalls. Besides his business ability, he had considerable musical talent, which he used for the enjoyment of area residents. He organized and conducted the Old Forge Band.

Smith came to the area from Honeoye Falls after his wife had spent three summers at Burnap's camp for the benefit of her health. He first bought a house in Old Forge, then decided to move to Eagle Bay where the only stable and on-going businesses were the hotel and railway station.

Seeing the little community's need for a store, he purchased property from Fred Yonkey, including a small building on the main road near East Avenue, which served as his store and the first year-round post office in Eagle Bay. Smith's application was filed with the Postmaster General April 29, 1919, and postal service in the store began the same year. Miss Little assisted with the postal duties.

Smith's business prospered and in 1920 he had a new building constructed by John Petersen. By 1925 business was better than ever, according to the August and September issues of *The Adirondack Eagle*. A summer storm caused a temporary slump and the *Eagle* article noted Smith's observations on the connection between weather and business:

> As soon as the sun shines fifteen minutes, the trails are dry, wild life out, all nature revived, and humans forget the unpleasant days and join with nature in general rejoicing. Happy and contented people are good spenders.

Smith and his helper served a lot of those "good spenders" in his store, called the Adirondack Art Shop and General Store, which carried "every delicacy of the season — cantaloupes, watermelons, fruits and vegetables."

Meanwhile, the in-store post office also was doing a booming business and Smith used the mail volume as an indicator of coming activity. So much mail was handled in the summer of 1925 that he confidently, and accurately, predicted that the hunting season would be "one great bombardment" by visitors.

The popular businessman has remained in the memories of Eagle Bay residents. One of these is Betty Nelson Spencer, who recalls visits to the store in her childhood. She remembers the post office in the front corner of the building and the cash-out counter toward the back. She notes that besides the window seat from which Jessie Liddle watched the passing scene, there was a big square heat register in the center of the store that became the winter seat. "I know countless pennies were swallowed up by that register," Mrs. Spencer adds.

The E. U. Smith store was sold to William McCurdy of Dolgeville in the early 30's and McCurdy operated it until 1945, when he sold it to Mary and Beryl Roach. The Roaches, who came from New Haven, New York, with their children, Robert and Patricia, operated the store as a delicatessen with groceries during their first year in Eagle Bay. In 1946 they built an addition and expanded the grocery line.

Beryl Roach became postmaster in 1947, serving for more than twenty years. His wife became post office clerk in 1952. In 1948 they added the post office wing on the east side of the building and two years later added the rear storeroom. In 1954 they joined the I.G.A. grocery chain, changing their operation to a supermarket. The entire store was remodeled in 1958. While Mary and Beryl Roach were working in the post office, their son and daughter-in-law, Robert and Ruth Roach, operated the store. Ruth later became postmaster.

Gordon and Ethel Freely bought the Smith-Roach grocery and general store in 1972 and renamed it the Friendly Market. They operated it only in the summers and in 1976 sold it to Richard and Connie Schmeer of Rochester. A family operation, it was renamed Schmeer Friendly Market. So when E. U. Smith built the general store in 1920, he was building what became a landmark in Eagle Bay.

Before E. U. Smith began operating the post office in his store in 1920, the mail was handled at summer post offices, including locations near the Cliff House and at the Eagle Bay Hotel. Wintertime service was uncertain until the railroad from Clearwater to Raquette Lake began operation, but summer service by the boats of the Fulton Navigation Company became available in the 1890's. The company, which in 1896 arranged for docking rights at the newly built Eagle Bay Hotel, operated a fleet which included, besides mail boats, vessels carrying freight and regularly scheduled passenger boats, as well as excursion boats.

An unusual mail service was the mail route which operated for many summers around the Fulton Chain of Lakes from Old Forge to Inlet on Fourth Lake and return. In the beginning, a steamer and in later years, a launch, was designated as a mail boat and made deliveries and pickups from camps and motels. Most of the mail was passed from hand to hand at the docks without the boats coming to a full stop. For several years Burt Youmans captained one of these boats.

Mail delivered in this manner was postmarked "Inlet and Old Forge R.P.O.," or Railway Post Office. Most of the postmarks included both the date and the letters TR with a number, such as TR. 4, signifying the train number. It came to be known as "the only service like it in the world" — a railway-post office run on a boat like a Rural Free Delivery route.

A deed agreement dated July 28, 1896, between William West Durant and Dwight B. Sperry, gave Durant the right to build and maintain a private wharf, a dock and a storehouse in a suitable and convenient place on Eagle Bay Hotel lots 134–137 (137 later being contested by Howard Weller and withdrawn), on Fourth Lake. The agreement covered:

> . . . the necessary approaches for his and their (Fulton Navigation Company) use and purposes in running a yacht or boat with steam power or otherwise, to and from said dock or wharf, on the Fulton Chain of Lakes together with a right-of-way and from said boathouse and dock and the highway running across said lots to Raquette Lake with teams, wagons, vehicles, loads or otherwise for his and their benefit and advantage, and his agents and representatives. (Recorded September 21, 1896, in Herkimer County)

The old Eagle Bay Hotel dock was used by steamers which plied the Fulton Chain after 1896 until the Navigation Company ended the operation in about 1926. In the early years, before the Raquette Lake Railway came through Eagle Bay, the steamers brought the mail regularly to the summer post office, which was moved to the Cliff House sometime after 1905. Mrs. Alice Lee was postmaster at that time. Available records do not show whether the office was moved back to the Eagle Bay Hotel before the year-round office was opened at the Smith Store.

The mail continued to be carried around the lakes as late as 1975. The boat crisscrossed the lakes, picking up and delivering mail first on one side and then on the other.

Beginning in 1929, the Burnaps operated the lake mail service. Their first boat was *Miss America*, with Don hired by his brother to be the operator. In 1950 Don bought a boat in Long Island and christened it *Miss USAMA* (U.S.A. Mail, pronounced "U-Sa-Me"). He ran this boat for about ten years and because it was too large for him to handle along with the mail, he hired a mail clerk. Many people were acquiring boats of their own in the 50's and so the passenger business in which Burnap engaged along with carrying the mail dwindled. He then bought a smaller boat, *Miss USAMA II*, which he operated for about ten years before acquiring an outboard. He ran this boat until 1975, when he lost his eyesight and sub-contracted for a while. The service of Don's four boats spanned a period of 46 years. Recalling his long service, Don tells this story:

> This was the only service like it in the world. In 1946 or after World War II, I got a letter from a man in Tokyo addressed 'To Captain of the Mail Boat, Only Service Like It In The World.' It came through in seven days right to the boat, which had a regular post office with RFD delivery. — The only kind of post office ever to deliver directly to a customer. It was started in 1901, I think. President Harrison was the instigator of it. When Burt Youmans piloted, it was the same type of post office.
>
> The government just didn't know what department to put this service under. First it was classified as railway mail. Then there was the problem of having to put *RFD* on this mail; so that's how it was. One time we had four mail clerks — two at a time.

Burnap said they made two runs each weekday and one on Sunday until World War II, when the Sunday trip was discontinued. Burnap left home at 6 a.m. and returned at 6:30 p.m. the route took him from Old Forge to Inlet and return. Although he often encountered heavy fog, he knew the way so well that he did not need a compass. He tried a compass only once and got lost, he recalls. After he got back on course, he found that all the fluid had leaked out of the compass, causing it to be inaccurate. After that, he always depended on his own "mental compass."

Burnap's route did not include Eagle Bay because after 1920 the community had a year-round post office. Its summer post office had been served by steamers until 1900, when train service began. Mail for Eagle Bay has been delivered by truck since the train was discontinued in 1933. The Eagle Bay post office has a star route year-round and in the summertime, two water routes — one on Twitchell Lake and the other on Big Moose Lake.

Since 1920 the following served as postmasters: E. U. Smith, in his store; Edward M. Youmans in the Youmans' building; Howard

Burkhard in the Youmans' building; Gertrude Merlau in the small corner building opposite the Friendly Market; Beryl Roach from 1947 to 1972 in his store in the former Smith building, and Ruth Roach (Mrs. Robert Roach) at the location attached to the Roach store from 1972.

The Tea Pot Dome

The Tea Pot Dome, a familiar Eagle Bay landmark, was one of the first buildings in the area with an all-steel frame. Built by Orr Liddle in the early 1920's for James Cervo, it is a structure, unusually large for a village the size of Eagle Bay. In the early days it housed Mrs. Cervo's restaurant — tea room, Brown's Movie House, and a sort of night club.

Brown's Movie House, which was in operation for many years, was popular with the young crowd in the summertime. Among the young people was Alfred Nelson, a Norwegian living in Eagle Bay. He would row across Fourth Lake to Inlet and pick up his girl friend, Frieda, a native of Germany. Despite the language barrier, he would do some courting as they rowed back across the lake to the movies at Brown's. After the show, he took her home to Inlet in his second round trip of the night. At the same time, other couples were coming in much the same manner to enjoy the movies projected on the screen by Burt Youmans, who worked the night shift in the theater as his second job.

During these years, Mrs. Cervo was busy serving her delicacies at noon and in the evenings, when music was provided for dancers. The whole enterprise was the idea of Cervo, the Eagle Bay Railway station agent.

During the early 30's, Jack Perry and Jack Kane rented The Dome, which they operated as a restaurant and dance hall.

Others who promoted entertainment in The Dome were the Kings of Utica, who ran a skating rink they called the Roller Dome, and "By" Jones, also of Utica, who ran a dance hall for teenagers. Jones's son Warren, and daughter, Shirley, were talented dancers and often enterained the customers, who paid "a dime a dance." In the late 40's, Mr. Prevost and his young wife ran a restaurant-night club for about two years. After the 40's, The Dome stood empty or had only transient tenants or owners.

In the early 60's, a band and entertainment group took over The Dome and immediately met with opposition from the village residents, who complained of noise. However, the group managed to stay on for a while. It was the last entertainment troupe to play at The Dome.

Over the years the Tea Pot Dome took on various names including LaChateau and the Half-Way House. Donald Gladwin of Utica owned the property for a time. In about 1975 Roger Dean leased

The Dome from Richard Shoemaker and remodeled its interior. Roger Dean and his wife, Betty, ran a home center from 1975 to 1978. After that the the building remained closed until being leased by the Joseph Mamoone Jr. family of Honeoye Falls, in 1980. The Mamoones, who had been coming to Old Forge as visitors for twenty years, moved there in 1977, later moving to Thendara. They gave The Dome a new name: *Mountain Emporium-Adirondack Spirits*. Their stock includes hardware, gifts, toys, cosmetics and general store merchandise, with a separate liquor store in the building.

So now the building has a different use and a different name. But no matter what it is called, to the natives it will always be The Dome.

The Old Trading Post

The Old Trading Post, long the most popular tourist attraction in the area, was operated by Frank Teich, a taxidermist who learned the skill through correspondence lessons. Stuffing animals became his obsessive hobby. He stuffed his dog and cat and preserved his horse's pelt. Later he bought stuffed animals wherever he could get them, and thus the Post came into being.

A former Wall Street brokerage clerk, Teich had set up a roadside stand and gift shop on Fourth Lake about 1915. Old-timers recall that the stand was located near the hotel which later became Northwoods Inn. The road through Eagle Bay had not yet been paved when he started his business.

The roadside businessman began to acquire other property. Deed records show that he purchased a piece of land from Howard Weller in 1925. The Teiches continued to buy land in Eagle Bay from 1925 until 1945. His mother, Catherine Teich, and his brother, Reinhold, also bought considerable land.

At the Trading Post, Frank assembled a fascinating collection of animal heads — some two thousand of them. These included Siamese twin calves, a Newfoundland hair seal, an English boar and many other animal heads that amazed tourists. From the famous Longhorn Saloon of San Antonio, Texas, Teich bought for display a head of a real Texas longhorn, with the longest set of horns known to exist.

Teich also enjoyed displaying his collection of antiques, the most valuable of which was an 1890 nickelodeon in working order. A large assortment of old post cards was also of interest to visitors. There was no admission charge but few persons left this unique museum without visiting the barroom or having a sandwich while gazing up at the unusual taxidermy display.

Teich ran a dance hall in his museum for many years, with the old nickelodeon furnishing the music. In the 1930's and 1940's, the streets were so crowded on summer nights with cars of visitors to the Trading Post that it was almost impossible to drive safely through the hamlet, and eager car parkers often overran the neighbors' lawns.

Betty Nelson Spencer in reminiscences of her childhood has this to say about the Trading Post:

> In our growing-up teen years, Dad never was the least bit concerned about our going to the Trading Post (or T.P., as we called it). Dad was a teetotaler and didn't approve of drinking for anyone, let alone his kids. But he knew there was no way anyone could sneak anything past Uncle Frank Teich and serve anything alcoholic to the Nelson kids. Peanuts and coke were our standing order, and Uncle Frank usually delivered them to our table himself.
>
> He was a good and generous man. As kids — most of our lives the only kids in Eagle Bay — we always had lots of stuff we had to peddle for church, scouts, school and other things, and Uncle Frank always bought!
>
> Before I was old enough to patronize the Trading Post, Uncle Frank used to have live bands to play for his dance hall in the summer. Hebe Traxell is one of the names that comes to mind. By the time we were teenagers, a jukebox was the source of the music. Uncle Frank always stocked a big box of long, black licorice sticks. We were allowed to go there to buy licorice ropes. In the early days there was a riding stable back of the Trading Post and Oscar Johnson had a shoe shop that stood near the Tavern.

While many did not approve the late night reveling at the T.P., no one denied that Frank Teich was good for Eagle Bay and good to its people. Tax-wise, the Teich family gave much financial support not only to Eagle Bay, but to Herkimer County and the Town of Webb. As a businessman, Frank contributed in many ways such as helping to sponsor the first fire engine. He rarely if ever attended a Park Association meeting, but when important issues were to be decided, he generously gave his rather numerous votes to a proxy who he thought would vote in the best interests of the community.

He had the good of both the community and individuals at heart and he was a good neighbor. Once in a severe wind storm the sign on a neighboring business place was blown down. The owner was awakened by the sound of hammer blows rather early in the morning and looked out to see Frank and a helper putting the downed sign back in place.

In 1969, after years of bringing tourism to Eagle Bay, Frank

E. U. Smith Building as it was when John Petersen built it. Credit Beyrl Roach.

Left to right: Not known, Lu Palmer, Smith's sister; Jesse Liddle; Smith; not known; last is Mrs. Moyer. Credit Helen Liddle.

Beryl and Mary Roach in front of their new postoffice addition to old Smith store. June 1972. Credit Mary Roach.

July 1951. Donald Burnap with his *Miss Usama No. I*. A mail and passenger boat. Don was owner-operator. He later owned *Miss Usama II*. Credit Don Burnap.

Burnap's mailboat 1952. Girls left to right: Donna, Beverly, Suzi (ballerina) Ficker. Credit Donna Holly.

Suzi on boat delivering and picking up mail, at camps along lake, between Old Forge and Inlet, N.Y. Credit Donna Holly.

Howard Burkhard — Real Estate-Insurance, Inlet, N.Y. Former Postmaster, Eagle Bay, N.Y. Credit Mary Evans.

Left Jack Perry, Right is Jack Kane, Peck's Chauffeur. These two fellows were involved in running the Tea Pot Dome. Credit Frieda Nelson.

Summer visitors in picture to left Burt Youman's buildings — to right The Teapot Dome with a new front. Credit Gloria Newton.

Frank Teich's original trading post, circa 1919. Credit Lon Snyder.

Frank Teich just came in from storing ice in his ice house. Ice was bought from village men who cut it from Fourth Lake. Credit Viola LeFevre.

Old Trading Post 1925, Frank Teich in doorway. Credit Blanche Zurl.

Old Trading Post 1930. In doorway Viola LeFevre and sons, Elton, Herbert and Wesley. Credit Blanche Zurl.

Vacationers taking advantage of Teich's riding academy. Credit Blanche Zurl.

The picture speaks for itself. Credit Viola LeFevre.

In old Trading Post behind bar — L. Frank Teich, R. Blanche Zurl. Customers not identified. Credit Blanche Zurl.

announced that he was putting the contents of The Trading Post up for auction. He had to do this because his health was failing.

On the auction days, crowds lined the streets and looked with something approaching awe at the thousands of items taken from the building to be sold. The old nickelodeon was the first to go and hundreds of other articles were snapped up quickly.

There were tears in the eyes of many people who realized what this sale was costing Frank in emotion. His animals and other oddities that he had gathered represented a life time of collecting, a fulfilling hobby.

Observers wondered afterwards why a group of history-minded residents did not come forward with an idea to preserve this building and its contents and turn it into a museum for the hamlet. But this was not to be. Two or three years later some who were new in businesses nearby exerted efforts to get the old building condemned. They succeeded and it was razed. So ended one of the most unusual tourist attractions in the Adirondacks and an end to Frank Teich's life's love and work. He passed away in 1981 after a long illness. His sister Viola Lefevre and one of her sons now reside on the Teich property.

The Floating Supermarket

The first direct food service to the inhabitants of Eagle Bay was provided by the Pickle Boat, which made trips from Old Forge around the Fulton Chain, stopping at camps and hotels. As unique a service as the mail boat, this floating grocery store was said to be the only one of its kind in the world.

Campers around Eagle Bay would meet the boat at the handiest dock and select their groceries. They would board the boat, file down one side and out the other, gathering armloads of produce and household supplies. They usually gave their orders for meats and fresh vegetables ahead of time.

It was Marks and Wilcox of Old Forge who really made the Pickle Boat an institution on Fourth Lake. Charles Wilcox, son of a Port Leyden engineer, was skipper of the boat for thirty-four years. His worst problems, he recalled in later years, were children who boarded the boat to buy a penny's worth of candy and spent so long selecting it that he often had to hurry them along as he started for his next port of call.

The Pickle Boat on Fourth Lake blew its last whistle in 1939. During the last years of the floating supermarket, area residents also were served by a grocery truck operated by the Guzzardos of Utica. They came semi-weekly or weekly with fresh vegetables, fruit, and fresh meat by order, to Eagle Bay and other points along Route 28. Even after the Guzzardo store in Eagle Bay opened in

1925, they continued peddling produce around the Park and other areas, especially to hotels and restaurants. This service was an important part of life in those days, before reliable refrigeration and modern stores.

Spencer Newton, Produce Man

Spencer Newton started work on the truck delivery route from Utica with Earl Owens. In 1927, in addition to the Marks and Wilcox Pickle Boat, Newton's boss had a boat which went around the lakes delivering fruits and vegetables. Newton went to work for C. E. Long in 1935 driving a truck from Utica to Big Moose, and then to Inlet passing through Eagle Bay twice on these trips. From the truck he delivered and sold meat, vegetables and fruit. He continued this until he went into the service during World War II.

After the war, Newton and his brother-in-law bought a truck and began a business of their own. They served hotels, restaurants, stores and private homes from Forestport to Raquette Lake including a side trip to Big Moose. In 1948 Gloria and Spencer Newton bought the old Telephone Office Building for $3,000 and began to make it into a home-store combination. Gloria ran a produce store in what later became the Newton living room. With a large supply of meat and vegetables, they served Kopp's Last Stand, Moosehead Hotel and Toboggan Inn, among others. Newton quotes some prices prevailing at the time:

Hamburg — 55¢ lb.; T-bone steak — 69¢ lb.; lettuce — 25¢ per head; tomatoes — 10¢ lb.

The Ice Supply

Another service remembered by many Park dwellers was the ice truck of Albert Urgan's. The iceman, who spoke several languages and was a decorated war veteran, had a regular schedule for his route. Residents needing ice placed a sign in the house window, turning the card so that the right-side-up message indicated whether the order was for a whole cake, a half cake or other quantity. Using tongs and pick, Urgan would bring in the ice, which had been cut from the lake in the winter and stored, and would place it in the customer's icebox.

Ice-cutting was a necessary part of the winter's work. The men shoveled snow from the ice so it would freeze harder and clearer. Then at the right time, a group worked together, hand-sawing the ice into large squares. They slid it down a trough to a sleigh, where another man would load it neatly.

Horse-drawn sleighs carried the newly cut ice to ice houses on shore. There the squares were packed in sawdust, which was good insulation, preserving the ice harvest through the summer months.

The Guzzardos' Store

The Eagle Bay business of the Guzzardos, which started out on wheels with the trucking of fresh vegetables, fruit and meat from their Utica store, turned into a local store in 1924. John Petersen constructed the Guzzardo building, with the store on the first floor and living quarters on the second floor.

Betty Nelson Spencer has this recollection:

> I can still see the store in my mind's eye, with the big bunches of bananas. The store had a porch which ran across the entire front, and this part was always full of fresh fruits and vegetables, mostly brought up each day from the Gussardos' Utica store. At night they put big screen fences across the front of the porch to preserve their wares from looters. Mr. and Mrs. Guzzardo had a large family. It seems some of the children's names were Vincent, Frank, Rose, Kathrine, Lucy, Joe and Tony.

One or more years during the depression and World War II the store was closed. After the war Joe came to the store with his wife, Hilda, and his father. After his father died, Joe and Hilda ran it for a few years in the summers only. They lived over the store and some of their children were born there.

Joe Guzzardo sold the business to Roger and Betty Dean of Syracuse in 1966. The Deans had bought a cottage in Lone Pine development near Eagle Bay in 1963 and had liked the area so well they decided to live there year-round. Betty ran the store in the summer of 1966 and they hired Virginia Ball to operate it during the following winter.

In 1967 Roger Dean retired from his job as meat buyer for the I.G.A. stores and came to Eagle Bay to take charge of the store as a full scale, year-round operation. Betty Dean recalls that there was very little winter business that year, with the first customer of the day often not appearing until noon. However, the following year brought a whole new aspect to winter business in the Adirondacks.

Betty remembers that year:

> Snowmobiling was a fast-growing new winter sport. Trails were groomed in the woods and winter business began to boom. More and more people began to come to the Adirondacks during the winters as well as in the summers. So the enterprise prospered. The business grew and space was added to the store. We lived in the apartment over the store until 1973. Then we added to our Lone Pine lake front property and winterized the building. We moved permanently to this residence. In 1974 we sold the store to Tim Hitchcock.

Under the Hitchcock management, the store name was changed to Tim's Foodland. Now a full supermarket, the store attracted customers from all around the Fulton Chain of Lakes as had Roach's Store, Guzzardos' and Dean's. Eagle Bay grocery stores have long attracted customers from Old Forge and Inlet.

The Corner Gift Shop

In the summer of 1947 John Petersen rented the corner building on the northeast corner of East Avenue. Using his skill as a craftsman, he made it into a gift shop for his wife, who named it *The Corner Gift Shop*. The specialty was a line of hand-carved birds and arrangements made by Helen Lay Strong, whose work is acclaimed nationally by the Audubon Society.

The shop attracted hotel guests from around the Fulton Chain, and the women from the Adirondack League Club created such a demand for Mrs. Strong's carving that it was difficult to keep them in stock. This was the first time her works had been put on public sale.

In the early summer of 1948 Petersen built a cottage-type building for his wife's gift shop on a point of land which he owned on the southwest corner of West Avenue and Eagle Bay highway. The name, Corner Gift Shop, was retained. Again Mrs. Strong's carvings were a specialty, along with other fine giftware and jewelry.

Salespeople during the Petersen ownership were Mrs. Pearl Burton, head salesperson; Mrs. Harry Kimmel; Mrs. Cleon Goodwin; Howard Chaney, art director in Clinton schools; Betty Nelson Spencer, and several others who contributed to the success of the business from 1948 to 1956.

After Petersen's death in 1950, his wife continued with the shop operation until her marriage to Herbert S. O'Brien in 1956. She then sold the business to Mrs. Gayle Pieper. Two years later Mrs. Pieper sold to Judge Lansing Tiffany and his wife, Mary, of Inlet. Mrs. Tiffany continued with the shop after her husband's death. After about twenty years as owner, she sold the shop to Dr. Wayne Choper in 1978.

The Lanterns Restaurant

In the late 1920's, Arthur and Emma Southard bought a piece of property facing Route 28 from Alexander and Ida Brush Turner. On this site Southard built an attractive restaurant, which in the beginning he called Twin Crow Inn.

Adjoining the restaurant the Southards built a two-story home from plans drawn by John Petersen. It was a mirror image of the two-story home which John had built for himself at the entrance to

Marks and Wilcox Pickle Boat. Credit Town of Webb Historical Society.

Spencer Newton and his grocery truck. Serving the lake region. Credit Spencer Newton.

Left Guzzardo's store 1932, built circa 1925; Harry Kimmel's gas pumps — center right: The electric sub-station. Credit Helen Liddle.

Corner Gift Shop 1948. Credit Author's collection.

Twinn Crow Inn; Blarney Stone; The Lanterns, etc. Restaurant established by Arthur Southard. Credit Standard Supply Co., Otter Lake.

Bud Kopp in his Liquor Store in Old Railway Building — Kopp's Last Stand. Credit Bud Kopp.

Eagle Bay. In the reversed plan, the rooms in the Southard house were on the opposite side from those in the Petersen house. For several years the Southards ran a successful restaurant.

Later there were changes in the name of this restaurant as it passed through the hands of several leasees and owners. It was known successively as The Blarney Stone, Halfway House and The Lanterns. Persons who have been associated with this restaurant include John Spilks, Mr. Lawless, Jim Ryan and Jerry Morgan. There was probably another owner before it was bought by Ed and Thelma Lindsey.

The Lindseys were naturals for such a business. Ed had long known the bar business, and Thelma knew all phases of the restaurant business from long experience. The Lindseys ran a thriving business at The Lanterns until Thelma died in 1976 and Ed died a few months afterwards.

Dick Lewis purchased The Lanterns from the Lindsey Estate December 1, 1977. He had worked at several of the better hotels in the area and was familiar with the restaurants and bar business. July 25, 1978, he married Christine Judson, a granddaughter of Roy Higby and daughter of William (Bill) and Patricia Higby Judson.

Earlier, Christine and her family had moved to Arizona, where she worked in some of the larger resort hotels in Scottsdale after finishing college. Lewis is a graduate of the State University College at Oswego. He is owner-bartender at the restaurant while Christine is owner-chef. Other family members involved in running The Lanterns are Dick's sister, Mary Beth Lewis, who helps in the summertime and at Thanksgiving and Christmas holidays, and Christine's sister, Sarah (Mrs. Donald Dew), of Oneida, who helps in the summer.

The Tavern

An interesting family from Ireland came to the Eagle Bay area in 1928. Dan Doran, who had established a gasoline-garage business in Utica, his two brothers, Mike and Jack, and two sisters, Eileen and Betty, had not been long from Ireland when they chose Eagle Bay as a place to establish a restaurant-bar and a gas station with certain limited automobile services. On May 28, 1928 Dan Doran purchased lot 227 on the east side of West Avenue of Eagle Bay Park from Thomas E. Howlan and his wife. According to a map accompanying the purchase, lot 227 fronted on the highway from Old Forge through Eagle Bay. On the same day Doran bought another parcel of land from the Howlans with fifty foot frontage on the State highway through Eagle Bay.

On the first parcel, the Dorans built their gasoline station and garage business which in 1950 became the Eagle Bay Volunteer Hose Fire House.

This was the first and only garage around which had a canopy in front to keep attendants and customers dry. In 1937 John Petersen built a rack for Doran on which to lift cars for grease jobs, another innovation in the area.

On the other parcel of land, Doran built The Tavern, a tidy building with an attractive bar designed and erected by Petersen. Operating Doran's Tavern in the 30's and early 40's were Harry DeMeza and Frank Hall. They were men of good taste who dressed well and conducted business efficiently. Then in 1946, Eugene H. Lauterbach and his wife, Katherine, bought The Tavern and gasoline-garage business from Doran. The Lauterbachs kept the business only three years, selling it in 1949 to Nick and Evelyn Pole from Utica. The Lauterbachs sold the garage to Eagle Bay Volunteer Hose Company in 1948. The volunteer company has continued as owners of this building and has added improvements over the years.

Evelyn and Nick Pole, in addition to the bar, ran The Tavern as a restaurant featuring "Chicken in the Ruff." The business thrived during the Pole ownership until the late '50's. Nicholas Pole deeded The Tavern to Evelyn Pole in 1960, and she sold it in 1961 to Prentice J. Wood and his wife. The Tavern was briefly owned by Gertrude Puffer Merlau and then reverted to Prentice Wood, who sold it to Richard Bock in 1971. Bock sold the business to Helen Simpson, an Old Forge native, and Gertrude Beckingham, also from Old Forge, in October, 1979. The two owners serve light lunches and legal beverages.

Although The Tavern has changed hands several times, the name has not changed. The format of the business has remained essentially the same — mostly light lunches and legal liquors.

Eagle Bay Railway Station

According to Henry A. Harter in his *The Fairy Tale Railroad*, it was not until 1901 that the railroad inspector listed the stations along the Raquette Lake Railway. The inspector says: "At Eagle Bay, which is near the head of Fourth Lake on the Fulton Chain, there is a new and convenient passenger and freight station." Other sources have said that the stations along the way were not open when the trains began runs on the line in 1900.

It seems logical to place the date of the opening of the Eagle Bay Station as 1901. The old warehouse was still standing in a fragile state in the summer of 1981. These two buildings are among the very oldest in Eagle Bay.

Tracing the history of the station of Eagle Bay, it was a participating station in all the railway's activities from 1901 until 1933. Since the spring of 1934, the building has been used as bar-restaurants. There have been many changes and renovations which are traced under the discussions of ownerships which follow, and through the series of pictures included.

The Raquette Lake Railway Station at Eagle Bay took on new life in 1934 when an enterprising young fellow named Bud Kopp strode into the village and bought the building from the Old Forge Bank.

He moved the building nearer the highway and immediately established a hot dog stand and liquor store. On a rock at the base of the Ledge property and behind the station, Bud painted a sign: "The World's Largest Hot Dog," the trade mark of his new venture.

Kopp also had a road sign put up carrying this slogan: "Remember, when you leave Eagle Bay, you are camping out." Inlet Chamber of Commerce officials were not exactly pleased with the message, so Bud accommodated them by taking down the sign. His hot dog stand prospered until World War II when he joined the armed forces.

He served thirty-eight months in the European theater as a mess sergeant and was discharged from Fort Dix in 1945. With his experience back of him, Bud came back to his liquor store and hot dog stand. He named it *Kopp's Last Stand* and at once changed the operation to a restaurant-bar business. Bud and his wife, Jane, were naturals for such a business. The public has never really known if all that good food was the result of Jane's skill or of Bud's know-how. The restaurant was one of the more popular eating places around from 1947 to 1970 under the management of the Kopps. Then Bud again branched out by buying a tract of land from Harry Kimmel and Leon Schopfer.

On this land he developed a cottage colony with a spacious home. On the development he built a swimming pool and planned to stock it with fish, but somehow he never supplied the pool with water, so finally he used it as an enclosure for pigs. Just what happened to the pigs is not recorded.

Bud has become one of the more popular builders in the area. In 1971 he built a laundermat in Eagle Bay for Jane to operate.

In 1968, Jane and Bud Kopp sold their restaurant in the converted Eagle Bay Railroad Station to John (Pat) and Chris Fogarty, who operated it as Fogarty's Tavern for eleven years. The Fogartys gave the place their own distinctive style and drew customers from a wide range of vacationers, hunters and friends. For a time it was called The Shamrock.

Joseph Whitbeck and his wife, Merle, from Syracuse, bought the building from the Fogartys in May, 1979. Immediately they closed the place for three months and began remodeling. The roofing was replaced and the lounge and kitchen were remodeled. The couple's children, Lloyd, Mandy and Russell, help with the operation of the restaurant. All have a sense of the history of the old station, which has been renamed Spike and Rail. Joseph, who formerly owned a construction business, has the know-how for upkeep of the place.

Domser's Coffee Cup

Children of the Eagle Bay area in the 1940's liked to gather on the front porch of a small building across the main highway from Guzzardo's Store. The attraction was a popcorn machine, the first in the area. Paul Domser, owner of the building which housed his small restaurant, operated the machine and dispensed the popcorn to his eager young customers.

The building, later to form the front part of Eckerson's Restaurant, was on land which Domser bought from Weller. It was operated as a small restaurant called the Coffee Cup by Mr. and Mrs. Domser for a number of years. They also sold newspapers, and during the summers had a substantial breakfast business.

The date when Domser or his daughter disposed of the business is not clear. But it passed through several owners, by lease perhaps, until January, 1967, when Ernest and Lois Eckerson bought the place from Rex and Margaret Baines of Utica. The Eckersons had been coming to their cottage in the Lone Pine area for several summers. When their son, David, decided he would like to start a broasted chicken restaurant, they took a lease on the place in 1966. Dave operated the business as Dave's Chicken Hut for three summers and Lois took it over in the summer of 1968 while David, then a college senior, went to Europe.

Lois resigned her position with E. W. Edwards of Syracuse in 1970 and the couple moved to Eagle Bay permanently. In 1971, they began a full-scale restaurant operation in the Hut, which had been enlarged two years earlier. In 1972 they renamed it Eckerson's and it soon became one of the best known eating places in the mountains. In 1980, the Eckersons sold their Lone Pine home to Bob and Jan Tanner.

John and Kathy Wright, both of whom hold associate in applied science degrees in hotel management from Paul Smith's College, purchased the restaurant from the Eckersons in 1976. The gift shop in the small building was disposed of by Lois Eckerson and the Wrights converted this room into a cocktail lounge. The 36- by 48-foot addition in 1969 became the main dining room. Operating it as a family restaurant, the Wrights have drawn diners from

The Tavern, owner 1950. Nick Pole Postcard portion.

Spike and Rail — originally Eagle Bay Station for Raquette Lake Railway. Then Kopp's Last Stand and other names in between. Credit J. Whitbeck.

A familiar winter scene in Eagle Bay. The building where Domser had his Coffee Cup — later The Hut — then Eckersons. Credit Mrs. Eckerson.

The Eckerson's Restaurant in the Heart of the Adirondacks. Credit Kathy Wright.

Still another form of winter sport and transportation — the snowmobile. Gathered at Eckerson's Restaurant. Credit Mrs. Eckerson.

Alfred Nelson built this after his lumber yard burned. Later it became Toboggan Inn. Credit Frieda Nelson.

Toboggan Inn, 1st Nelson's lumber yard. 1980 Hard Times Cafe and Saloon.

Barb's Do-Nut Shop. Barbara Wood and two daughters. Credit Mrs. Wood.

Harry Kimmel at his Harry's Super Service. Credit Helen Liddle collection.

throughout the Fulton Chain of Lakes areas and on summer evenings in peak times, long lines of patrons are on hand waiting to be seated.

An Unusual Toboggan

Prentice and Al Wood, an ambitious young couple experienced in food service, came to Eagle Bay looking for a place to establish a restaurant. Prentice Wood's grandfather, a brother of Alonzo Wood, was believed to have been the first child born in Raquette Lake. Standing vacant for several years was the two-story building which Alfred Nelson had built in his lumber yard to replace a small building that had burned in the early 30's. Prentice and Al bought the place from Nelson in 1948 and set about remodeling the place into a restaurant downstairs with living quarters on the second floor.

They named their new business *Toboggan Inn* with a toboggan replica placed across the roof of the front porch. The novel name caught on, as did Prentice and Al's good food. *The Toboggan* quickly became one of the "in" places to eat in the mountains. The salad bar was the first of its kind in the area.

In the mid 70's the Inn passed into the hands of Carl and Doris Shorey Evans. After they operated the restaurant under the *Toboggan* name and format for two years, the property returned to the ownership of Mr. and Mrs. Wood. It then stood vacant for at least two years.

Scott Thompson, an enterprising young man, bought Toboggan Inn from Prentice Wood on July 8, 1980, and renamed it Hard Times Cafe and Saloon.

Stonecutter from Sweden

In the late 1930's a stocky man with bushy hair and piercing eyes, Carl Hansen, came from Sweden to Eagle Bay. He began working for John Petersen and other area people doing mostly stone masonry.

Allen Wilcox, for whom Hansen did extensive work, said that he was one of the finest stonecutters and masons in the area. There are many places in Eagle Bay where his work serves as a monument to him. He cut the stones for the beautiful fireplace in the Indian Room, the cocktail lounge of the former Mohawk Hotel. On the same premises he cut the stones for the elaborate veranda at Mohawk Hotel, and built the steps, walk and railings at Margaret and Allen Wilcox's magnificent home.

Carl Hansen enjoyed his skilled occupation but he was a lonely man, living around folks for whom he worked. While working for Petersen, he had a room in the garage apartment. One day he asked John if he might buy a small piece of land on the south end of the Peterson three acre tract on Route 28 just at the entrance to the village. John owed Carl some wage money, not really enough to pay for the land, but they made a deal. The wage money paid the price of the land and Petersen gave Carl scraps of lumber from buildings he had erected. So Carl built himself a small liveable house, for which the Petersens contributed odds and ends of furnishings. Carl lived in this little "make-do" home for almost ten years.

The Donut Shop

Hansen sold his place to Barbara and Ernest Woods. Ernest says his grandfather was the first child born in Raquette Lake, and was a brother of Alonzo Wood. In May 1969, the Wood family began a small food business in a trailer parked in the woods alongside their home.

They did so well with the business that in 1972 they added a donut shop to their house. Then state authorities told the Woods that their addition was six feet over on the state property. They had to tear down the building and relocate the donut shop in front of their home. The business prospered. It seems Barbara's donuts, pizza, and barbecue sandwiches, along with her pies and other homebaked goodies, filled a long-felt need among summer vacationers. All of the Wood family, including Ernest, Barbara, Tammy and Bonnie, help in this small fast-food enterprise. But Barbara gives credit also to her friends and neighbors. She says, "that's what 'God's Country' is all about: Good people, helping people."

Eagle Bay Service Company, Inc.

It is believed by residents who were here at the time that the first part of Eagle Bay Service Company, a gas station, was built in about 1926, or shortly after the Eagle Bay road was paved. The original building consisted of what is now the office. Through the years as the business grew, the three bays were added. The last bay was completed and in use before 1950.

Old pictures in Helen Liddle's collection show that Phil Panella's name was on the business in 1929 and W. L. (Army) Armstrong's name was on the building in 1931. Dan Doran is believed to have operated it after Armstrong. Mr. Moore, who operated the Elk Tourist Lodge, now Mountainside Lodge, ran the Eagle Bay Service Station for some time. Marks and Wilcox of Old Forge bought the station during those years. They owned it when Harry Kimmel took it over and ran it as Harry's Super Service. At this time Frank Vogt worked for Kimmel at the Station during the summers.

Eagle Bay Service Co. Inc. Eagle Cliff and Ledge Road property is directly behind the garage. Business owned by Robert Hansen in 1981. Credit David Schultz.

Virginia Ball and daughter Sally. Ginger was once a telephone operator at Eagle Bay Exchange. Telephone building — later Spencer Newton's property circa 1942. Credit Blanche Zurl.

North Star Restaurant at Eagle Bay just across the Hamilton County Line.

Kimmel took Charles Hansen as his partner during the late 1950's. When Kimmel retired in 1965 and moved to Florida, Hansen bought the property. He ran the business himself for four years. In 1969 he took Robert Hansen as his partner and they operated the station together. After Charles Hansen died in 1972, Robert Hansen bought his share and has since owned the entire business. For a number of years it was run as an Oldsmobile and Chevrolet dealership. It is operated now as a family business with Robert Hansen as the manager; sons Ronald and Norman as mechanics, and Eleanor, Robert's wife, as bookkeeper.

The Eagle Bay Electrical Substation

The Eagle Bay Substation was built in about 1931 by the Old Forge Electric Company. The transformers were placed on the roof of the small brick building located on the northwest corner of Route 28 and the Big Moose Road. The company hired someone to stay at the building most of the time to read meters and do repair work. Electrical appliances were also sold there.

Some of the men who worked at the substation were Eugene Terwilliger, Clifford Puffer and Dominic Fredette. Harry Kimmel, who ran a service station (gas pumps only) between the substation and Guzzardo's store, no doubt worked in the substation during the time before he leased Harry's Super Service, which became Eagle Bay Service, Inc.

Youmans' Electrical and Plumbing Shop

In connection with his work as electrician and plumber, Burt Youmans established a shop where he sold all needed electrical and plumbing supplies. In addition he sold paint and other supplies helpful to maintenance of hotels and cottages. For many years Burt's bulldog companion kept watch over the shop when Burt was not on the job. When Harold and his wife, Louise, came to live in Eagle Bay in the 40's, Harold (Yock) went into business with his father. Burt also had a woodworking shop after his son Eddie had given up the post office and his little store in that area. It was in this woodworking shop that Burt made his wood bases for lamps which became so popular.

During his father's illness Yock took over the electrical and plumbing shop and continues (1981) to operate it. He and Louise have an apartment over the shop, and the other apartment over the woodworking shop they rent, as they do the garage apartment and Burt's mobile home. At his father's death, Yock became owner of the entire complex.

From many sources the author has tried to document the first store in Eagle Bay. There seems to be no documentary papers, but Louise and Yock say that the east side of their building was an icehouse at one time, while the west side, where they live, was at one time a store. Burt remodeled these buildings after he bought the property, but much of the old buildings remain in the complex. Louise and Yock have all the verification needed for the location of an old store, and an icehouse since Burt told them this, and Yock has lived there since early childhood. Who owned this original store, and what type it was has not been verified.

The Telephone Company

A telephone exchange was established in Eagle Bay before 1925. This exchange has served Eagle Bay, Big Moose and Inlet since its beginning.

Before the dial system, the girls who served as operators over the years stayed in two buildings at different locations in the Park. Usually a house mother was with them. Later they stayed in the telephone building which adjoins Burt Youman's shop and home, and in 1981, owned by Spencer and Gloria Newton.

Among people who worked in the telephone office were Hazel White, Gert Puffer Merlau, Vera Sperry, Hazel McLaughlin, Mrs. Smith, Virginia Ball Cusack, and others.

The North Star

As has been said before the Herkimer-Hamilton County lines cross through Eagle Bay a short distance north of the village.

Joe Payne, one of Inlet's well known builders, bought land near the Hamilton county line in 1950 and on this land he built a gas station with an apartment above it. The Paynes operated the station until 1970. In 1974 they sold it to Edward Doggett. Doggett operated the garage as a snowmachine-chainsaw-small equipment repair and sales shop for several years, leasing it in 1980 to Drake's Distributors for the distribution of beverages in the area; and to Cole Enterprises for auto repair and gasoline sales.

In 1950 on the same tract of land Joe Payne also built the North Star Motel just north of the gas station. He sold the motel to Mr. Vosburg in 1959. It then passed through several other ownerships and in 1981 is owned by Rocky Postiglion.

Also in the 50's Robert J. Harter of Parish, friend of Beryl Roach, bought from the Cliff House owners a small lot near the North Star Motel property on which he built the North Star Restaurant.

Harter did not own the restaurant for many years before he sold it, to Charles Fleciano, who then sold to Richard Cross. It has been sold and resold a few times since. It was last purchased on July 14,

1981 by Steven and Paula Martini who operate it by serving breakfast and light lunches.

Unique Gift and Craft Shop

There have been gift shops in Eagle Bay since E. U. Smith's sister, Lu Palmer had one in the Little Corner Building across from E. U. Smith's store. *Unique* owned by Betty and Ted Harwood is what its name implies — totally different. It is an innovation in gift shops of the area.

In a building which has served as at least two enterprises for the Harwoods, they have created a charming shop with unusual items not to be found elsewhere.

Much of Betty's merchandise is handcrafted. Some of it is totally different. From little glass Christmas trees to unusual handmade wall-hangings one can find many eye pleasing gifts at *Unique*. This little shop is the last business place on the right hand side of Route 28 south toward Old Forge.

George Delmarsh — Arch Sr.'s father. Progenitor of the clan. Credit Delmarsh collection.

Cedar Island dock and landing. Credit Arch Delmarsh III.

CHAPTER VII

Eagle Bay Area Private Estates

The development of private estates in the Eagle Bay area came several years after the Raquette Lake area developments, and were on a smaller, but no less luxurious scale. Dollar Island does not properly fall into the classification of an estate, nor does the Anderson place, although both are beautiful examples of early Adirondack architecture, Paownyc and Albedor are certainly worthy of the estate label. Their developers-owners were of the millionaire group of men who were searching for the quiet and beauty offered them by this area of God's Country. They spent their money lavishly to build that which would add beauty and harmony to what God had provided from nature. In recent years Neal Ottaway has developed the Old Yacht Club property into an estate that surpasses many older estates in natural and developmental beauty. The difference is that on much of the Ottaway development he has built rental facilities which complement his private estate.

Beautiful Cedar Island

Fred Hess, who is known by most students of Fulton Chain history as the "progenitor of Inlet's architectural development," roamed the Adirondacks for more than forty years, leaving his imprint upon much of the area. In the early 1870's Hess built a bark shanty on Cedar Island near the head of Fourth Lake and directly across the lake from Eagle Point. He built this shanty for the sake of a sick friend and when the friend recovered and returned to his home, Fred Hess stayed on. He had been permanently won to the woods.

He loved to work with hammer and nails and took pride in improving his island camp. At about the time Alonzo Wood built his hotel on the North Shore of the lake, Hess erected one on the island where he had built his shanty and called it Cedar Island House. It was one of the first resorts on Fourth Lake and was ideally situated for the boat transportation of the day. It became popular with sportsmen and attracted an excellent clientele.

Hess was a great fisherman and hunter and was prone to turn his attention to those sports rather than to running his Cedar Island House. Philo Wood was, in the early days, Hess's desk clerk. Often when he came down to his desk in the early morning he would find

Hess gone. Investigation soon disclosed that the boss was off on a hunting or fishing trip with some of his guests. The records are not clear whether Hess "lost" or sold his hotel, but by 1894 it was owned by Joseph Porter.

Joseph Porter of New Haven, Conn., a meat packer, purchased Cedar Island from Wm. Seward Webb and, in 1894, a ten-acre tract of the Fourth Lake allotment, which Webb had purchased from Adirondack Timber and Mineral Company, Ravand Hawley president, in 1891. Porter was a very business-like man and hired a manager for Cedar Island House. When he brought his family to the hotel, he paid his hotel bill just as the guests did.

According to the map of Eagle Bay area the ten-acre purchase made by Porter from Webb in 1894 included the Cedar Island right-of-way in the Eagle Point allotment.

Arch Delmarsh Number I

David H. Beetle in his book *Up Old Forge Way* tells that Arch Delmarsh at the age of 21, son of a Greig sawmill operator, "trekked 18 miles over wilderness roads to the Forge, boarded the night boat, got off at Cedar Island and hired out to Fred Hess as a teamster at $1 a day and board." This was about 1891. Delmarsh became famous as a guide and later managed the Cedar Island Hotel several years for Joseph Porter.

When Arch Delmarsh was operating Cedar Island, the hotel accommodated about one hundred persons. There were two large cottages and four smaller ones adapted to families preferring a camp by themselves. Other than the living quarters, the Cedar Island House provided an office building, billiard room, bowling alley, boathouse and a large assembly room.

Pure water from a mountain spring was piped across the lake and was the sole supply for the Island which was well wooded and comprised about three acres of land. There was a boathouse equipped with Adirondack boats, canoes and rowboats. Experienced guides were on hand at all times. An advertisement gives this information:

> The Island is only ¾ mile from the mainland at Eagle Bay so that a trip in a rowboat or in one of the frequent steamers on the lake leads to many delightful excursions to the lakes and mountains in the vicinity. Raquette Lake, Big Moose Lake and smaller lakes may be reached by half a day's trip in small boats and over short carries, and trains take day excursions to Blue Mountain Lake and the more remote places.

After Arch Delmarsh bought Rocky Point, his brother Eri ran the Cedar Island Hotel for a few years until it was sold to Otto

Berg. Then Eri went to Limekiln and ran Limekiln Inn. The Max Berg Associates operated Cedar Isles as a very successful girls' camp for a number of years.

Don Burnap's Story

Donald Burnap tells the story of the Cedar Island girls on a hike up Bald Mountain. A group of them got lost and came to Burnap's Camp. They asked him to take them back to the Island in his boat. When he landed at the Island, the girls jumped from the boat and scattered. They did not want Mrs. Berg to know they had been lost. But Burnap kept their back-packs as a guarantee of his pay. Mrs. Berg paid him six dollars for bringing the girls to the Island, and asked him to go back for the packs. When he returned she wanted to pay him only three dollars for the second trip, but Don insisted on his six dollars which she finally paid him.

Berg sold the Island to a New York company, which operated it as Camp Ten-Rab. During the depression the Ten-Rab Corporation failed. Moses Cohen of Old Forge held the mortgage and foreclosed. Dr. Longstaff bought it in 1933 from Cohen.

When the camp burned in the summer of 1934, Dr. Longstaff rebuilt it and operated it as a boys' camp until 1950. At that time he sold it to Mr. Campbell from New Jersey, who ran it for one year; then let the Island come back to Dr. Longstaff. Mr. Swan, a former counselor under Dr. Longstaff, leased it. Later it was leased to another man. Then it lay idle until Suzanne Farrell and her husband, Paul Mejia, bought it from Dr. Longstaff in 1970.

Dr. Longstaff, a dentist on Long Island during the winter months, had built, over several years, an enviable record for his skill in operating summer camps for boys and girls. Cedar Island was no exception. Every possible activity was made available to Cedar Isles campers. Their sailboating attracted much attention from residents around the head of Fourth Lake, as the colored sails of the boys' boats livened the beauty of the lake. Besides the boating, there were two stables and the riding ring located on the mainland in Eagle Bay Park and connected with many miles of riding trails.

A Ballerina Buys Cedar Island

In the summers of the 1950's a young girl, talented and destined for world acclaim often sat daydreaming on the sands of Eagle Bay Park beach. She dreamed of what it might be like to live on beautiful Cedar Island in Fourth Lake waters. While she gazed at the beauty before her, and wished that someday it might all be hers, her two sisters busied themselves with swimming and other more realistic amusements which the lovely beach offered.

The little dreamer was Suzanne Farrell, who was to become principal ballerina for New York City Ballet. Her sisters, both talented and eager for life, became noted in their own way. Donna became a ballet teacher, and later married Paul Mineker. She chose motherhood over a career and is the mother of three sons, Steven, Kenneth and Christopher. The other sister became a pianist, but also chose motherhood over a career. She is Beverly Ann (Mrs. Lyle) Leeson and has three young daughters, Laura, Kathryn and Rebecca. The Leesons' home is in Rutherford, New Jersey; the Minekers live in Camillus, but have a summer home in the Eagle Bay area near Palmer Point.

In the summers of the '50s, while their mother, Donna Holly, was busy in Cincinnati, Ohio, these girls visited their grandmother, Frances VonHolle, who owned Buckeye Abode in Eagle Bay Park on Lakeview Avenue. Donna Holly also often visited Eagle Bay during the summers.

Suzanne Farrell's dream of owning Cedar Island came true on December 4, 1970, when she and her husband, Paul Mejia, completed the purchase of the property from Dr. George Longstaff. Paul Mejia tells the story this way:

> My wife had known the Fourth Lake area since she was a little girl. I did not become familiar with the area until we were married in 1969. My first sight of Cedar Island was from the top of Rocky Mountain in 1969, at which time we also learned it was for sale. We immediately decided to buy the Island. As far as we were concerned. Cedar Island is the most beautiful place on earth. At the moment it is only a home for the summer. In 1979 we completed a beautiful dance studio on the Island. The studio is a joy to use. Even though our schedules keep us from spending much time there, we feel that even one week's stay gives us the equivalent of four weeks' vacation any other place.

Suzanne Farrell, a native of Cincinnati, Ohio, made her debut with the New York City Ballet as an apprentice dancer in "The Nutcracker." In 1961, she was invited to join the company and she began a rapid rise to prominence. In a few years she was promoted to principal dancer. Many roles have been created for her during her career with the New York City Ballet.

In 1970, Miss Farrell joined Maurice Bejart's Ballet of the 20th Century in Brussels, Belgium. Five years later, she rejoined the New York City Ballet. She has appeared many times as guest artist both in this country and abroad, and has received numerous prestigious awards.

Paul Mejia began studying ballet at the age of eleven when he entered the School of American Ballet in New York City. As a student he danced in "The Nutcracker." He joined the New York City Ballet in 1965 and in 1970, joined Maurice Bejart's Ballet of the 20th Century.

Building Preserved and Renovated

When the couple bought Cedar Island in 1970, they found that the island, after being vacant for several years, was naturally in a state of disrepair. Miss Farrell's and Mejia's artistic temperaments and their love for the island brought interesting changes. They have preserved and renovated the beautiful old stone building. It has been made into their living quarters, simply and tastefully decorated in furnishings and accessories which blend with the island environment.

Miss Farrell comes to the island whenever her schedule permits. In the newly completed dance studio, she can practice at leisure while looking out upon one of the most beautiful and restful views in all of the Adirondacks. Walkways and bridges have been built over the entire area so one may easily get from one island to the other. There are other sleeping cottages in convenient locations, and in the summers, the couple's friends visit them from time to time. Miss Farrell performs each summer in Saratoga Springs with the New York City Ballet.

The couple has an Adirondack pleasure barge and other boats for travelling back and forth to either Eagle Bay dock or to the Inlet dock. They also use the Bird Seaplane Service.

They prefer to swim and relax from their busy schedules when they are on the island. Dancing is their way of life which has left no time for hobbies.

So only three-fourths mile from Eagle Bay, surrounded by the waters of Fourth Lake, lies a spot that nature and geology have endowed with unusual beauty. This spot serves Miss Suzanne Farrell, an artistic and beautiful creation herself.

Dollar Island

The study of the geological formation of the Adirondack Mountains lends emphasis to the feeling that God favored this portion of His creation. The mountains, often triple rims of them, circling the placid blue waters of the lakes, the thousands of square miles of land covered with numerous varieties of stately trees, lush growths of ferns and wild flowers, an abundance of wildlife, and birds of many kinds all attest to the richness of nature with which this region is favored. Fourth Lake is one of the most richly endowed

Cedar Island. Credit Arch Delmarsh III.

Cedar Island, circa 1900. Credit Mary Evans collection.

Cedar Isle Boys' Camp. Boy's rifle practice. Credit George Longstaff collection.

Cedar Isle Boys' Camp. Caroline Longstaff Nelson in the boat. Credit Dr. Longstaff collection.

1952 sailboats from Cedar Isle Camp taken from "Suits-Us." Credit Donna Mineker.

1950 Boys camp on Cedar Island from boat in Fourth Lake. Credit Donna Mineker.

Suzanne Farrell's family: Mother, Donna, holding Suzanne, Donna Jr. standing, Father, holding Beverly. Credit Donna Holly.

Suzanne Farrell in her dance studio on Cedar Island. Credit Farrell/Mejia.

Suzanne enjoys a swim. Credit Farrell/Mejia.

Paul Mejia relaxing on Cedar Island. Credit Mejia collection.

Frances von Holle, in her beloved Eagle Bay Park. Credit Donna Holly.

Dollar Island House. Credit Fallis collection.

areas. An especially beautiful feature of Fourth Lake is its varied islands dotting the placid blue waters.

The Eagle Bay story is concerned with two of these — Dollar Island and Cedar Island. Both lie directly opposite Eagle Bay and have long been connected with the business life of the village. Cedar Island with its hotel, built by Fred Hess, and this business later transformed first to a camp for girls and later to one for boys, has maintained a close relationship with Eagle Bay. Docking facilities for the island boats, an Eagle Bay post office address, later a riding stable at Eagle Point, and shopping for occupants' needs have all connected Cedar Island directly with Eagle Bay. Inlet and Eagle Bay have a dual claim to Dollar and Cedar Islands. The occupants share their business with both villages. The beauty is shared by all who see them from either shore.

It seems an unlikely coincidence that Joseph Porter, a meat packer from New Haven, Connecticut, bought 10 acres of land of the Eagle Bay Allotment from Wm. Seward Webb February 19-22, 1894, with the right to use the water spring on lot 137 adjoining the Eagle Bay Hotel property, and on July 5, 1894, Dr. Edward S. Gaylord, a dentist also from New Haven, bought Dollar Island from Wm. Seward Webb with the same water rights from the spring on lot 137 — the David Wood Survey of 1893. These two men must have known each other and must have influenced each other in buying these adjacent islands. Certainly it is not coincidence that Fred Hess built the first house on each Island.

Careful research has not revealed the year in which Fred Hess built Dollar Island House. However, his framed picture has hung on the wall of the Dollar Island House living room for many years with a handwritten inscription: "FRED HESS, THE MAN WHO BUILT DOLLAR ISLAND HOUSE." Hess, who built Cedar Island House in about 1882, first occupied Cedar Island in the 1870's. Research has not revealed from whom or if he bought the Island, but other historians have said that he built Cedar Island House in the early 1880's. Neither has a record of his sale of Cedar Island been found. David Beetle, in his book *Up Old Forge Way*, simply said he "either lost or sold his hotel by 1894."

The question remains as to whether Fred Hess had built Dollar Island House before or after Dr. Gaylord purchased the island, though it was probably after the Gaylord purchase. The house is of log construction with block ends joining the logs, rather than tongue and groove construction. Cedar Island House was built first, but since it burned in 1934, Dollar Island House is the oldest of the Island buildings.

Dr. Gaylord and his wife, Harriett, were married prior to 1876. It was on August 30, 1876, that Harriet B. Gaylord in a very brief will bequeathed to her husband, Edward S. Gaylord, "all my property at the time of decease." Harriet Gaylord died February 17, 1911, according to the records of Hamilton County; so she really had sixteen summers to enjoy the beauty of Dollar Island. Dr. Gaylord continued coming to the island for several years after his wife's death. In 1915 he hired Edith Irene Smith as his nurse-housekeeper, and she remained with him until his death January 3, 1926.

In his will, dated July 17, 1925, a copy of which is filed in the Hamilton County Courthouse, Dr. Gaylord recognized the long service of Miss Smith thus:

> In recognition of faithful services of Edith Irene Smith, since 1915 as housekeeper and nurse, I give to her the sum of Ten Thousand Dollars ($10,000) and my Adirondack camp, known as Dollar Island, including entire contents; my radio set; my Brunswick phonograph with records; walnut library table; such solid silver as she desires; photograph and engravings not otherwise designated, rugs, large mirror in the parlor; also such furniture as she may select. E.S.G.

Thus it was that in 1926 Edith Smith of New Haven, Connecticut, became the owner of Dollar Island. An interesting sequence of ownership of Dollar Island is listed before 1895.

Dr. Edward S. Gaylord bought the Island from William Seward Webb July 5, 1894. He sold the Island to Paul C. Skiff September 25, 1894. Skiff sold the Island to Harriet B. Gaylord on the same day. This was perhaps a legal maneuver by Dr. Gaylord to get the property into his wife's name without making it an outright gift. In her will made in 1876, Mrs. Gaylord left all her property to Dr. Gaylord. The legal documents referred to are on file in the Hamilton County Courthouse in Lake Pleasant.

This documentation has varified that Edith Smith was the sole owner of Dollar Island from 1926 until 1960, when she sold it to Dr. Frank C. Vogt. Besides these 34 years, she of course had spent summers there as Dr. Gaylord's nurse and housekeeper from 1915, making a total of 45 years on the island. Edith Smith loved Dollar Island and braved the hazards of living alone there without electricity. The people of Eagle Bay and Inlet were aware of Miss Smith's situation and knew when she was on the island alone. Whenever she needed something, she would hang a tablecloth or sheet on a pole in her small yard to attract attention of local boaters, who always responded to her call for help.

Miss Smith was a close friend of Harry and Madeleine Clark, who ran a boat livery on the old Anderson place. She often spent her last night of the season in the area with the Clarks. When she sold the place to Dr. Frank Vogt, she told of the type of entertainment they often had on the island during the summers when Dr. Gaylord was alive. They had a rather large dock and when they had company, the doctor would get out his Brunswick phonograph and records and set it up outside. The guests would dance on the dock to the phonograph music. Another form of entertainment was for chairs to be brought out on the dock, where all would sit and listen to the numerous orchestras that played at the hotels around Fourth Lake during the summer. The orchestras' music would blend in a swirl of sweet sounds that were enjoyed by the Dollar Island listeners.

Dr. Frank Vogt, who had spent his summers in Eagle Bay Park until he began his college work which led to his M.D., bought Dollar Island from Edith Smith, September 9, 1960. In 1966, Dr. Vogt transferred Dollar Island title to his first wife, Evelyn. In the same year, the title to the Island was transferred back to Dr. Vogt, who has owned this beauty spot since.

No attempt has been made to renovate the old house into a modern show place. Vogt has added some conveniences without taking from the historic flavor of the place. He installed a six volt battery system whereby occupants can switch on electric lights whenever or wherever there might be danger in darkened areas. Refrigeration and cooking facilities are operated with propane gas. A beautiful antique wood heater still adorns the living room — a very rare heater indeed. It is assumed that the heater has been in the house since it was built. Frank and Jean Vogt are appreciative of the old house and its contents. Mrs. Vogt was excited about finding upstairs the old Brunswick phonograph mentioned in Dr. Gaylord's will. They have now found a proper needle for it and can play some of the very old records found with the machine.

In 1934, during the fire on Cedar Island, Frank Vogt was working for Captain George Dallard, who owned boats at Eagle Bay. Vogt helped Captain Dallard in the rescue of boy campers from the Island.

When helping to rescue the campers from Cedar Island during the fire, Frank Vogt saw sparks flying from Cedar Isles to Dollar Island House. As soon as possible he took his three horse power motor boat and went over to Dollar Island. He climbed onto the roof and began to smother out the sparks that were beginning to burn the cedar shingles. It was a tough task for one teen-ager, but Frank put out the last of the sparks and thus saved the beautiful old building. He had always loved Dollar Island and became a proud owner of the historic site. Dr. Vogt died December 26, 1981. His wife, Jean, still resides in their West Caldwell, New Jersey, home.

The Frank Anderson-Harry Clark Place

The Frank Anderson place, lot number 133 of the David Wood Survey, is one of the older, more romantic places in the Eagle Bay area. It was first occupied by Jonathan Meeker of steamboat *Hunter* fame. He built a shanty on the shore, and tied up his *Hunter* there at night. This was in the early 1880's. According to records, Wm. Seward Webb became owner of this small tract of land when he purchased most of Township 8 from Ravand K. Hawley.

Frank P. Anderson of Upper Montclair County, New Jersey, purchased Lot 133 from William Seward Webb and his wife, Eliza Osgood Webb, for three hundred fifty dollars, November 9, 1893.

The Anderson family was in possession of this place from 1893 until Harry Clark of Eagle Bay bought the place from Maude E. Anderson, Brooklyn, November 6, 1948. Then June 22, 1951 Harry Clarke made a deed transferring the property to himself and his wife, Madeleine. Only two names have been on lot 133 title from 1893 until 1981 — Anderson and Clark.

Edith Smith, an owner of Dollar Island, gave Madeleine Clark some bits of interesting history of the Anderson ownership and occupancy. The Andersons were piano manufacturers. They opened the camp at Eagle Bay religiously the first of July and closed it Labor Day. In the early days there was no road into the camp; so they and all they brought from Old Forge came in by steamer. Anderson knew many of the great musical performers of his time and a few of them came to Fourth Lake to visit him and his family. Miss Smith told Madeleine what wonderful times they had. They strung Japanese lanterns from the trees along the lake front for outdoor parties, often masquerades. There was always someone to play the piano. The great Caruso was a guest of the Andersons. He often sang at the parties, and could easily be heard over the lake at Eagle Bay Hotel. Miss Smith said practically the whole woods around would be filled with people from the various hotels listening to Caruso's great voice — a free concert.

Mrs. Clark said only a short time ago she discovered some of the old Japanese lanterns stored away in the boathouse. Also, she found in the house a walking stick with Frank Anderson's initials on it, and the date 1888. She says she believes the camp was built between 1884 and 1888. However, the recorded deed gives the date of the Anderson purchase from Webb as 1893.

Harry Clark first came to the Fulton Chain of Lakes area about 1914–15. He was driver for Shanahan, department store owner from Syracuse. Shanahan owned a car, but did not drive it on the mountain roads. They came up in a wagon or carriage to the camp they owned on Fifth Lake which is still standing. The roads were mostly sand with turn-outs, and the Eagle Bay-Inlet road did not go beyond Sixth Lake at that time.

Harry went to Syracuse University, where he studied engineering. Later he was associated with a New York real estate company. When he closed the New York and Syracuse offices, he came back to the Adirondacks where he met Madeleine at the Mohawk Hotel. Soon they were married and bought their first boat, *The Hacker*, custom-built by J. L. Hacker.

Before their marriage, Harry ran the *U-GO-I-GO II* for Allen Wilcox, who had bought it from Ivan Brush. Madeleine was a lover of horses, and did a lot of riding and golfing at the Mohawk Hotel. Since Harry was a natural for boats, sensitive to every engine sound, they went into the charter-sightseeing boat business. They had three boats. The last they bought, *Geraldine 5*, was the last boat built by Jack Rivet. The Clarks transformed the Anderson property into a business — a working boat yard where people docked their boats, stored them, and others rented or chartered the Clark boats for pleasure. Mrs. Clark, after Harry's death, was operating the business in the summer of 1981. She ran a riding stable in Eagle Bay for several years.

Paownyc

Gracing the shores of Fourth Lake in the Eagle Bay area is the luxurious family colony of Paownyc established in 1908 by Oliver M. Edwards of Syracuse.

According to *THE AMERICANA — BIOGRAPHIES, 1930*, Oliver Murray Edwards was an American inventor, manufacturer, merchant, poet and publisher born in Ephratah, Fulton County, in 1862. He was the son of Eleazer Wells Edwards and Amy Murray Edwards. His grandfather and father were prominent merchants in Johnstown. His father later moved to Syracuse, where he established the firm of E. W. Edwards and Sons. Daniel and Oliver Murray were partners with their father in the Syracuse firm until the latter withdrew and entered business for himself.

This branch of the Edwards family was established in America by Talmadge Edwards who with his brother Daniel came from his home near the English border of Wales before the Revolutionary War. It is family tradition that Daniel was killed in the American War for Independence. Talmadge Edwards first settled in Connecticut where he lived for a number of years before moving with his wife and son, John, to Johnstown, where he began the business of tanning and dressing leather which led to the glove industry in Johnstown. John Edwards grew to manhood there and took an active interest in Fulton County public affairs and was later elected to the United States House of Representatives in 1836. The Paownyc line of Edwards descends from John's son, Daniel, born in Johnstown. Daniel married Sally Maria Wells, whose father Eleaser Wells owned the Colonial mansion, Johnson Hall, once property of Sir William Johnson, but which now belongs to the State of New York. Their son, Eleazer Wells Edwards, became the father of Daniel M. and Oliver M. Edwards.

When Oliver M. Edwards withdrew from the E. W. Edwards and Sons mercantile business in Syracuse, he began the manufacturing of several of his inventions which led to a large enterprise.

He invented the Edwards window fixtures, metal sash for use on railway and motor cars, and the padlocks sold under the trade name of "Omeco." He held the patents on the extension platform trap doors now in worldwide use on steam and electric railroad cars. He manufactured special steel equipment for banks and public buildings, and the steel office furniture that bore his name. These various manufacturing interests were carried on by the O. M. Edwards Company, Incorporated, Syracuse, of which he was chairman of the board and in which his three sons were his partners. He was president of the Oliver Murray Edwards Realty Corporation; and the owner of the Oliver Music Company and the Revilo Press, all of Syracuse.

In addition to his numerous business interests and his continued activity as an inventor, Mr. Edwards was the author of a considerable quantity of verse, much of which was set to music by well known composers. His verses, written over a period of years for the entertainment of his family and intimate friends, were long known to the public only in such instances as they were used as songs, but he was eventually persuaded to publish a selection from his writings which appeared before the public as 'From Depths Unknown' (1928).

The Rev. Robert Hugh Morris of Philadelphia once said of O. M. Edwards:

> As for the verses themselves . . . his thoughts like his words lilt along . . If you doubt Mr. Edwards' poetic gifts, sit in the soft starlight on a July night on a veranda of his camp on Fourth Lake and hear him recite some of his verses and you'll know you've heard not only a versifier of parts, but a true poet-at-heart.

THE AMERICAN — BIOGRAPHIES noted that; "His summer home was Camp Paownyc, Eagle Bay, Fourth Lake of Fulton Chain."

Mr. Edwards was very much a family man, and when he went looking for a summer home, he was interested in finding an ideal

Dr. Edward S. Gaylord owned Dollar Island from 1894 until his death 1926. Credit Dr. Frank Vogt.

Fred Hess — Woodsman, Guide, Builder "The Man Who Built Dollar Island House." Credit Dr. Frank Vogt.

The Dollar Island Dock. Credit Author's collection.

Showing log construction of Dollar Island House. Credit the author.

Dr. Frank Vogt — owner of Dollar Island House, 1981. Credit Frank Vogt collection.

Close-up front of Dollar Island House. Note second floor log construction. Moss packed between logs. Credit Author's collection.

The old Anderson Place. Later the Harry Clark residence. Credit Author collection.

Harry Clark's boat, the *Hacker*. Credit Madeleine Clark.

Oliver M. Edwards of Paownyc. Credit Edwards collection.

Paownyc — The Edwards Estate, Fourth Lake — the main lodge and boathouse. Credit Author's collection.

place to establish a retreat, not just for his immediate family, but for the future families of his children and his grandchildren.

The first property in the Eagle Bay area bought by Edwards was the cottage and land owned by Dr. G. L. Mooney of Syracuse. Edwards named the camp Paownyc, which was the trademark of his company. The letters in Paownyc stand for the three big railroads which were his first and best customers: Pennsylvania, Ontario Western, and New York Central. The presidents of the lines were friends of his and visited at Paownyc from time to time.

To carry out his dream of a family colony, Edwards added other land to his original camp until 1917-18 the families owned 1,200 feet of lake front. Since the first purchase in 1908, Paownyc has been in the O. M. Edwards family. Most of the family who occupy the vast estate were born after Paownyc was built. As the Edwards children were married and began their families, O. M. Edwards had a home built for each new family.

The original cottage is occupied by the Harold Edwards family. This place had eight bedrooms, bath, boathouse and billiard room. The main house which is built over the boathouse has six bedrooms. It has a 50 by 50 foot living room and six boat slips. Family weddings have often been held in this large living room. The Patricia Smith-David Slater wedding was held there September 7, 1980.

When the Edwards children were growing up and even after they had their own families, they all gathered for their meals in the large dining room of the main cottage. Thus, O. M. Edwards did realize his dream of a close family complex. For dinner there were as many as fifty family members around the dining room table.

Mr. and Mrs. Evie Van Arnum of Inlet were employed by the O. M. Edwards family. Mrs. Van Arnum did the cooking for the family when they were at Paownyc in the summer. Van Arnum was caretaker and general supervisor of the estate. Van Arnum's father built the beautiful fireplace in the J. J. Edwards' home. The Van Arnums lived at Paownyc in the summer.

Supplies Shipped Daily

From Syracuse the Edwards families reached Paownyc by the Raquette Lake Railway to Eagle Bay or by steamer 12 miles through First, Second, Third and Fourth Lakes. All groceries and supplies, including beef, were shipped from Syracuse daily and either picked up at the railway station at Eagle Bay or brought to Paownyc around the Lakes by steamer. Milk for the children was brought from Syracuse each day in five-gallon containers.

In the early days on the estate there were two large boilers, two generators and a gas-making plant. Paownyc also had its own fire pump and fire connections. The water was pumped up from the lake and the drinking water was chlorinated by a chlorinating machine which remains on the estate.

Also on the grounds is the original saw with which ice was cut from the lake in the winter and stored for summer use. There was a woodworking and machine shop on the place, and the original incinerator is still on the grounds. Paownyc was a totally self-contained estate. It was run by the Edwards's Syracuse Company with Mr. Edwards at Paownyc in the summer conducting business by telephone.

O. M. Edwards was an enthusiastic boatman. The *Naiad*, which won a record as the world's fastest boat, was purchased by Edwards. He won many races on Fourth Lake with it. Eventually The *Naiad* was sold to Big Moose, probably as a fire boat.

The original boat, *Josephine*, which belonged to O. M. Edwards, Sr., is over 70 years old and is in a fine state of preservation. The *Omeco*, of the same age, was J. J. Edwards' boat, and is also in excellent condition.

Famous Visitors

Many famous people were visitors at Paownyc over the years. Among them was a close friend of Mr. Edwards, the world-renowned Billy Sunday. He and Edwards had known each other during Billy Sunday's baseball days. Edwards was not only a boating fan, he also was a baseball fan; so he and Billy Sunday spent many happy summer days together on the beautiful front porch of Paownyc's main lodge. In those quiet times Sunday would often break into his favorite song, *Over the Bar*. J. J. Jr. enjoyed the company of Billy Sunday's son, who was only three years or so older than he. Among other prominent guests were railroad presidents including Mr. Crowley, head of the New York Central. Also visiting this Edwards' hideaway was George Rankin, president of the Louisville & Southern Railroad.

Another favorite Edwards visitor was Col. E. A. Simmons, a New York publisher, who was persuaded by O. M. Edwards to build himself a place nearby. When Simmons bought the land and started the Albedor, he warned Edwards that his would be a much larger cottage than any Edwards owned, and of course it was, but Edwards had a whole colony of cottages, all occupied by his own family members. Simmons conceded he could not top that record.

Of the Edwards children who settled in the summer places were Joseph, the oldest, Harold, Oliver, Amy Childs and Louise Smith. Fine homes were no novelty to these Edwards children. In Syracuse they lived in the best homes.

Oliver M. Edwards married Josephine Reton, whose family founded the glove industry at Gloversville. The Retons were from France.

The Edwards family occupancy and ownership of Paownyc spans five generations. J. J. Edwards, Jr., the oldest grandchild, has two sons, and Oliver Edwards, Jr. has one son. J. J. Edwards, Jr. now has two very young grandsons, the first boys to be born into the Edwards family in over 20 years.

The family holdings are now incorporated. Five families are involved. There are five directors, one for each family.

O. M. Edwards passed away in 1938. Later each family head purchased his own place. Each spring the directors meet to decide what upkeep work needs to be done. While this property lies in Hamilton County, the Edwards address and main village contact is as much Eagle Bay as Inlet, so there is a dual claim to this one-of-a-kind family colony. It has spanned two World Wars, a great depression and is still thriving.

Fabulous Albedor

The fabulous estate of Albedor is an eye-pleasing part of the Eagle Bay-Inlet area. Despite County lines, the two hamlets in God's Country share the beauty of Albedor. Many stories have been written about the estate, its original owners and the sisters for whom it was named. The information in this section comes lovingly from one who shared the joys of this beautiful summer home with her sisters and parents. She is Betty Simmons Fenton. Here is her story:

> Growing up in New York City and as head of the Simmons-Boardman Publishing Company, Colonel E. A. Simmons felt the need for a home in the country for his family's summer vacations and his own relaxation. Friendship with O. M. Edwards and Mrs. Simmons' happy summers at Big Moose during her youth gave Colonel Simmons and his wife, Ida, the inspiration to choose beautiful Fourth Lake as the likely spot on which to build their summer estate.
>
> Under the architectural plans of Mrs. Simmons, construction was started in 1927 and completed in 1928. Named for their three daughters, Aline, Betty and Doris, Albedor spread over many acres and contained many buildings other than the main house: a laundry, icehouse, garage with an apartment for the caretaker, and also a tennis court. The best area of all, though, was the playground with three life-size playhouses complete with sanitary and cooking facilities, where the three

girls could even entertain adults at (grown-up) tables and chairs. Not to be forgotten was the play store, the *Albedor Supply,* which sold miniature replicas of all national brand products with sales rung up on a tiny cash register which actually worked. Wintertime fun was not neglected, as a toboggan slide was erected on the opposite side of the property from the playground and many brisk hours were spent snowshoeing on frozen Fourth Lake.

After the main house was completed, attention was turned to the boat house, which boasted a huge entire second floor room for dancing and entertainment, complete with stage. In 1931, the colonel and his wife were making plans for an anniversary celebration in October, but his death on September 30 of that year put an end to any festivities.

Mrs. Simmons carried on the estate alone and in 1936 put her architectural talents to use once again by having another home constructed on the property for her oldest daughter, Aline, who was then married and the mother of two.

Faced with rising costs and children not able to spend time with her during the summers, in 1950 Mrs. Simmons reluctantly decided to sell Albedor. Unfortunately she passed away September 20, 1951, so did not live to meet any new owners. The estate was willed to a Brooklyn Orphan Asylum, which in turn sold it to private owners, of whom over the years there were several, until Mr. and Mrs. Hans Holl purchased Albedor and turned it into a charming hotel. It has remained publicly operated until the present day. The oldest daughter's home was sold separately and is still a private home, owned at present by the Trinkaus family of Trinkaus Manor Restaurant in Oriskany. As to the namesakes of Albedor, Aline was struck by a car in Orlando, Florida, and killed instantly on November 22, 1963, the day of the Kennedy assassination. Doris is now Mrs. Fred Hatter and resides in Melbourne, Florida, and Betty has a home on Third Lake, Old Forge, with her husband, Merle Fenton. Of eleven grandchildren, two grandsons of Colonel Simmons now reside in Old Forge with their families, the sons of Betty and Merle.

The successive sales of the Albedor since Mrs. Simmons' death reveal that some of the owners have been the orphanage, which got it by will from Mrs. Simmons, the Foley brothers and their sister, Mildred, of Old Forge and Utica, James C. Capron of Boonville, and Mr. and Mrs. Clark McKee of Eagle Bay. Mrs. McKee said she had great plans for "that beautiful place," but it was too large. Mr. McKee wanted more freedom from such a large holding; so they sold it.

Albedor looking from Fourth Lake toward land. Credit Mrs. Hans Holl.

Winter 1928–29 at Albedor. Left to right, the nurse, Aline, Mrs. Simmons and the Colonel. Credit Betty Simmons Fenton.

At Albedor 1930, Colonel Simmons and his daughters. Left to right: Doris, Betty, Aline, and Colonel Simmons. Credit Betty Simmons Fenton.

Albedor — main entrance hall — entering from the north the main entrance hall is about 30' square. Finished throughout in natural red fir. The stairs were designed by Mrs. Simmons. The main open stairway has sweeping bark-covered rails. Credit Betty Simmons Fenton.

Albedor — Fireplace in living room, conversation piece, massive pink structure, full ceiling height and 10 feet wide. It is composed of only 13 stones, all hammered by hand from one huge boulder found on the estate. The stone mantel shelf, one piece, is over 12 feet long and weighs nearly two tons. Fire logs five feet long are used in the opening. The inglenook formed about the fireplace makes it cozy.

Albedor — Mrs. Simmons in one corner of living room. Credit Betty Simmons Fenton.

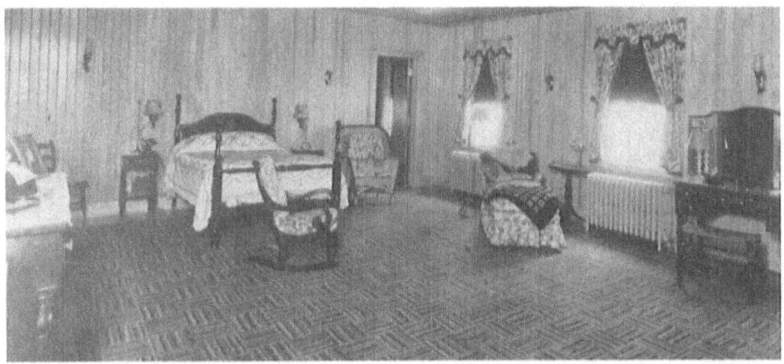

Albedor — Mrs. Simmons' bedroom — second floor. Credit Betty Simmons Fenton.

An area newspaper dated May 6, 1956, printed an article headlined thus: *Holl Buys Albedor On Fourth Lake.* The article cites the sale as being "the biggest Adirondack hotel transaction in recent years." Hans Holl, a veteran hotel man, purchased Albedor, which was built in the late 20's, as a summer estate of the late Colonel E. A. Simmons, millionaire publisher, the news story said. The Albedor estate was described as 30 acres of forest property with 12 buildings. Purchase and building of the estate was estimated to have cost Simmons about $500,000. The Holls' purchase price was listed as being in the neighborhood of $80,000. Anna Holl, wife of Hans Holl, was listed as co-owner.

Howard Burkard, Inlet realtor, handled the sale for James Capron of Boonville. The article gives this description of the property:

> The main lodge contains 20 big rooms. The living room is 65 feet along the front of the building with huge picture windows that give a panoramic view of much of Fourth Lake. The two-story boat house has a game room, a ballroom and a stage on the second floor. On the ground level there are slips for motorboats, rowboats and canoes. It is much larger than most camps in the area. Albedor is situated on the north shore of hotel-lined Fourth Lake and is next to Rocky Point Inn on the Eagle Bay side of the Inn.

The Holls began at once to convert this beautiful estate into a charming hotel and restaurant. With their expertise in hotel and restaurant business, Anna and Hans Holl soon established Albedor as one of the finest hotel-restaurants in the Adirondacks without detracting from the original beauty of the estate. The areas around the seven large stone fireplaces were surrounded by attractive, comfortable chairs, where friendly groups might relax and chat the evening away. Among the ground attractions, use was made of the tennis courts, the large outdoor recreation room, indoor and outdoor badminton courts, the large library, and television was installed. Boating, fishing, swimming and golfing facilities were at hand.

Albedor has 800 feet of water front. It is surrounded by 28 acres of beautiful forest frequented by partridge and deer, as well as other game and wildlife. In the winter, the new owners held Albedor open for those who enjoyed skiing and skating and the wonderland of snow-covered ground and trees. They operated the hotel on the European plan and offered the superb cuisine for which the Holls had long been noted. Among attractions for Albedor guests were the beautiful spacious bedrooms. The interior of the bedrooms is unique in that each, like all the rooms, is finished entirely with wood paneling with a velvety finish on its natural grain, and is entirely free of plaster. No nails or other such items show in the entire finishing. The Holl family operated Albedor with outstanding success from 1956 until Mr. Holl's health failed in the mid-60's. In the spring of 1966 they sold the Albedor to Dr. and Mrs. Harold Frendt of Jim Thorpe, Pennsylvania.

While traveling to and from dog races in Lake Placid, Dr. Frendt had become acquainted with and had greatly admired Albedor. He and Mrs. Frendt spent their honeymoon there in 1959. Mrs. Frendt says that their stay at the Albedor with Hans and Anna Holl as their hosts was a most memorable experience. The excellent food and the luxurious accommodations lingered in their memory.

So it was that when Holl's health failed, Dr. and Mrs. Frendt purchased the estate in April, 1966. Mr. Holl died the following fall. The Frendts had opened Albedor in May of 1966, only a month after the purchase, a quick transition for them from Pennsylvania to the beauty spot in the Adirondacks.

Dr. Frendt was a breeder of Siberian Huskies and participated in races in New York, New England and Canada. In order to promote this Adirondack area for winter enthusiasts, Frendt held sled dog races in February of 1968. The races were held from the Albedor and twenty teams from all over the country vied in a five-mile race around the perimeter of Fourth Lake. Ed Sylvain of Quebec was the winner. This was an interesting venture both to the many spectators lining the course and for the dog trainers who returned to the area for winter workouts. During the summer of 1968 the Frendts had opened the large ballroom over the boat house for entertainment. This attracted the "over forty" young crowd.

In the early 70's snowmobiling was introduced to the Central Adirondacks. The natural beauty of the area and the foresight of local planning committees in grooming the trails for the snowmobiles caused this sport to quickly become the most popular of winter activities. Businesses that had previously closed at the end of the summer season now remained open.

At the time of its construction, Albedor had been completely winterized and was offering every facility to both the summer and winter visitor. There were no expensive renovations and this was another plus for the owners. Cross-country skiing also attracted many people to the North Country. Mrs. Frendt adds her personal reaction:

> From every angle, we feel that the Central Adirondacks is one of the most beautiful areas in the country, abounding in every advantage nature has to offer.

The Ledge Road Property

In a resort area like Eagle Bay property often changes hands; yet at the same time there has been almost constant ownership of some. Property on the ledge overlooking Eagle Bay was included in the sale of Township 8 to Wm. Seward Webb by Ravand K. Hawley in 1891. Webb sold the property to William J. Thistlethwaite and wife in December, 1902, starting a round robin of transactions. Thistlethwaite sold the land to the Adirondack Development Corporation July 9, 1918.

Howard Weller bought the same piece of property from the Adirondack Development Corporation November 5, 1921. Then July 15, 1926, Weller and his wife, Florence, sold a portion of the land to Angie Furlong. Mrs. Furlong, a sister of John and Fred Petersen, held the property until July 27, 1940, when she sold it to Denton-Waterbury of Whitesboro. Russell Miller bought the land from Denton-Waterbury in 1942 and owned it for five years, except for a portion which he sold to Jack Kinney. Kinney owned his part of the land until 1951, when he sold it to Mabel and Cleon Goodwin. The Goodwins in 1966 sold it to Otto and Irma Wolf of Hilton. Mr. Wolf died in 1977, but Mrs. Wolfe owned the property in 1981. There are several camps built on this Ledge Road property, including The Crow's Nest, and there have been a number of owners involved. The camp which Kinney sold to the Goodwins was the last camp at the end of the Ledge Road, a charming little log cabin.

The Ledge Road property has long attracted attention in the Eagle Bay area. It stretches on a rocky ledge from the Big Moose Road back beyond the location of the old Eagle Bay Railroad Station. In Weller's *Adirondack Eagle* of July 25, 1925 he gives space to the description of much of this property and lists some of the lots which had been sold. John Petersen was the contractor involved in some of these sales. Mrs. Crowe from Detroit, Michigan, who had the Crow's Nest built, lived in that place for a number of years. In 1951 she sold it to Cleo and Julia Stephenson of Ohio. In 1955 the Stephensons sold the Crow's Nest to Kenneth Slater of Hilton, and his sister, Eleanor Zielenski of Rochester.

Slater sold it in 1976 and it has changed hands twice since then. Others who have owned property on Ledge Road over the years are Ray and Alice Smith and James A. Wilkins. Kenneth Thomas, of Buffalo, owns a camp off the Big Moose Road on Ledge Road. These and other properties purchased on Ledge Road are evidence that Weller was an outstanding real estate promoter and shows the attraction of the Eagle Bay area.

The Hidden Camp

One of the most fascinating older camps in the Eagle Bay area is tucked away almost completely out of sight in the woods just off Big Moose Road about three-tenths of a mile from the village. Although not a large camp, it has served several prominent people. Cleon and Mabel Goodwin of Hilton, 1981 owners, say the camp was built in 1925. Ben Sperry owned the property as part of the Eagle Bay Hotel land and built the camp for his sister. The structure has a large living room-dining room, two bedrooms downstairs, kitchen, bathroom, and two porches. Inside around two sides of the living room there is a balcony. Divided into two parts, the balcony serves as extra bedrooms. A large brick, rather than the usual granite, fireplace forms the center attraction of the living room. Water from the camp is pumped from Eagle Creek, which runs in front of the place. Drinking water is brought in from other sources.

Former owners and tenants of the hidden camp have been: Ben Sperry and his wife, Mabel; Mildred Kellog Case, Guilderland; Margaret Talmade, Esperance; Roswell M. Case, Esperance; Mildred I. Case; Donald Case and his wife, Madeline, of Old Forge. In 1957 the Cases sold the property to Charles and Marian Kofmeihl, who built the red and white cottage on a front lot of property owned by David Schultz and Herbert O'Brien of San Antonio, Texas. This cottage was formerly owned by Audrey Brownell.

In 1965 Kofmeihl sold the Sperry Camp to Edward and Doris Brickle.

The Edward Brickle Family

Many families who moved to Eagle Bay long after the formation of Eagle Bay Park Association have contributed in different ways to the growth and development of the hamlet. From Fairport came the Edward Brickle family. In 1946 they bought a lot on the Big Moose Road from William Cusack. Brickle built his cottage himself.

The Brickles sold their home and business in Fairport in 1954 and moved to Eagle Bay permanently. They added improvements and winterized their camp, making it into an attractive home for year-round use. Brickle bought a lot across the Big Moose Road from Alfred Nelson on which he dug his water well.

Brickle went to work first for Lawrence Payne of Inlet and Mrs. Brickle worked two summers for Beryl Roach in his grocery store. Then in 1957, Brickle started an electrical contracting business and did all the wiring for Camp Gorham when the property was first purchased by the Rochester Y.M.C.A. Since the start of his business

168   God's Country

at Eagle Bay and even after his retirement, Brickle did all the electrical work at Camp Eagle Cove. For many years he did the electrical work for Miss Mildred Foley at Northwoods Inn, and also for the Turner Camps. He went as far away as Boonville to wire the Medical Center there.

The Brickles bought the small cottage next door to their home from Mrs. Lawrence Creighton. This is still a part of the Brickle holdings. They at one time owned a lot on Lakeview Avenue and all of the Don Case property on Big Moose Road, which was once Ben Sperry property and part of Eagle Bay Hotel holdings. They bought the Don Case property from Charles Kofmeihl in August 1965. The Brickles sold this interesting piece of property to Cleon and Mabel Goodwin in September 1966. The Goodwins sold, in the fall of 1981, to the Don Fosters of Hilton.

Four children of the Brickle family were part of Eagle Bay young crowd until they married and moved away: Jean Moss, Marion Knight, Edward G. Brickle and Donald J. Brickle.

Fulton Chain Yacht Association Property

The Fulton Chain Yacht Association bought from William J. and Gwendolyn Thistlethwaite a tract of land of the Thistlethwaite allotment which lay

> from the line of low water mark on Fourth Lake, then northwesterly, westerly and northly along this low water mark to the mouth of Eagle Creek, then up Eagle Creek along center line as (creek) winds and turns, to the lands of Thistlethwaite Allotment and lands of New York State . . . This tract included approximately 34½ acres. The Yacht Club was given the right to dredge and clear the creek of any obstruction.

The Yacht Association gave Thistlethwaite a mortgage for $4,000. Thistlethwaite assigned this mortgage to Citizens Trust Company of Utica, which immediately assigned the mortgage to Thomas Buchanan of Yonkers. Then in March 1910 The Fulton Chain Yacht Association gave a $25,000 mortgage to Charles S. Symonds as trustee to secure that amount of payment of bonds. July 26, 1920 Etta J. Buchanan, executrix for the estate of Thomas Buchanan, gave notice of "commencement for foreclosure procedures" against the Yacht Association.

Carroll A. Thomas, trustee, in action of foreclosure executed a referee's deed. On Jaunary 31, 1921, Howard Weller took over the whole tract by referee deed for the sum of $3,625. In 1925 Weller sold the property to Robert Earl, who owned it for a few years and then sold it in the 1930s to Jackson-Perkins of the Perkins Rose

Company, Newark. The two Perkins boys came to Eagle Bay for several summers, and then went to war in the 40's. After returning from World War II, the boys were interested in making careers for themselves, so Jackson-Perkins put the property up for sale.

John Petersen introduced Neal Ottaway of Yorkville to the Jackson-Perkins property. So it was in 1945 this piece of God's Country took on new life when Ottaway bought it. Across Eagle Creek from the old club was a tract of land owned by Mrs. Remington Howard, whose deceased husband was a nephew of Judge Remington, who had a summer home in Eagle Bay Park. On the Howard property were a few log rental cottages that had fallen into a state of disrepair. Neal was an ambitious younger man. In 1949 he bought the Howard land from Bill Cusack, local realtor.

The Cottage Colony — His Kingdom

Neal's work was now laid out before him — work that would challenge him for years to come. He tackled the work by priorities.

On the original Howard property in Lone Pine, Neal sold, to several prominent people, cottages which he had built in place of the Howard cabins. John Piersma bought some of the Howard land from Neal, then sold a home site to Al (Smitty) Smith, a former NYS policeman, who built a home there.

Neal Ottaway then built cottages around the old Yacht Club property. These new cottages were ideal for rental property. Now not only was his "paradise" secure; his "kingdom" was built around him.

The Ottaway children became sports enthusiasts. Marian became ski and swimming instructor at the Mohawk Hotel. Jeanne also worked at the Mohawk as the children's hostess and helper. She graduated in nursing and is in administration at Monterey, CA hospital. James worked at Big Moose with the Dunn boys and became one of the area's first barefoot water skiers. James Ottaway was named to the 1981 United States International muzzle-loading team. He won the silver medal in the national metric matches in Colesville, N.J., taking second place in a match for original (antique) rifle percussion pistols. He competed in Bisley, England and was an alternate on the U.S. revolver squad in the world championship, where he excelled.

Who is Neal Ottaway? Instrumental in the development of one of the most beautiful subdivisions of summer homes in the entire area, he began as a garage owner in Yorkville. Then according to Neal, he and John Piersma built an aircraft hanger at Marcy and called it the Utica Aircraft Inc. There they had both a flying school and flying service.

Living room in the hidden camp 1980 owned by Mabel and Cleon Goodwin. Note the balcony. Credit Mabel Goodwin.

The original Yacht Association House Ottaway replaced. Credit Neal Ottaway collection.

Beautiful new lodge built by Neal Ottaw on the original Yacht Club Associatio property called "His Paradise." Crec Neal Ottaway collection.

This Yacht Club Association old boathouse has been replaced. Credit Neal Ottaway collection.

3erta and Neal Ottaway. Credit taway collection.

The cottage colony which Ottaway has developed along Eagle Creek. Credit Ottaway collection.

Ottaway and Piersma later moved their flying business to Oneida County Airport, where they went into twin engine planes and flew longer shuttle flights to the larger airlines. They sold this business after a twenty-five year partnership and it became Valley Aircraft. Piersma continued his hobby and owns three planes, including a seaplane which, during the summers when he isn't flying, is parked on the lake in front of the lovely home which he built on the Howard property in the Lone Pine area of Eagle Bay.

When Ottaway retired, he razed the Yacht Club buildings and he and Stuart Nelson built a fabulous new home on the same ground. This home is pictured in a group labeled "His Paradise." Nelson built the unusually beautiful fireplace in the living room.

The Ottaways have a home in Florida and a motor home which they have used to travel to California and other parts of the United States to visit their children. Yet, it is in their part of "God's Country" on Fourth Lake and Eagle Creek that the Ottaways find their greatest contentment.

CHAPTER VIII

Longstaff Camps
Summer Mecca for Girls and Boys

Moss Lake, Prestigious Girls' Camp
Joseph Grady in his book, *The Adirondacks — A Story of a Wilderness*, says that as early as the Civil War period, Moss Lake first bore the name Whipple Lake from O. W. Whipple of Utica. An artist, Professor Morse, spent several summers in the early 1870's in a bark shanty on this lovely Adirondack lake, and during that time it acquired the name Morse Lake. Grady assumes that Moss Lake is a contraction of Morse to the simpler pronunciation. However, old-timers who know the lake well believe the name Moss Lake was derived from the heavy build-up of a mossy growth. Whatever the origin of the name, Moss Lake brought certain fame, and much economic benefit to the Eagle Bay area.

Longstaffs Buy a Lake
Dr. and Mrs. Herbert Longstaff bought Moss Lake in 1918 from a four-family club. The Longstaffs first had the idea of selling the Mohawk and building at Moss Lake. However, since the Mohawk was established as a popular hotel, and continued to make money, their enthusiasm faded, and they talked of selling the lake. Young George Longstaff had fallen in love with Moss Lake and persuaded his parents to let him try to make it self-supporting. They decided to let their son try his wings. In 1923 Young George opened a girls' camp on the lake. He had been studying the rapid development of summer camps in the Eastern States for both boys and girls, and chose to begin with girls. He advertised in nationally popular youth magazines. By the time he had roads and living facilities established on the property, he had a good staff selected and 20 girls to attend the first summer.

As the years went by Moss Lake became one of the nation's most prestigious camps for girls. Internationally known familes sent their girls to Dr. George Longstaff's camp at Moss Lake. Among them was Sara Roosevelt, granddaughter of President Franklin Delano Roosevelt. Over a long period of years, the clientele became more and more select as more girls wanted to come. The enrollment finally topped 150. So this beautiful round lake became a summer mecca for girls of wealthy, prominent families. The girls were devoted to Moss Lake Camp which was said to have the largest camp recreation hall, if not in the world, certainly in the United States. The girls lovingly called the hall "Madison Square Garden." At least two basketball games and an archery tournament could be held in the hall at the same time. Moss Lake is a round, clear lake with an island of its own. The girls' camp bordered both sides of the Eagle Bay-Big Moose Road about three miles from Eagle Bay. The lake lies south of the road.

Famous Instructors for Moss Lake

George Longstaff earned a degree in dentistry and became a practicing dentist on Long Island. His success in running camps, according to Dr. Longstaff, lay in the selection of his staff. His modesty prevents his taking the credit. Below are some of the people to whom he gives credit. The "big names" for the mid 30's, most of whom remained with the camp for an average of twenty years, included persons familiar to the national sports scene.

For swimming, which was one of the leading sports at Moss Lake, there was John Zinnoch, a top performer in his day, who with Handley, was a founder of the New York State Women's Swimming Association. Zinnoch held a tight rein on Moss Lake swimming activities and turned out some expert swimmers.

In riding there was more than one famous instructor. First there was Baretto de Souza, author of many books on equitation and an outstanding instructor. Then came Alexis Selihoff, a colonel in the Russian Imperial Army, and the military head of Fillis Academy in Petrograd. Other colonels from the Czar's cavalry were Nicholas Shishkin and George Otaroff, who was replaced by Frank Carroll before the end of the 30's. All of these riding instructors left their mark on the equestrian program at Moss Lake. Through the first ten years of the "Good Hands" class in the National Horse Show, first place went to Moss Lake girls or to winter pupils of these instructors.

Included in the sports was fencing, somewhat unusual for girls. J. Martinez Castello, probably the top fencing master in the world, and N.Y.A.C. coach, was in charge. Castello was an author and the owner of the country's largest fencing equipment house. He also was coach of the N.Y.U. fencing team who were perennial champions. In archery, Andrew Brush gave instruction to the Moss Lake girls for many summers. He was a top competitor in the early days and was the country's outstanding coach in the 30's.

Dancing, especially ballet, was a popular form of activity for the Moss Lake girls. Heading this activity at Moss Lake for about fifteen years was Helmy Smirnova, who came to America with the last Russian Imperial Ballet. Her uncle was the Russian consul in New York City. He gave Helmy $3,000 when the first World War broke out and told her he would be back in a few months, but she never saw him again. Smirnova was followed by Anneliese von Oettingen who was with Moss Lake for 23 years. Her daughter says:

> She was the ballet specialist at Moss Lake from 1949, when she first came to the Eagle Bay area with her two children, Tyll and Cornelia, until 1972. The two months of camp ballet training were concluded with a Ballet Recital that included *Goldilocks, Peter Pan, Underwater Fantasy, The Little Match Girl, Travels Around the World*, which area residents anticipated and attended. Madison Square at Moss Lake was packed with singing campers and parents, visitors, other instructors, some of whom never missed a recital. Anneliese 'brought the house down' with these professionally created performances.

Anneliese recalled that the discipline at the Camp made amateurs into pros. She said that Dr. Longstaff always demanded the best instruction, and to obtain that he hired only professionals — the internationally known instructors who were great specialists in their field, teaching such talented, receptive girls — more than 135 of them each summer. Not only were they trained in sports and the arts, they were given the opportunity to understand and maintain high social and moral standards.

The Moss Lake girls were each summer a familiar part of the Eagle Bay scene. They occasionally hiked to the village as an outing, visiting the various stores, always accompanied by some of the staff. Also they used the area riding trails for their journeys on horseback. Eagle Bay, for years, had the advantage of the closeness of this camp which played host to nationally and internationally famous families' offspring. Over the years children of former campers attended Moss Lake, even to the third generation. The founder hears from his "former girls" who continue to nurture a deep love and loyalty to Moss Lake.

After the 1969 season Dr. Longstaff leased Moss Lake to Robert and Jane Rider, with an option to buy. Mrs. Rider had been a camper and a counsellor. The three Rider daughters followed Jane to Moss Lake as campers. Thus Dr. Longstaff felt assured the camp was in good hands and would ensure its operation for at least another generation. Mr. Zinnoch and two head counsellors were still with the organization. Three years later Longstaff transferred title to the Riders. Two weeks after the transfer, the Riders wrote the Moss Lake families to announce the closing of the camp and their sale of the property. Dr. Longstaff had proved the value of

Dr. George H. Longstaff, Dentist, and Administrator of summer camps for Girls and Boys. Founder of Moss Lake Camp for Girls. Credit Mrs. George Longstaff.

Moss Lake Recreation Room. Credit Doris Lamphear.

Moss Lake Camp. Credit Doris Lamphear.

Moss Lake Girls take to the water. Counselors look on. Credit Dr. George Longstaff collection.

Moss Lake Camp as a recreational and educational institution. It seems sad that it was consigned to such an early demise.

Cascade Lake Bought By Longstaff

As trustee under the deed made by Charles Snyder and his wife, Eva, the Ilion National Bank and Trust Company sold Cascade Lake Tract, parcel No. I and II to Dr. George Longstaff, July 1, 1937. Four hundred sixty-one acres of this land lies in the Town of Inlet and 18.49 acres in the Town of Webb. The land sale described in the deed contains a total of 480.29 acres. The Cascade property was part of the Township 8 sale made by Ravand K. Hawley of the Adirondack Timber and Mineral Company to William Seward Webb, May 1891.

It is interesting to note that this same land was a part conveyed and described in a deed to Charles E. Snyder by Ferris Meigs of Tupper Lake, the sole surviving member of a joint stock association — by the name of Adirondack Timber and Mineral Company — the deed bearing the date June 20, 1929.

Parcel No. II of the Cascade Lake property lay in Township 41, Totten Crossfield's purchase in the Town of Long Lake and contained 75 acres of land which according to the deed was to be held as wild forest land never to be lumbered. It was the same land "set over to the severalty to Charles E. Snyder by deed in partition between him and the people of the State of New York, dated November 17th, 1902."

This parcel was described erroneously in the deed, and Snyder had it corrected by another deed.

With the above described large acreage of land and the rather palatial home built by the Snyders, Cascade Lake seemed another ideal place for a summer camp. The lake is unusually beautiful — long and narrow with cliffs as high as 200 feet. It is flanked by a corridor named by Charles Snyder, *Druid's Hall.*

Also gracing this beautiful spot in God's Country is Cascade Brook which makes a breathtaking leap from just above the lake for a forty foot drop — a hissing, singing, tumbling, beautiful waterfall. Lovely mountains, Cascade Range, form a background for the glittering lake and are a paradise for the more seasoned hunter.

An ideal mecca for boys and girls, Cascade was opened as an all-boys' camp by Longstaff, a sort of companion for Moss Lake. A few years previously he had opened the Cedar Isles Camp on Fourth Lake across from Eagle Point.

Dr. Longstaff ran the Cascade Camp for three or four years. Then came Pearl Harbor, and he converted the camp into a co-ed camp for very young children. He doubted his ability to maintain

Cascade Lake Boys' Camp. Lawyer Charles Snyder former home in background. Credit George Longstaff collection.

Prize Winning Cascade Lake riding team at Sagamore. Credit George Longstaff collection.

his staff standards with so many of the older counsellors going into service. He put all the returning men and all the boys on Cedar Isles, and thus had one good camp. He staffed Cascade with one married couple and several women. It worked out rather well, but Longstaff lacked a vital interest in co-education; so he leased the place to Fritz Kleeman, who ran a girls' camp for about five years. When Kleeman had it, he emphasized equestrian skill, and his girls were noted for their showmanship at annual horse shows. After Kleeman gave up his lease, Dr. Longstaff sold the property to two families from New York City. They operated it as a girls' camp for about four or five years and then the state took Cascade Lake property over under their eminent domain powers. Whether they did this at the invitation of the owners or as the state's spontaneous idea, research failed to determine. Anyway, that beautiful spot is in the Forever Wild category. The palatial home has been destroyed. Some say this is good; others say God's beauty spots should be used to the fullest.

The Indians at Moss Lake
May 13, 1974

Sunday, May 12, 1974, was a typical spring day. The residents of Eagle Bay passed the day in their usual pursuits. Many travelled along Big Moose Road to the neighboring village for commerce or socializing, and as they passed the Moss Lake site of the recently sold former girls' camp, there was a tug of nostalgia for the many years when the daughters of the prominent and famous spent their summers there.

The grounds were beautiful and the various buildings had been constructed at a time when pride of workmanship was at its finest. They were different now only in the respect that they no longer had electricity or telephones connected. Many wondered how it would be by the end of summer, as the buildings would be gone by then, removed by the state.

In 1969, Dr. George Longstaff, founder of the camp, had leased the Moss Lake property to Robert and Jane Rider of Bridgewater, Delaware, with the thought that it would be operated as it had been. Three years later the Riders elected to buy the property, and only a few weeks after their purchase they sold it to the Nature Conservancy, a non-profit organization which had the state's approval to hold the property for later sale to the Adirondack Park. The Moss Lake site was one of four tracts of privately owned land purchased by the state in August of 1973. The beautiful landmark was slated to fade into local history with the scheduled final removal of the buildings.

The Indian Occupation

The threat of rain which had been menacing the local residents that day made good its promise. By nightfall, there was a heavy downpour which continued unabated throughout the night. When the rain was at its heaviest, at about 3 Monday morning, April 13, 1972, the Indians came.

They arrived in all manner of vehicles — cars, vans, trucks and the like. The Indians continued coming until well into the day. They were seen driving along the road to the Moss Lake site in vehicles laden with all sorts of supplies — one van was seen with boxes of cereal tied on top; others had mattresses and bedding visible. They came in "family units" and brought with them chickens, ducks, goats, a few head of cattle and horses, the usual farm animals, and their dogs. They felled trees to block all roads and trails to the area; and at each blocked ingress posted two to four men to stand guard, insuring that no one might gain access.

Many of the women and children took shelter in the buildings of the girls' camp, while most of the men gathered firewood and erected wigwams and tepees around the grounds. These were Mohawks, but there were representatives of the Oneida, Onondaga, Seneca, Cayuga and Cherokee tribes.

The Indians named the camp Ganienkeh, meaning Land of the Flint. The seizure of the land had been planned by the Indians in detail for more than a year and a half. Having no prior knowledge of this planned invasion, the local residents awoke to a most unusual week. By general agreement, they decided to try to live as harmoniously as possible with their new neighbors. A few things were necessary, however, in order to assure this, such as access to Big Moose Road. Authorities, having been notified, proceeded cautiously; all efforts at arbitration necessarily had to be more than tactful, diplomatic and discreet. First to visit the encampment was Conservation Officer William Merleau, but no effort was made to evict the Indians.

Visits were paid by State Police, namely Senior Investigator, Richard J. Gildersleeve. His stated purpose was to gather information, but no further action was planned at that time.

Community reaction was mainly concerned with tourism, a principal source of revenue. Hunting and fishing had always been popular with those who lived in the area, but with the advent of easier access via local aircraft and snowmobiles and the like, year after year the area increased in popularity with sportsmen throughout the United States and Canada. Many sportsmen, ignorant of the recent occupation of the Moss Lake site, were turned away from trails into the woodlands by blockades with two to four Indians standing as sentries.

Kakwirakeron, a spokesman for the Group, Tom Cook, president of the American Indian Press Association, and Louis Hall, another spokesman for the group, would speak to authorities from the gate house flanked at all times by four Indian guards. Kakwirakeron told reporters that the Indians had brought food with them and they intended to plant crops in the spring. They hoped to clear some of the land and intended to restore buffalo grazing there. Residents of the Town of Webb assisted the settlers in finding water and other facilities as measures to safeguard them against possible injury.

The summer months passed with a certain amount of tension, but for the most part uneventfully until the early autumn, when a series of events took place which greatly altered the atmosphere and the attitudes of the local residents and all concerned.

Spraying Bullets

On Monday, October 28, 1974, two brothers, Steven A. Drake, 22, and Michael Drake, 20, of Inlet, were driving along Big Moose Road from Moss Lake to Eagle Bay when at 5:15 p.m. shots rang out from the encampment which bordered the highway on either side. One bullet struck the driver, Steven Drake, in the shoulder. Steven's brother, Michael, slid over his brother and drove the remainder of the distance to Eagle Bay. From there Steven was rushed to Old Forge Medical Center and then to St. Luke's-Memorial Hospital in New Hartford.

At 8:45 the same evening, the Madigan family, Roger and June, of Johnson Road, Geneva, were returning home from a vacation trip and decided to dine in Big Moose. Upon returning via the Big Moose Road, their automobile was fired upon "several times" as they passed the Indian encampment; at least six bullets hit their car. One bullet came through the car and lodged in the spine of Aprile A. Madigan, age nine, a fourth grade student. She was rushed to Old Forge Medical Center for emergency treatment. For many weeks, her condition was described as critical.

In both instances, the Indians charged that they were fired upon from the passing cars by the passengers and that they had fired back only in self defense. A meticulous search was made by the State Police and other officials, with particular awareness of the minority as the Indians were categorized. The result showed no evidence of firearms in either of the vehicles concerned.

Following these unfortunate incidents, the residents of the nearby communities reacted with shock, and fear, as did State Police and other officials. State Police were immediately stationed around the clock at either end of the Big Moose Road which cut directly through the center of the occupied area.

Also, during this early period of tension, the people living at Big Moose — whose only access out of the area was along this same road — initiated an organization which included all the people living in or near the affected area. Thus, COPCA — *CO*ncerned *P*ersons of the *C*entral *A*dirondacks — came into being.

Two items were the basic goal of COPCA:

1) The return of Moss Lake, Bubb Lake and Sis Lake areas to the jurisdiction of the State of New York, the owner of these properties. This includes the departure of the Indians from these properties at least until such time as their claims have been adjudicated by proper legal process.

2) The presentation of facts about the Moss Lake encampment that are unknown to the general public, or facts that have been, due to one thing or another, distorted so as to mislead the general public.

There followed letters to various officials and numerous attempts to contact the Indians and engage in mutually satisfactory dialogue. The investigation of the shooting got nowhere; officials were not allowed on the grounds and in spite of repeated expressions of regret on the part of the Indians about the grave injuries to the Madigan child, nothing was resolved. In May of 1979, Miss Madigan and her father were awarded $157,000 by the State of New York. This amount was less than the medical expenses that resulted from the shooting incident some five years earlier.

There were a number of legal skirmishes, but nothing more of great consequence. The people living in the area wanted to avoid the kind of confrontation which had happened a few years before at Wounded Knee; so they proceeded cautiously.

There will probably never be a real answer to the problems that took place in the Moss Lake area from 1974 through 1979. There can only be a reporting of the known facts.

The Moss Lake site had never been used for farming, as the terrain was much too rough and difficult to cultivate. The occupying Indians soon learned that their efforts to clear the land by chopping down many of the huge trees growing there were to no avail.

On May 14, 1977, it was announced that an agreement had been reached between the State of New York and the Indians to end the three-year occupation of Moss Lake. This agreement was reached on May 13, the anniversary of the initial occupation. The Mohawks were granted titular rights to 5,000 acres in Macombs State Park and 700 acres in Minor Lake Dam State Park in Clinton County.

Because the state may not give away property without some form of return, the Indians agreed to build and make accessible to visitors a model village in which Mohawk lore and life patterns would be highlighted.

Since no farming or stock raising was permissible on state property, the peace treaty envisioned private lands should be bought with privately donated funds, next to the parklands, for farming purposes. The treaty also called for the Mohawks to begin leaving Moss Lake in Herkimer County no later than August 1, 1977 and to complete their migration within ninety days.

On Sunday, January 14, 1978, State Police ended more than three years of duty at the Mohawk Indian campsite at Moss Lake. They left mobile units to cover the territory instead of the fixed post.

After several delays and extensions, the Mohawks finally began to leave Moss Lake for their new home. They left in groups over a few months. The last four Indian men left on July 31, 1978. The state completed the clean-up. Thus ended the Indian occupation of Moss Lake and that beautiful area of God's Country was returned to "The Forever Wild Land."

"Reach into the sky and feel the warmth of the sun — the cleansing of the rain — the caress of the wind.

Walk with kindness and love for all. Reach beyond what you are to what you can be. Learn from those before and give to those who follow."

Anneliese von Oettingen — Ballet Camp — P.O. Box 155, Eagle Bay, N. Y. 13331

CHAPTER IX

People – Life Blood of a Community

People build a community with their physical strength — lumber-brick-steel — and with their mental and moral strength in ideas, decisions and actions. Eagle Bay has had its share of dedicated builders. Most came from other places, found the area to their liking, and did their part to develop it.

There were skilled craftsmen, shopkeepers, grocers, restaurateurs, real estate brokers, railroad men, mechanics, car dealers, ballet teachers and artists. There were hard-working immigrants, congenial summer residents, good neighbors and leaders with broad vision, along with a few "colorful characters."

Orr Liddle

Orr Liddle, from Wevertown, was one of the early community builders in the literal sense. As a contractor he built the Tea Pot Dome in Eagle Bay, a girls' camp on Cedar Island, a boys' camp on Woods Point, Eagle Cove and buildings in the Raquette Lake and Big Moose area.

Liddle came first to Thendara, where his uncle, John Wakely, had built and was running a hotel that later became Van Auken's Tavern. Liddle married Pearle Giles in 1905 and they lived in Thendara until 1910.

In 1909 Liddle bought lots facing the Eagle Bay-Inlet road, which, according to a 1909 map of the Thistlethwaite Allotment, was the only privately owned section on the road through Eagle Bay. The Liddle house stands today in much the original state. The Liddles were known for their neighborliness. The story is told that when an Indian family, the Traversys, lived in Eagle Bay, one of their children died. In their sorrow they turned to Mrs. Liddle and she helped prepare the child for burial and comforted the family.

One of the Liddle daughters, Helen, has long served in many capacities in hotel industry of the Eagle Bay area and has a keen grasp of area history. The Liddles had four children, Ernest, Jessie (deceased), Helen and Elizabeth.

John Petersen, Woodsman

Another prominent builder-contractor of Eagle Bay was John Petersen, who was born in Utica in 1884, son of Danish immigrants, Hans and Marie Clausen Petersen. When he reached young manhood he joined his two older brothers in the building business in Utica, but because he was not advanced beyond apprenticeship in the construction company, he decided to break away and start out on his own. In the early 1900's he did much of the hand-finishing work on the interior of Kamp Kilkare near Raquette Lake.

As early as 1917 John and his brother, Fred, had bought land from Howard Weller in Eagle Bay Park, but it was not until after World War I, about 1919, that John began building in the Park. Numerous buildings, including many homes and businesses along Route 28 bear the Petersen mark. The two-story home at the west entrance to Eagle Bay, owned by Dr. Wayne Choper, was at one time the Petersen home, later the Petersen Tourist Lodge and finally Harnett's Lodge.

His love for fine wood and his construction work were the center of his life. His happiest moments were spent sitting at his desk creating a building plan and then selecting lumber for it and putting it all together. The carpenters who worked for him found him a demanding but just taskmaster.

During World War I, about 1917, Petersen spent some time in Baltimore, Maryland, in building work for the government and was sent briefly to Texas on a building inspection trip. While he was in Houston on government assignment he met Clara Vaughan Hatcher, who twenty years later was to become his wife.

John was an individualist and a strong man physically, mentally and spiritually. Lifting and carrying a railroad tie was no great task for him and carrying a two hundred pound deer from the woods was an annual joy. Bearing a devastating illness with courage became his daily routine for almost ten years. His six foot, two inch height with a lean 185 pound frame made him a stand-out among men. He died in May 1950.

Alfred Nelson from Norway

Yet another builder arrived in the area in 1914. In that year Andrew Grindland, living on Fourth Lake, sponsored one of his countrymen, 20-year-old Alfred Nelson of Norway. Eager to earn a livelihood, the young man was welcomed at the Grindland home and worked for a while for his sponsor, later coming to Eagle Bay. He worked a few years for John Petersen before going it alone in the building trade, which was booming in the little "upstart" development of Eagle Bay.

In 1923 a young German girl, Frieda Pfahl, arrived in Syracuse, under sponsorship of her uncle. He got her a job with the Kaufman family, Syracusans, who had a summer home in Inlet. Frieda and Alfred met in the summer of 1924 and despite a language barrier, they let Cupid take over and were married November 14, 1925. Alfred built a house for himself and Frieda in the heart of the Park and they had three daughters and a son, one daughter having died early in their marriage.

His son, Stuart, joined Alfred in the building business and they worked with their construction crews for many years. His children remember him thus:

> Basically he was a very religious man. Hardly a day went by that he didn't begin it by reading the Bible as he ate breakfast. He was undaunted by the difficulty of any task. We often marveled at the superhuman strength he could muster when needed — putting a full-size bathtub on his back and carrying it upstairs alone . . . or rowing a boat down the lake, towing a log that was to become the main support beam for the length of his shop, which later became Toboggan Inn. . . . He weathered many hardships. In 1930 his shop — his livelihood — burned to the ground. During the Depression, many of his debtors went through bankruptcy and left him holding the bag. But he went to his deathbed eternally optimistic, and declaring there was no place in the world that could hold a candle to the United States of America, the land of opportunity if you were willing to work.

Their Children

Their children are now married and living busy, successful lives of their own. Paula married Charles Gray. They have five children, Charles, Karen, Annie, Phylis, and Bobby. Betty married Raymond Spencer and their children are Dan, Dave and Carrol. Ruth married Albert Brussel and their children are Lynn, Juli, Betsy, and William. Stuart married Mary Ann Lum, and their children are Kim, Richard, and Kristen.

Alfred died April 12, 1974. He and Frieda had been married 49 years. In his last years he and Stuart's son, Richard, spent hours in the cellar making bird houses. No doubt he was in this way trying to instill in his grandson some of his love for creating things from wood.

Seth Burton Youmans, Man of Talent

Another skilled craftsman was Burt Youmans, who came to Eagle Bay from Old Forge in 1923. He was a man of many talents,

Orr Liddle — established first permanent year-round home in Eagle Bay. Builder, contractor. Credit Helen Liddle collection.

Mrs. Orr Liddle — was known for he neighborliness; a mother devoted to h family and home. Credit Helen Liddle co lection.

John Peter Petersen, a typical pose. Always his pipe. Credit Author's collection.

John and Clara Petersen in Uti Thanksgiving, 1937. Credit Author's c lection.

John P. Petersen Home — built 1926. Later Petersen's Lodge, then Hartnett's Lodge; 1980 owned by Dr. Wayne Choper, 1982, "The Eagle's Nest."

Left to right Mrs. and Mr. Moyer and Alfred Nelson checking thickness of ice. Credit Frieda Nelson.

Sucker Brook camp for the hardy hunter. Left to right George Allen, Alfred Nelson, Ivan Brush. Credit Frieda Nelson.

Alfred and Frieda Nelson November 13, 1965. Their 40th Wedding Anniversary. Credit Ruth Nelson Brussell.

Minnie Rebner Youmans, circa late 30's. Credit Yock Youmans.

Seated Burt Youmans, rear left to right, Edward Youmans, grandson Gary; Yock — taken the year before Burt died. Credit Edward Youmans.

Patricia Youmans Selbach; daughter of Yock and Louise Youmans. Credit Yock Youmans.

Edward Youmans' sons: left to right Gary, business in Florida, Maurice called Maury, attended Syracuse U., played professional football, real estate, Florida. Jim teaches English and Drama. Credit Edward Youmans.

an expert in electrical and plumbing work. His first project in Eagle Bay was for the Inlet Utility Company, building the electrical line to Inlet. With the help of his son, Yock, he installed the water system for Eagle Bay Park and did the electrical and plumbing work for buildings as they were erected in the Park after 1923. He also did sheet metal work, installed roofing and made stove pipe and metal items.

Burt, a native of Oneida, had started work in Old Forge at the age of 17 building guide boats for Ben Parsons. Later he was a captain on the Fulton Chain steamboats and on one of his trips carried Chester Gillette from Inlet to Old Forge on his way to jail in Herkimer County. Gillette was later convicted of the murder of his girl friend on Big Moose Lake. Youmans was the last pilot to work for the Navigation Company before the runs were discontinued. He ran a garage in Old Forge for some years before moving to Eagle Bay.

During his first years in the community, he lived in Eagle Bay Hotel. He bought his first land in 1926 from Howard Weller and two years later bought property from the Ilion Trust Company on which he later placed a mobile home. In 1938 he purchased the lot between the mobile home and Eagle Bay Service from Charles Snyder.

Burt's wife was the former Minnie Rebner, whom he met while working at the Bald Mountain House in his early youth. They were married in 1905. Their sons were Harold (Yock), who took over his father's business, and Edward, a former Eagle Bay postmaster.

Youmans had two special hobbies. One was the raising of bulldogs — he was never without one as a happy companion — and the other was using his lathe and machinery for creative woodwork. Many in the Eagle Bay area treasure the wood-based lamps he crafted from soild blocks of black cherry or other choice wood. These lamps became collector's items even during his lifetime.

Burt died at age 90 at his home in Eagle Bay — a lifetime that reached from the days of the guide boat to jet travel.

The Searings, Summer Residents

In the summer of 1921, while he was a sophomore in Colgate University, Robert Searing came to Eagle Bay to work for Howard Weller.

Searing thought he was coming to a job as a civil engineer, but he spent most of the summer digging ditches. It was during this summer that work really got under way constructing the roads throughout Eagle Bay Park. Lots were being staked out and sold. Searing purchased a beautiful wooded lot on Central Avenue on which he and his wife, Alvina, built a camp.

At this time, the organization of Eagle Bay Park was just getting under way. When Weller first opened the Park for sale of lots, he endeavored to sell lots throughout the park area rather than on the lakefront. In about 1924 he did open up three lakefront lots directly behind the beach. Richard Searing, Bob's father, bought two of these lots. Alvina Searing notes that John Petersen built their camp on the last of these two lots, and his brother, Fred Petersen, built their camp on Central Avenue. Both brothers were excellent builders, Mrs. Searing noted.

William Cusack, Modern Weller

In the 1940's William Cusack Sr. took over the Howard Weller real estate business. Eagle Bay Park people who turned their "for rent" cottages over to Cusack were almost certain to have a full, rental period.

Cusack's parents had come to the Eagle Bay area for many years during Bill's growing-up years, staying at the Mohawk for a vacation. Bill's education took him into teaching in the industrial arts field and in the later years of his career, Cusack taught in the Utica School System. During this time he, his wife, Shirley, and their son, Bill Jr., lived during the summers in a cottage which they owned in Eagle Bay Park.

After his retirement, he bought the log cabin, real estate office and home combination which Weller had built a few years before. Bill and Shirley operated the real estate business and Bill Jr. went to college and became a doctor. Then Shirley's health failed, and suddenly Bill was alone. He continued his real estate business and his winter trips to Florida.

Later he married Virginia Pellor Ball. Virginia qualified for a broker's license and for a few years she and Bill continued to operate the business. In the early 70's Bill retired and they moved permanently to Florida.

Dedericks, Marchants and Mearns

The family of James Dederick — his wife Kate, son Ralph, then 17, Lillian Marchant and her husband, Richard, first came to Eagle Bay in 1917. They came to inspect a lot in the Joy tract which Dederick had purchased sight unseen. They landed at the Eagle Bay dock, where Howard Weller was trying to get his motorboat started. Since it was a lovely beach and a good place to camp, they got permission from Weller to pitch tents.

The only roads at that time in Eagle Bay Park were East Avenue and Lakeview Avenue from the East Avenue junction to the Fourth Lake beach. The Dedericks liked the location so well that they

Log Cottage — Weller had this built and used it as a home and real estate office. Bill Cusack bought it from Weller estate or directly from Weller. Credit O'Brien.

At Golden Beach — Raquette Lake, 1933-34, Eagle Bay Park Outing. First row James Dederick, Mrs. Kate Myer, Ralph Dederick, Shirley Marchant. 2nd row Dr. Griffiths, Miss Anne Gudmundsen, Mrs. Mildred Vogt, Darton Marchant. Dr. Francis Vogt, Mrs. Kate Dederick, Mrs. Lillian Marchant. Credit Shirley Mearns.

Dederick Camp (Hudson River Lodge) on Lakeview Ave. Memorial Weekend, 1919. Standing in front, left to right Charles Marchant, James Dederick. On steps Ralph Dederick, Mrs. Lillian Marchant. In back Mrs. Kate Dederick (3 others unknown). Credit Shirley Mearns.

Eagle Bay Beach 1932 James Dederick, Mrs. Lillian Marchant, Shirley Marchant; standing John Gudmundsen. Credit Shirley Mearns.

selected a lot on Lakeview Avenue at the junction of what is now Central Avenue. Weller's asking price for the lot was $200. Eventually Weller agreed to accept Dederick's Joy tract lot and $175 for the Eagle Bay lot.

World War I intervened and nothing was done about building a camp on the lot until the spring of 1919, when a Mr. Featerly was engaged to do the work. The Dederick family came to Eagle Bay on Decoration Day, 1919, to inspect the building. At this time they found that the most tenacious inhabitants of Eagle Bay were the black flies and punkies. With only mosquito netting to repel the bugs, they found this a far from pleasant weekend. Not discouraged, the family returned for an August vacation and found the large front porch had been screened.

First Water System

The first few years following the Dedericks' arrival there was no water piped into the Park. There was a pump on Central Avenue (not yet a road) about halfway toward the Eagle Bay-Old Forge highway from Lakeview. Residents had to go to the pump to get water for camp use. Ralph Dederick recalls that the water pipes were laid in the early 20's. At this time a water storage tank was placed on Eagle Cliff so there would be pressure for the water mains laid in the Park. The pump was tended by John Gorman, who was a deputy sheriff of Herkimer County and the Eagle Bay Park policeman.

Eagle Bay in the beginning had no fire-fighting equipment. In the summer of 1923 a camp on West Avenue burned down in mid-afternoon. Ralph Dederick went to the Eagle Bay Hotel and borrowed some fire hose, which he carried in a wheelbarrow to the Park water main on Central Avenue. There he and Weller hooked up the hose and dragged it over to West Avenue to wet down the remains of the cabin. Dederick recalls that the first fire department in Eagle Bay was formed after World War II. Until then Eagle Bay depended on the Inlet fire department. For the new department, Eagle Bay men bought an old Army fire engine.

The Dedrick Camp, Hudson River Lodge, has been the summer haven for four generations of the family. Shirley Marchant Mearns, granddaughter of James Dederick, has been spending her summers in Hudson River Lodge all her life. She particularly remembers the Eagle Bay Park family dinners, held usually twice during the summer — the Fourth of July and Labor Day. Mrs. Mearns also vividly remembers the Eagle Bay night watchman, who walked around the Park in the wee hours and often rested on the birch bench in Hudson River Lodge front yard.

The Dedricks, Marchants and Mearnses are repeatedly mentioned as Park residents who know Eagle Bay Park best and whose names are firmly woven into the social fabric of the area.

T. W. Fuller of Marks and Fuller

"Let's get off and say hello to E. U. Smith," Theodore Fuller suggested to his father, William, one summer day in 1919 as they sat looking out a train window.

The Raquette Lake Railway train had pulled into the Eagle Bay Station, and across the road passengers could see the store sign, "E. U. Smith." The Fullers, on vacation from Rochester, went over to greet the storekeeper and never got back on the train. Before the visit was over, Ted had bought a lot in the Weller development of Eagle Bay Park, on which he later built a log cabin that was to serve his family as a summer home for many years.

Ted joined the Marine Corps in 1917, serving with the 23rd Machine Gun Company in the Battle of Belleau Woods in France. On return to civilian life, the World War I veteran took a job as clerk in the company of Marks and Fuller, believed to be the oldest commercial photographic supply firm in the world. It was founded in 1860 by Henry Marks in a small upstairs shop on State Street in Rochester.

George Eastman, who later founded Eastman Kodak of Rochester, bought his first supplies from Marks in 1877, when Marks was doing a bigger business in picture frames than in photographic supplies. Eastman was an unknown inventor at the time when he bought less than $50 worth of chemicals and instruments from Marks. Perhaps that is why it is said that without Henry Marks, Eastman Kodak Company might not have been born. And without Eastman Kodak, Marks and Fuller certainly would not have developed into the million dollar Rochester business it became.

William J. Fuller, who started work for Marks in 1878 as a sixteen-year-old, became a partner in the firm in 1902. Six years later Theodore Roosevelt's name was added to Marks and Fuller's growing list of notable customers. Roosevelt regularly sent his film to the company for processing and after word got around Washington of the President's preference, the firm was flooded with orders from senators, representatives and foreign dignitaries.

Marks died in 1912 and the elder Fuller in 1934. At that time Ted Fuller took over as company president, serving until retiring in 1968. He was a summer resident of Eagle Bay until his death June 2, 1979.

For many years Fuller distributed his photographic supplies from the extra building on the grounds of the Corner Gift Shop.

Bridge Club at Weller Cabin, 1939, 1st row Mrs. Flora Weller, Mrs. Millie Vogt, Mrs. Kate Dederick, Mrs. Harriet Remington Sulgar; 2nd row Mrs. Lillian Marchant, Mrs. Pearl Burton, unknown, Mrs. Alvina Searing, Mrs. Bea McCurdy, Mrs. Mildred McKee, Mrs. Marguerite Fuller, Mrs. Kate Myer. Credit Shirley Mearns.

Theodore Fuller of Marks an Fuller. Summer resident of Eag Bay Park over 60 years. Cred Marguerite Fuller.

Perhaps the first log cabin built in Eagle Bay Park was this one of Ted Fuller's. In the late 40's John Petersen built a log-siding elaborate home for them on the lake front in the park. Daughter Peggy on the steps. Owned 1981 by L. Beauchamp. Credit Mrs. Ted Fuller.

Shellwood — interior of the Fuller home. Credit Mrs. Ted Fuller.

Left to right: Janet Fuller Blakeman, Marguerite Fuller, Peggy Fuller Dardene, at Shellwood Lodge, Eagle Bay. Credit Fuller collection.

He rented this place from the John Petersens. Besides being a popular distributor of photo supplies, he took postcard photographs of Adirondack area scenes and distributed them through the businesses in and around Eagle Bay. Philip Dardenne, Fuller's son-in-law, was vice-president of the company.

Fuller's wife, Marguerite, and his daughters, Peggy and Janet, were leading members of the summer colony. Peggy was married to Dardenne and Janet became the wife of George Blakeman, an Inlet native. Philip and Peggy are both deceased.

Henry Smith

Henry Smith was Eagle Bay's singing carpenter. Although a resident of the Loomis Road in Inlet, he did most of his work in Eagle Bay. A man of unfailing good humor and optimism, he found time to sing, no matter how complex or difficult the work. His songs were always of a religious nature, and whenever something went wrong, instead of uttering a string of cuss words as many of his occupation did, Henry just sang louder.

For years Smith was John Petersen's right hand man in the building business. Petersen depended on him for many jobs that he would not trust to others. Respect and admiration for each other made them fast friends.

Born in Syracuse in 1887, Smith married Mabel Wescott of Eaton in 1910, and in 1927 they and their son, Perry, moved to Inlet. Henry became a devoted member of the Church of the Lakes in Inlet, serving as an usher and Sunday School teacher. He died July 29, 1979.

The Gitelmans and Sturmans

Long-time Eagle Bay residents have fond memories of summer people of years gone by. Judge and Mrs. Jacob Gitelman of Rochester were among them. Mrs. Gitelman, who earned prestige as an artist, painted a portrait of Betty Nelson Spencer, a village native then six years old. Betty remembers sitting long hours, along with Betty Ann or Joyce Davern, who posed with her.

Other cottagers were the Leon Sturman family on Central Avenue. As orthodox Jews, they did no work on the Sabbath. So Pauline Nelson was paid to light the burner on Saturaday morning enabling the Sturmans to heat water.

Judge and Mrs. Peck

Judge and Mrs. Samuel Peck of New York City brought youngsters growing up in Eagle Bay a glimpse of a very different world. The couple spent summers in a Swiss chalet which John Petersen had designed and built for them on East Avenue. The property included a cement driveway, the only one in the village, where Eagle Bay children learned to roller-skate and ride bicycles when the owners were not in residence.

A feature of the property was a lawn ornament, a little green troll — one of those creatures of Teutonic folklore who inhabited caves or hills. The troll appeared when the Pecks did, as a sort of herald to their arrival. An observer remarked that the judge looked rather like a large troll. He was a short, heavy man with a ruddy face.

Across the street from the chalet was the Pecks' carriage house, built in chalet style also. John Kane, their chauffeur, lived upstairs. The cars kept in the carriage house were elegant, "the likes of which no one before or since saw in Eagle Bay." One was a limousine equipped with a speaker horn so the judge and his wife, riding in the enclosed back seat, could talk to the driver. Another nicety was the vase of flowers in each car.

Mrs. Peck, who wore a bright red wig, had been a musician with opera companies. She had an upright piano on which she said she had played accompaniment for the famous singer, Lillian Russell.

After Mrs. Peck died, July 2, 1939, her estate, including the Eagle Bay Park property, went into the hands of her Syracuse lawyer, John Tuck. The chalet was sold and passed through the hands of various owners. The carriage house was remodeled by Petersen. A living room with a fireplace, a kitchen and other first floor accommodations were added. Owners since 1939 have included the A. J. Youst family, Ed and Marje Mantor and Allen and Dorothy Smith, who again remodeled the carriage house. In 1981 it was bought by John and Kathy Wright.

The Ike Chapells

On Eagle Point Road nestled among spruce, birch, hickory, maple, hemlock, beech, pine and balsam is an unusually lovely Adirondack cottage, built in 1938–1939. This cottage belongs to a family that has contributed over twenty-five years of dedicated service to Eagle Bay Park.

Ike Chapell and his wife, Marion lived in Honeoye Falls. They were involved with the educational system there and later in Rochester. In a camper made by Chapell, they came camping at Golden Beach near Raquette Lake several years before it became a State Park. In 1931 they stopped at Eagle Bay to see a lot on Eagle Point Road which had been purchased from Howard Weller by their friend Stan Stever. Stever had decided not to go through with his deal with Weller; so Chapell took up the mortgage on the lot and paid Stever some of what had been paid to Weller.

In 1932 Alfred Nelson cut the logs for Chapell's cottage, split the logs in half, took them to the sawmill, had them planed and edged with the bark left on the outer side. On Chapell's lot, Nelson stacked and covered the logs, and there they lay until 1938 when Chapell began his building of Camp Ro-Do-Wa. The camp reflects the names of his grandsons, children of his only daughter — Robert, Don and Wayne.

Nelson helped with the plans for the Camp, but this was primarily an owner building project. Mr. Chapell worked at the project over a few years before it was completed but they began living in it in the summer of 1939. Ro-Do-Wa reflects the personal, loving work of the owner. There are many other camps in Eagle Bay Park that have been built by the owners, but this camp is rather special, since Chapell, the owner has taken a special interest in the business of Eagle Bay Park Association. For well over twenty years he acted as secretary-treasurer of the Association, and has served at different times as a director. Also the camp is unique in log structure. There are a few log camps in the Park, and several log siding structures, but few have the log siding with the original outside bark still in excellent condition.

Henry Thibado

An old-timer who won the hearts of many Eagle Bay area people was Henry Thibado who was born in Indian Lake, but spent his early childhood in Raquette Lake. Thibado, as one long time resident remembers him, was honest, dependable, a hard worker and a fine carpetner.

He was a well known and excellent guide, "toting" hunters and their supplies to hunting camps deep in the woods. A caretaker for many camps in the Inlet-Eagle Bay area, he bought a large tract of land off the Uncas road. This land was well wooded, and Henry Thibado took advantage of his vast number of fine trees, cutting only those which needed harvesting. From these trees he sold fiewood and raw lumber to local residents. When he delivered a load of firewood one of his sons was usually with him.

Henry Thibado received the Purple Heart as a World War I veteran. In 1920 he married Hattie Payne. They moved to Inlet, where they lived for about thirty years before moving, in the early 50's, to a home on the Big Moose Road in Eagle Bay. Henry and Hattie Thibado had six children, four of whom still live in the Inlet, Eagle Bay, Old Forge area and are following in their father's footsteps as contributing, loyal citizens to their respective neighborhoods. Henry Thibado died in 1957 and it has been said that his passing left a void, not only in the lives of his wife and children, but in the lives of all who knew and depended on this fine man's skilled workmanship.

Ivan Brush of the U-GO-I-GO and U-GO-I-GO II

One of the lonely, single men of Eagle Bay was Ivan Brush. His parents were the original owners of the Brush Camps and of the very popular boats, U-GO-I-GO Nos. I and II. Ivan was the captain of No. 2 and when he retired from running his pleasure and sightseeing boat, he came to Eagle Bay Park and built himself a small camp.

He talked to only those people whom he liked and trusted. At times he would appear at the front door, be invited in and simply sit silently, often for an hour at a time. Other times Ivan might spend his time telling his best liked neighbor how badly someone had treated him. More often than not, however, Ivan simply wanted to sit with someone as company. He was "a silent, gentle man."

Betty Spencer comments:

> As I look back today and reflect on some of the stalwart Eagle Bay people, however, I can only wish that more people today had the grit of some of these early people — Slim Carkhoff, Ivan Brush, Amos Hudd, Carl Hansen, and a few others. They seemed to have so little, but they asked nothing of anyone. They were eager and willing to work for whatever minimum needs they had. 'Welfare' was not any part of their vocabulary. Life must have been difficult for them, but these men did not complain. So in their own way they were an inspiration to many others who had so much.

Slim Belonged to All Eagle Bay

Slim (William) Carkhoff was one of the colorful characters of Eagle Bay. Described as a strange but gentle man, he had several physical problems, caused by blood poisoning early in life — or so the story went. He limped, his hands shook, and his speech was slurred.

Slim was an inventor of sorts, very mechanical despite his handicaps. From an old truck chassis he made a machine to cut wood and drill wells. Howard Weller, in an early issue of the *Adirondack Eagle*, recommended Slim as a fine worker, especially good with a paint brush, always willing to do more than he was paid to do.

Residents remember Slim's delightful sense of humor. He painted the doors of the firehouse and presented this succinct bill: "2 doors, 2 coats, 2 bucks."

An ambitious man, not given to taking handouts, he lived life in his own style, almost as a hermit. This life style included an annual bath in Fourth Lake on the first warm day of spring. He and his clothing took their bath together by the lather and dunk system.

The Swiss Chalet built circa 1926 by John P. Petersen for Judge and Mrs. Samuel Peck of N.Y.C. Picture taken 1932: Left to right Hilda Smith, Helen Liddle, Elizabeth Liddle. Credit Helen Liddle.

The Ike Chapell home on Eagle Point Road. Credit Ike Chapell.

ke and Marion Chapell 50th wedding anniver-
ry. Credit Ike Chapell.

John Rogers presenting Henry Thibado, right, with a merit of honor. Credit Mrs. Alfred Thibado.

an Brush's *U-Go-I-Go II* rechris-
ned *The Nat Foster* by Allen Wilcox
en he bought it from Ivan. Later
ydocked and made into this cot-
ge. Credit David Schultz.

Slim Carkoff was an inventor. Here is his version of an automobile. He used this for transportation. Slim was a personality one could not forget. Credit Frieda Nelson.

Ole Olson

Ole Olson who lived in an Eagle Bay cottage is remembered for his violent death in an incident that shook the community in 1934. Olson was blown to bits during a quarrel with a friend. The quarrel led to a tussle on a bed and had a grim finale.

Ole no doubt had forgotten that he had placed a case of dynamite under the bed. The movements of the two fighters set off an explosion. Ole's limbs were scattered about and nothing remained of the cottage except kindling wood.

Alonzo J. Snyder, Hotel Guest

Alonzo Snyder, an Adirondack vacationer for 60 summers, first came to the Eagle Bay area in 1919 as a guest at the Onondaga Hotel, which later became Foley's Northwoods Inn. He stayed there each summer for a number of years and then began vacationing at Becker's, which was owned by Mr. and Mrs. Fred Becker, Mrs. Freda Westfall's parents.

Snyder and his friends came from New York City by train to Utica, thence to Thendara and then by the Raquette Lake Railroad to the Fairview Station. In the earliest times Snyder spent in the area, Frank Teich owned and operated a small shop near Fairview. The Fairview Station was nearest to Onondaga and Becker's. During these early years, until 1926, the roads were dangerous and all but impassable by car.

After several summers at Becker's, Snyder went to the Mohawk in 1933, when the Wilcoxes began operating the hotel. He continued his visits through 1979, in later years renting Pawnee cottage from Marietta Schultz Kelley. Snyder died at his home in New Jersey in the late fall of 1979.

Anneliese von Oettingen
Ballet Camp — Eagle Bay, New York

Anneliese von Oettingen — international ballerina, choreographer, teacher of ballet — is a cultural and talented asset to the Adirondack area. In 1973, after Moss Lake Camp for Girls closed, Anneliese established a School of Ballet based in Eagle Bay, but including Inlet and Old Forge. This school is attended each summer by groups of students coming from many states, though most are students of her internationally known School of Ballet in Cincinnati, Ohio, where she has six suburban schools and a Ballet Company. Not only is this a well known school of ballet, but it is also attended by a number of athletes who are given a special program of training and exercise, including those athletes suffering from sports injuries.

Alonzo Snyder made the Eagle Bay area his summer home from 1911 until 1979. He loved God's Country. Credit Alonzo J. Snyder.

Alonzo Snyder's tent — 1911 at the Onondaga Hotel. Credit A. Snyder.

Anneliese von Oettinger studied and performed in Berlin, London, Potsdam and throughout central Europe before coming to the United States in 1947. In London she studied with Nicolas Legat, who was formerly with the Imperial School of Ballet in St. Petersburg and who taught Pavlova and Nijinski. She was licensed to conduct a School of Ballet in Germany, with professional certification in Ballet, Pointe, Modern Dance, Tap, Character Dance, Acrobatics, Music Appreciation, History of Dance, Choreography, and Anatomy of the Dancer. Anneliese incorporates all of her experience in these fields in the Eagle Bay Ballet Camp. Students enjoy the unique approach to these aspects of dance. There are sessions for children, teens, adults, professional dancers, and athletes. Members of her staff at Eagle Bay are Dr. Rebecca Wiester, Anneliese's daughter, Cornelia Berns, and Jody Katsanis.

Anneliese has been successful teaching and training athletes. Among them are Allison Reid, the 17-year-old, who recently won the 1981 women's Pentathlon championship of the United States; Brad Cousino of the New York Giants and Ken Avery of the Kansas City Chiefs; and the United States ice skaters who participated in the 1980 Olympics held in Lake Placid. Anneliese has had a busy life not only teaching ballet but also training and teaching roller skaters, ice skaters, linebackers, marathon runners, swimmers, high jumpers, circus performers (horseback riders), movie stars and actors, pentathlon athletes, as well as the disabled (blind, deaf, slow learners).

Anneliese gives personal attention to each student in a "family atmosphere." To be close to the natural beauty of the Adirondacks is inspirational and revitalizing. For those who have not yet experienced the close kinship of Art and Nature, it is their opportunity to clear away the distractions of the automated world in which they live and to concentrate on the elements of life.

At her Ballet Camp in Eagle Bay, Anneliese offers these dancers, who number about 45 each summer, a great variety of additional activities such as hiking, swimming, canoe trips, outings on other lakes, visits to museums, and attending performances of the New York City Ballet at Saratoga Springs.

The Anneliese von Oettingen Ballet Company occasionally performs at the Community Arts Center in Old Forge. These ballets are original compositions with the choreography created by Anneliese and performed only by her Ballet Company.

"Eagle Bay is the ideal environment for the active artist, Anneliese. She is not an architect of buildings, but an architect of artistic mouments: Monuments of Nature and Art, permanent within each of her students," notes a critic of her work.

An Artist in Eagle Bay

Jay and Shirley Garbutt in 1962 bought "Trails End" camp on Central Avenue in Eagle Bay Park. The camp was built about 1924 for Bob and Alvina Searing.

"Jay Garbutt's creative imagination and artistic skill coupled with experience have earned him an important role at Conklin, Labs and Beebe Inc. for 34 years," says the CLB tribute to Garbutt, Jr. He has worked as an artist, lay-out, art buyer and for years as the one responsible for all aspects of print advertising for CLB, lending his talents to various national consumer and trade accounts, including those in diamonds, footwear and food industries.

Garbutt retired as senior art director for CLB in Syracuse. In winter, he and his family reside in Phoenix. In summer they conduct their Slabwood Fence Gallery, where he displays his art work on his slab wood fence, in their Eagle Bay Park home.

Donna — Eagle Bay's Teenage Ballet Teacher

Donna Ficker Mineker, talented teacher of ballet and tap, who is a sister of Suzanne Farrell, principal ballerina of the New York City Ballet, spent most of the summers of the 1950's in Eagle Bay with her grandmother, Frances von Holle, and her aunt, Helen Brittingham. For several years Donna had studied dance in Cincinnati. She missed her dancing during the summers in Eagle Bay.

In 1954, when she was only fourteen, Donna had a creative idea which she put into action. Through the efforts of the Eagle Bay Ladies Fire Auxiliary and Stuart Nelson, the fire chief, she obtained the use of the Eagle Bay Fire Hall for dance classes.

She let the teenagers of the village know her plans. Her enrollment exceeded her expectations as her classes grew in number and in excitement. In 1955 her previous students from 1954 were on hand for summer dance classes. There was also an influx of enrollees from Inlet and Old Forge. Again her summer dance program was successful.

In her third summer, 1956, she found her efforts even more gratifying. She decided to show the public what her pupils had accomplished. Donna and her dancers staged a "petite gala." The resident students who did not participate in the dance classes worked as "apprentice troupers" selling tickets for the review. The program netted over $200 which was given to the firemen by the Auxiliary in Donna's name.

It was during this time that Donna met Paul Mineker whom she later married. Before marriage she went to Juilliard School of Music from which she earned an M.A. degree in dance. She also has recently completed her certification as dental hygienist. In the

DONNA FICKER PRESENTS HER DANCE PUPILS IN "THE SLEEPY TOWN EXPRESS"
Sunday evening, August 26, 1956 Seven o'clock

EAGLE BAY FIRE HALL

This is the story of three children who have invited their friends to their home for an evening of fun. Finally their mother sends their playmates home and the children go to bed. While asleep the Fairy Princess comes and awakens them, telling them she can take them to a land of fun where they will meet Nursery Rhyme characters, dolls, animals, etc. Of course this is only a dream, but all in all the children had an enjoyable evening.

Scene I Children's Bedroom

Children: Michele Kopp, Debbie Winslow, Spencer Newton
Playmates: Marianne Guzzardo, Linda Guzzardo, Marla Guzzardo, Martha Ball, Donna Ball, Pam Harwood, Penny Harwood, Beth Ann Newton, Joanna Hansen
Mother: Sue Ficker
Fairy Princess: Sue Ficker

Scene II Sleepy Town

Mary Quite Contrary: Penny Harwood
Flowers: Beth Ann Newton, Joanna Hansen
Jack: Charlie Winslow
Jill: Gretchen Windhausen
Butterflies: Donna Ball, Marianne Guzzardo

Scene III Toyland

Mouse: Marla Guzzardo
Elf: Linda Guzzardo
Dancing Doll: Pam Harwood
Gypsy Doll: Martha Ball

*** *** *** *** ***

Other children served as "apprentice troupers" selling tickets and doing other vital chores.

BEVERLY FICKER, ACCOMPANIST

STORY, CHOREOGRAPHER AND COSTUMES; DONNA FICKER

SPECIAL APPRECIATION TO: Lewis Mulchy, for his assistance and the Eagle Bay Firemen for permission to use the Fire Hall.

Anneliese von Oettingen, internationally known teacher of ballet. Credit Anneliese von Oettingen.

Court Dance "Pavanne" from "Dances Through the Centuries." Left to right Karin Miller, Kurt Yabuk, Beverly Strelau, all solists of A. von Oettingen Ballet Co. at Eagle Bay. Choregraphy Anneliese von Oettingen, music by Gluck. Credit Ms. von Oettingen.

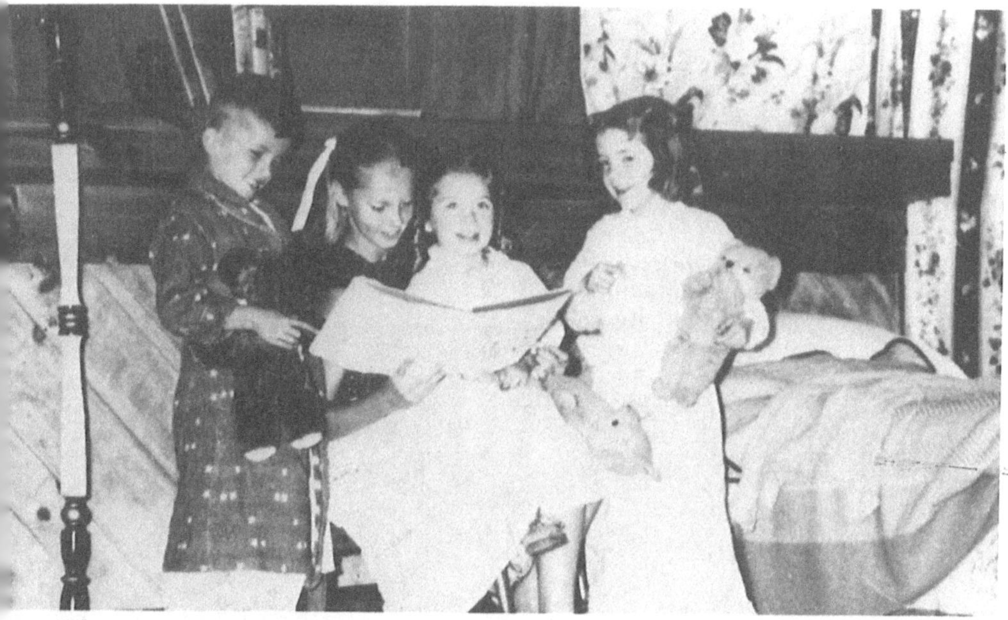

"Sleepy Town Express" choreography by Donna Ficker. Left to right Spencer Newton, Suzanne Farrell in early teens, Debbie Winslow, Michele Kopp. Credit Jane Kopp.

Donna Ficker Mineker — at age 16 as Fairy in Sleepy Town Express which she staged in the Eagle Bay fire hall. Credit Donna Mineker.

The author's two favorite men. Good helpers; good companions — Herbert O'Brien, husband; David Schultz, son.

Theodore R. Fallis and his son, Theodore P. on Eagle Bay dock. Credit Theodore M. Fallis.

Mrs. Theodore R. Fallis, left, daughter, Theodora; right, Theodore No. 2. Picture shows Eagle Bay Creek entrance into Fourth Lake.

winter she is at home in Camillus, where she has a dance school and also works for a dentist. In addition she is the mother of three teenage sons. The Minekers spend the summers in their Eagle Bay area cottage and Donna teaches dance at Old Forge Art Center.

Reminiscence of the First Camps in Eagle Bay

No one knows for sure which was the first camp built in Eagle Bay Park, but, research discloses the following facts.

Theodore R. Fallis, born in 1855, married young Mary Dussalt, both of Little Falls, in 1898. They spent their honeymoon in Eagle Bay. Theodore Fallis was a manufacturer of cigars and always took a supply along with him on vacation trips; so on his honeymoon he sold cigars to the old Eagle Bay Hotel, where they stayed.

The honeymooners fell in love with the Eagle Bay area and returned often on vacation trips with their daughter Theodora and son Theodore P. On July 18, 1918 Fallis bought twenty feet of right-of-way over lots 254–255 entering on East Avenue from Howard Weller.

Theodore M. Fallis, grandson of this honeymooning couple, lived summers in the Eagle Bay Camp, Dorla, until he was eight. He says his father, Theodore P., told him the old camp was there before any other in the park. It is standing much as it was in the earliest days of the park and perhaps was built long before the elder Fallis bought the property. Since this statement cannot be documented it is safe to say the camp was one of the first in the Park.

There are wide age spans in the Fallis' line. Theodore M., 24 in 1981, is young enough to have been Theodore R.'s great-grandson. A deep love for the woods, mountains and lakes was instilled into him and the one thing he wants most is to some day be able to buy the old camp.

The history of the land transaction of the camp shows Theodore R. Fallis and his son, Theodore P. Fallis, owned this piece of God's Country from 1918 until September 25, 1964. At that time Theodore P. sold the old camp to John and Mary Slagel, who deeded it to their daughter and her husband, Carol and Norman Burak, on September 20, 1977. The Slagels and Buraks have added a modern kitchen and other conveniences to the old home. The tree growing through the porch roof as seen in the picture has been removed.

Many older residents believe that the camp which was owned first by Mrs. Littlejohn, later by her niece, Gertrude Wikander, is the oldest camp. On a map made by Weller in 1917, the Littlejohns' two lots are shown, and according to John Petersen, he and his brother Fred, lived in a small cabin that was on the property at that time.

This cabin later became the downstairs part of Wikander's enlarged camp.

Other People

The biographies in this chapter are of those people whom the author had the good fortune to know personally and well. When all the biographies were done, it was felt the chapter would be incomplete without the addition of other names.

The names of all the people connected with the Raquette Lake Railroad at Eagle Bay were not available. It is known that C. G. Ward, engineer for the railroad construction company, lived in Eagle Bay. Just where he lived is not known. In 1905 William Pulling came to Eagle Bay as stationmaster. Here at the station he met Mrs. Pulling when she arrived by train to begin summer work at one of the hotels. They were married while Mr. Pulling was still stationmaster at Eagle Bay. In 1907 W. A. Pulling was transferred to the Raquette Lake Station and James Cervo took over in Eagle Bay as stationmaster when Pulling left.

Traversys and Guinands owned the property which later became the George and Pearl Burton property. Pearl Burton Coats sold the historic old place to Murray Dunn in the '70's.

For many years the Ortner family owned a home on Eagle Point. Later after her husband's death, Marie Ortner sold the home and had a place built farther around on Eagle Point Road. Her son, Carl, has owned this place since his mother's death.

Mr. and Mrs. Mark Gais were residents of Eagle Bay Park for many years. They were a kind and gentle couple, always interested in their neighbors' well-being. Another family in the Park during the 30's and early 40's was the Reed family. They had two lovely daughters, Elaine and Kathy, who were popular with the younger crowd.

The Sid Parkers and their daughter were long a part of the Eagle Bay scene. They sold their home in the late 60's to the Paul Kelley, Jr. family, whose members for several years were a happy addition to the summer population. Among other Park families during these early years were the "By" Jones family, mentioned in connection with the Tea Pot Dome and Mr. Tartaglia, who bought property on the lake near Pearl Burton Coat's home. Tartaglia's daughter, Mrs. John J. Barry, owns the home. John Barry died in the summer of 1981. The Martin J. Nunn family of Rome, long-time Eagle Bay summer visitors, built a lovely home on lake frontage land next to the Searing property.

William Hamel, hunting companion of John Petersen, built a home on the lake front between the Petersen home and Kelley's. Hamel later sold this to the Matthews family.

Lina Lou Kellog, long-time Park resident in early years, was given her home, *Faerie Lodge,* by John Gudmunsen, whose wife was a life-long friend of Lina Lou's mother.

Clarence Pylman, long time in the Adirondack area, chose the Big Moose Road on which to build a lovely year-round home for his family. Another resident of Eagle Bay since the early '20's is Viola Lefevre. She continues to come to Eagle Bay during the summer and lives on the Frank Teich property. Her son, Elton, and his wife, Ruth, also have a home in Eagle Bay. Blanche Pellor Zurl has long been a summer resident of Eagle Bay and worked at The Trading Post during its best days. Sadie Hinman was a waitress in the Trading Post for many years. Her husband, Louis, worked as a maintenance man in the area. They owned two places on Forrest Lane.

Then there were Lewis and Mary Mulchy. Mary was for years housekeeper and supervisor of laundry for Rocky Point Inn. Louie, a maintenance man, was employed by The Mohawk Inn for many years. They owned a two-story home on Forrest Lane across from the Hinmans.

Dorothy and Amos Sullivan came to Eagle Bay as vacationers in the late 30's and about 1945 bought land from John Petersen on which he built them an attractive cottage facing Route 28. He later sold adjoining land to Dorothy's mother, Mrs. Hazel Vanderlinde, and built for her a home like the Sullivans'. Amos Sullivan passed away in the summer of 1981.

Since their marriage, John Breakey, and his wife, Jane, have lived in their home at the intersection of East and Lakeview Avenue. Their son, Jon, has grown to manhood in Eagle Bay.

Carrie Beutner's mother, Mrs. Miller, at her death, left her lakefront home on Eagle Point road facing the lake, to Carrie. The Beutner family came to this cottage many summers. The two daughters and son were well liked young people in the Park. Mrs. Beutner's brother, Fred Miller, was owner of this cottage in 1981.

Charles and Martha Barkauskas, with their son and daughter, live in Martha's grandfather's old home which they have extensively remodeled. Mr. Pellor, her gandfather, was for many years a summer resident of Eagle Bay. He taught school at different places in winter.

Mr. and Mrs. Leon Beauchamp in 1981 were owners of the Ted Fuller lovely log camp built in 1920 which marks it as one of the older camps in the Park. The Beauchamps have remodeled the camp.

Note: It is the hope of the author that this listing of some of the long-time residents of Eagle Bay will give the reader an idea of how many people have lived in and loved this corner of God's Country.

CHAPTER X

Aviators in Adirondack Skies

Aviators at Eagle Bay Harbor

The pioneers in aviation reflected the romance and excitement of this form of transportation and recreation both in their innovative approach to flying and in their private lives. Their early efforts laid the foundation for today's more sophisticated operation.

Pilots working out of Adirondack bases say that the men who flew from Eagle Bay and Fourth Lake were the very best of their day. From the Eagle Bay base they took tourism off the ground as they skimmed over the beautiful mountains and lakes in a great scenic adventure.

Brussel, Van Auken and the Stinson

"We flipped a half dollar and lost." With this quip E. Albert Brussel tells how he and Harold Van Auken reached their decision to buy a plane and start a chartered air service in the Adirondacks. They had been mulling the idea for two months and the coin toss by which they "lost" the choice of further delay prompted them to go ahead.

The day of decision was in early July, 1929, in Old Forge. Had they made up their minds earlier, they would have had the first chartered plane to fly the region. As it was, George Hand of Syracuse brought a Curtiss-Robin to the Adirondacks earlier that summer and for about a month flew the area. But the plane was destroyed by fire on Raquette Lake and he was forced to abandon the enterprise.

Undaunted by Hand's misfortune, Brussel and Van Auken held to their plans for an air service and founded the Central Adirondack Aviation Corporation.

With Jack Morton, the first pilot for the new corporation, Brussel arrived in Detroit July 11 to buy a plane and then went to the plant in Wayne, Michigan, to take delivery. There they saw the brand new four-passenger Stinson SM2AC "Detroiter" with a 225 horsepower Wright J6-7 cylinder Whirlwind engine and a fixed pitch propeller. The aircraft was equipped with wheels and flown to Mount Clement, Michigan, where Morton replaced the wheels with pontoons. The plane was the first ever to be equipped with Fairchild floats.

Morton flew to Buffalo and on to Fourth Lake. With characteristic humor, when they were over the Utica Airport, Morton dropped a parachute with a note attached. The note said they were low on fuel and he was bringing the Stinson down on Lake Delta near Rome. He added a postscript that they were going on to Fourth Lake anyway.

On landing in Fourth Lake, the "Detroiter" docked at the Eagle Bay Hotel, which became the corporation's base of operations. On its maiden flight the plane carried the first express cargo to the Adirondacks — 300 pounds consisting of a cylinder block, head, pistons and connecting rods for Fulton Navigation Company.

As soon as they reached Eagle Bay, the spirited pilot took Brussel's partner, Harold Van Auken, for a flight. He then took his girl friend up for a ride; then the owners' wives were given a preview of the Stinson's capabilities.

Mrs. Brussel described her first flight with Jack Morton:

> He was very enthusiastic about the plane and wanted to show what it could do. He proceeded to perform rolls, loops and other stunts. About the time he leveled off, he noticed that Mrs. Brussel looked pretty "green." He apologized, not knowing that it was her first flight. Needless to say, they haven't been able to get Mrs. Brussel higher than the Empire State Building since that time.

The Central Adirondack Aviation Corporation soon developed a rushing business flying tourists around the Fulton Chain and ferrying fishermen and hunters to remote areas. Passengers enjoyed the view and the comfortable rear seat, which held two and was made entirely of wicker.

The Pilots and Crew

After a year as company pilot, Morton was replaced by "Skeet" Sliter of Canada-Caroga Lakes area, who also stayed a year. Sliter was succeeded by Merrill Phoenix from Syracuse, who flew at an early age and stayed with the company for its duration.

The final crew member was Albert (Red) Panella who served as groundman. He handled sales and helped in maintenance and servicing the plane. A licensed pilot himself, Red taught co-owner Al Brussel to fly the Stinson. Brussel did not elect to get a commercial license.

New ideas came with the new Stinson and new service to the Adirondacks. Experimentation in fish planting was started. The Rapshaw Club, a prominent sportsmen's organization, used the plane to stock Beaver River. The fish were transported by train to Old Forge in tanks, then flown to Beaver River, where, while in flight, they were dropped, with a survival rate of 75 to 90 percent. The idea proved successful and has been used extensively throughout the country in other remote areas.

The Depression Strikes

The fledgling company started in 1929 soon encountered a great obstacle to success — the Depression. The fateful coin toss responsible for the pioneering efforts undertaken by Brussel and Van Auken, preceded the Black Thursday by only three months. The epidemic of economic ruin found its way to the Central Adirondacks, where even in that beautiful setting no one was immune. With declining business and general financial malaise throughout the community, it was decided to sell the plane. Reluctantly Brussel and Van Auken placed an advertisement in an aeronautics trade journal, and in 1934 this brought Chester McLean of the Panhandle Air Transport Company (PATCO) to Old Forge to purchase the Stinson.

With a change in ownership, arrangements were made to fly the plane from Old Forge to Seattle, then to Juneau, Alaska, PATCO headquarters. The plane was stored in Brussel's garage at the time of the sale, as the Fulton Chain was still covered with ice. A set of wheel gear to replace the Fairchild floats was installed by Merrill Phoenix. The plane was towed onto the beach at First Lake and the wings were assembled for takeoff. The floats were shipped by express to New York and through the Panama Canal to Seattle.

The Stinson in Alaska

On March 28, 1934 Jack Howard, a pilot and hotel owner from Seattle, Washington, along with Chester McLean of PATCO, readied for takeoff. Lucille Van Auken, sister of Harold Van Auken, former co-owner of CAAC, expressed her wish to fly cross-country in the Stinson. An experienced traveler, she had crossed the country many times, but never in an aircraft. After much discussion, it was decided she could go and she was given a total of fifteen minutes in which to get ready. Intrepid traveler that she was, she made it. The Stinson departed Old Forge and the Adirondacks the same day and made thirteen stopovers before reaching Seattle. One was a lengthy layover in Fargo, North Dakota, because of a blizzard on Easter Sunday.

Upon arriving in Seattle, McLean and Miss Van Auken had to wait yet another six weeks for the arrival of the floats, which were being shipped through the Panama Canal. Once the floats were attached, the "Detroiter" went on to Juneau.

McLean flew the Stinson for PATCO, taking fur traders, miners and the like into the Alaskan northlands. Lucille Van Auken elected to return cross-country by bus.

After the Stinson years, there were other air services chartered in the Adirondacks somewhat filling the void. For years area residents wondered what had become of the four passenger "Detroiter" after its sale to PATCO.

Then, in 1969, Norton (Buster) Bird, who operated a charter plane service in Inlet stopped by to see his old friend, Al Brussel. Bird had with him a book by Archie Satterfield, *Alaskan Bush Pilots in the Flat Country.* In it were a story and several pictures on McLean and PATCO. Immediately Brussel recognized his old plane, comparing the numbers shown on the aircraft with those in his own flight log book. The article recounted the purchase of the Stinson in the Adirondacks and its service in the Alaskan flat country. One of the photographs showed a downed and wrecked Stinson. The article mentioned that the plane had been sold to the University of Washington for classroom demonstrations. So the pioneering Stinson, which had led the way for other chartered services in the Adirondacks, had not outlived its usefulness. It was still contributing to the improvement of aviation.

Merrill Phoenix

Merrill Phoenix soloed when he was 18 and started flying for the Central Adirondack Aviation Corporation when he was 21. Few pilots have had such extensive firsthand experience in the evolution of aircraft. He first took the controls in 1928, a period not far beyond the days of the dashing long white scarves that were the mark of the early birdmen. As Phoenix's career advanced, planes became safer with more sophisticated equipment and instruments. The leather helmets and jackets worn by the pioneers eventually gave way to cabin aircraft.

But earlier, unpressurized cabins and long hours aloft took their toll on many pilots. Phoenix suffered a gradual hearing loss from the great number of flying hours under these conditions. However, he lost none of his expertise.

Phoenix was not only a competent pilot, but was accomplished in all phases of air and ground mechanics and procedures. And he gave the planes he flew loving care. Typically, one winter when Al Brussel stored the Central Adirondack Aviation's Stinson in his garage in Thendara, Phoenix stripped it down and gave it a complete overhaul.

The pioneer, whose license number was 10988, first took to air without much instruction. He recalls it this way:

> The pilot training I received was most informal and in ex-

change for helping build a hangar, washing airplanes and such. One day at the Hinsdale farm, which later was Syracuse's Amboy, a good friend, Ernie Hannam, told me to take the plane around for landing or two — his brand new OX5 Waco. That was the real beginning of my flying activities. Dual time as student was not recorded, but it was just a very few hours.

During World War II, Phoenix was one of the earliest ferry pilots, flying the large bombers for the Royal Air Force. With Montreal as a starting point, he ferried planes from Canada, to Scotland and Egypt for the Allied forces. These were American bombers, a far cry from the Stinson he had piloted in the Adirondacks in the 30's. In the ferrying operation, the pilots, radio men and navigators, as well as the flight engineers, were personnel of the 45th Group, R.A.F., Ferry or Transport Command. The mission involved an almost worldwide movement of aircraft, people and supplies. "It was a rare experience for such as me," Phoenix comments. Back from ferrying duty, Phoenix conducted seaplane activities at Bill Dunay's from the Wood Hotel dock. Beginning in 1947, he operated under the name of Phoenix Adirondack Flights with a YKC Waco, a 225 horsepower craft.

Allen Wilcox, hotelman who flew with Phoenix both before and after the pilot's wartime service, pays tribute to his skill:

> Merrill Phoenix was an expert in relation to landings and takeoff from Beaver Lake. This lake was surrounded by trees — a small lake — and the minimum distance for takeoffs and landings in small seaplanes. The type of landing was sometimes called a "falling leaf" landing, setting a plane down with very little forward motion — a slide-slip landing. On Beaver Lake Merrill took off in the pattern of a horseshoe. When he turned in the horseshoe curve, it was called a "step off takeoff."

When Phoenix was not flying he kept the plane parked under the Fifth Lake bridge or at the Wood Hotel. Both he and his aircraft were familiar figures in the Adirondacks.

Until 1955, when he gave up seaplaning in the area, his blue and yellow Waco was flying about every activity a Central Adirondack seaplane was capable of doing, Phoenix says. Bus Bird of Sixth Lake took over the aircraft with spare parts in 1955 and used it for several seasons. A long-time friend of the Adirondacks and its people, Phoenix returns regularly for vacations and visits.

Harold (Scotty) Scott

From time to time a dynamic person, whom it is impossible not to notice, emerges on the scene. Such a man was Harold Scott,

Curtiss Robin Plane at Eagle Bay July 11, 1929. Credit Al Brussel collection.

Harold Van Auken, Jack Morton, pilot, and Al Brussel 1929. Credit Brussel collection.

Left Mrs. Al Brussel, son Albert. Center Mrs. H. Van Auken, right her son. Ready for a take-off in the new Stinson — 1929. Credit Al Brussel collection.

An Eagle Bay first — 1932 — loading Stinson aircraft with fish hatchery cans of fingerlings to be flown to Witchopple and Big Crooked and be planted there; termed a success by Prof. Hartnett of Rap Shaw Club. Seaplane NC 452H — Stinson Model SM 2AC Wright J6-7 225 H.P. Fairchild floats. Credit Merrill Phoenix.

Eagle Bay based Stinson "Detroiter" 225 H.P. Wright — Fairchild floats — J6-7 motor at east end of Witchopple Lake — Merrill Phoenix and Prof. Hartnett (Rap Shaw Club leader) after arrival from Eagle Bay Aug. 1932 — Aircraft License NC 452H Stinson Model SM2AC. Credit Merrill Phoenix.

Stinson "Detroiter" Wright J6-7 225 H.P. Fairchild pontoons loading freight — from #4 end of Beaver River flow to go to Witchopple Lake "Rap Shaw Club" Nov. 1932. Credit Merrill Phoenix, pilot.

Hunters use seaplane to travel to and from Eagle Bay, 4th Lake. Displaying the six pointer is Stinson pilot, Merrill Phoenix, Nov. 1932. Credit Merrill Phoenix.

November 1933 Eagle Bay a different sight than summertime. Here is low water, snow on the sand beach and snow on the seaplane. Seaplane NC452H — Stinson Model SM2AC Fairchild floats. Credit Merrill Phoenix.

Stinson Monoplane Wright J6-7 225 horsepower — Fairchild pontoons. Eagle Bay Beach — Hunting party standing by, 1933. Credit Merrill Phoenix.

Van Auken and Brussell's Stinson in Alaska. Note number and flight log. Credit Al Brussell collection.

Merrill Phoenix relaxing in the home of friends.

1946 Harold Scott designed, built and successfully used the original seaplane fish tank equipment. It is being used here. Ausable Lakes fish planting from air — a trial run — water only. Credit Merrill Phoenix.

1946 at Beaver River Flow awaiting some passengers from the Rap Shaw Club dock. Credit Merrill Phoenix.

1946 The Eagle Bay WACO seaplane NC2258 had many uses and planting fish from the air was one. This by arrangements with a private club. Loading fish tank in plane. Ausable Lakes. Credit Merrill Phoenix.

1946 hunting season means carrying al[l] sorts of equipment, supplies and hunt[t]ers. The hunters come out with tw[o] good size bucks. Credit Merrill Phoenix

e Mobile with skiis, built by Scotty in 1925. sing a Harley Davidson Motorcycle engine nd an airplane propeller, Little Falls. Credit orothy Scott.

Scotty on Fourth Lake, circa 1930. Credit Mrs. Dorothy Scott.

Scotty with his mascot "Boots" summer 1936. Credit Dorothy Scott.

pioneer aviator of New York State's Mohawk Valley and the Central Adirondacks.

Scotty was born in Little Falls in 1900, son of Andrew and Mary Scott, and as a boy was caught up in the excitement of the newfangled flying machine. When he was very young, he saw Harry Atwood flying non-stop from Albany to Buffalo, a breath-taking feat. On that day Scotty resolved that some day he, too, would be a flier.

All through his school and college days Scotty kept his goal in mind and after attending Niagara University, he worked as a stock clerk to save $400 for the flying course at the Sweeney School of Aviation in Kansas City, Missouri. On completing the course in the summer of 1926, he bought a World War I surplus plane, with George Van Buren, projectionist in a Little Falls movie theater, as his partner. They purchased the plane, described as a standard J-1 airplane with a new Curtis OX5 motor, from Nicholas Beazley Airplane Company of Marshall, Missouri.

With Claude Norris, of Nabor, North Carolina, also a recent graduate of the Sweeney school, Scotty flew the open-cockpit plane back to Little Falls. Total flying time was fourteen hours, but because of treacherous winds over Ohio, the young airmen many times were forced to land after covering only fifty miles in a day.

The main cause of the delay was not the strong winds, but the strange appetites of some pigs at LaFayette, Indiana. Scotty set down in a farm field near there while he and Norris had lunch with a friend. On returning to the plane, they found that the pigs too had been eating lunch — they had devoured the fabric coverings off the aircraft. Scotty spent two weeks on repairs to put the plane back in flying form.

So nearly three weeks had passed from the date of purchase — August 11, 1926 — until Scott and Norris landed on Seymour Field, west of Little Falls. Before heading for the field the early evening of July 31, the young aviator circled over his mother's house.

The Little Falls *Evening Times* the next day said, "Arrival of the plane was an event of great interest to local residents because Mr. Scott is the first Little Falls boy to own and fly a plane in this vicinity." Scotty's long flying career was under way.

Two major events occurred in his life in 1930. He married Dorothy McIntyre of Dolgeville on June 4, and he moved to Inlet, where he became one of the first pilots to fly the Adirondacks. He switched from wheels to pontoons and started flying charter trips, often taking off from the Mohawk on Fourth Lake to Allen Wilcox's property at Beaver Lake. He also flew passengers to any place which had a lake a half mile or more across so he could land. His plane was a gold and red Waco, which he parked under the Fifth Lake bridge next to his Inlet home.

"Adirondack flying isn't especially hard," Scotty used to say. "You just have to know the country and watch out for bumps. A north-south wind sweeping over the ridges makes some nasty air pockets."

He did indeed know the country, even being able on at least one occasion to fly in the dark. The story goes that a Beaver River boy suffered a deep gash on his knee and Scotty received an emergency call for a doctor in the middle of the night. He picked up Dr. Fred Cole of Inlet and took off in the black night — no lights anywhere. By the light of a single lamp in the window of the Beaver River cabin, he "felt his way down" and landed. Asked about his daring and accuracy in this and other difficult situations, Scotty replied, "It is the same principle as coming into a dark room you know and reaching for the light."

Harold Scott is said to have been the first to land a pontoon plane on an ice-covered lake, a convenient thing to be able to do, especially when picking up a hunter stranded in the woods after a lake suddenly became iced-over. Scotty invented a simple, sure way to locate a landing site on a frozen lake. He always carried a supply of stones in the cockpit and he would hurl these down at the lake until he found a spot thin enough for the stones to penetrate. In that place in the lake he would safely bring his pontooned plane down. The stone-dropping of course, required flying at a low altitude. The technique was a boon to winter aviation. There was the story of another pilot who ignored the innovation and Scotty had a photograph of the plane. It landed upside down on the lake.

Scotty and Jim Cheyne, who first worked with him as a mechanic, flew many hunters into remote areas which were safer for hunters than the more crowded areas. And on other flights Scott and Cheyne kept on the lookout for lost hunters. "If you're lost, go to a clearing and wave a white handkerchief. We'll find you," was Scotty's advice.

With Allen Wilcox as an occasional observer, Scotty flew fire patrols as well as many patrols looking for lost hunters. Forest rangers also often flew with him over burning sections to estimate the extent of a fire. Sometimes the flier discovered and reported a fire before it had been spotted from the observatory.

Restocking the lakes with trout fingerlings was another of Scotty's services. From a truck carrying pails of young fish, the fish and ample water were transferred to the plane and placed in a fish tank which Scott invented. Scotty then flew low over the lake while Jim Cheyne or another helper opened the tank, planting the fish like sowing wheat.

In twenty years of flying the Adirondack lakes, the pioneer pilot made numerous forced landings, but always there was a lake nearby. He was meticulous in maintenance and so never had to spend time with a sick motor. Only once did he have a close call, the time he landed on Beaver Lake with a broken rod in his engine. The resourceful birdman looked around until he found a towel rod attached to a camp stove, fashioned it into shape, worked it into the motor, and made it back to Inlet, where there was still enough light for a safe landing.

Herb Helms of Helms Aero Service at Long Lake remembers Scotty's barnstorming when Herb was still in high school. He and a friend would always try to get the first ride when Scotty came for the annual Long Lake celebration because they thought the first one was the longest. "It was in his old but beautiful open-cockpit Waco straight wing," Helms recalls. "I'm sure this had a lot do do with my becoming a pilot later on. The pilots who flew at that time from Fourth Lake were the very best," Helms recalls.

Scott, who was described by author David H. Beetle as "good looking, clear-eyed, slim and cautious," often had a favorite passenger beside him. The passenger was Boots, a Boston Terrier, who was as much at home in the plane as the average dog is with his head out the window of a car. Boots knew that he was welcome to go when Scotty took off with no human sightseers aboard. He would run around and beg for his goggles, and then climb onto the wing of the plane, teasing to get into the cockpit. The flying dog apparently liked to live dangerously, as assistants to Scotty sometimes had to grab his paw to keep him from falling over the side. When this happened, according to a newspaper account in 1936, Boots calmly took his paw away from the man riding with him and watched the Adirondack scenery go by. At the time of the news account, he already had chalked up about a hundred hours in the air.

Flying sightseers had its humorous incidents. One recalled by Scotty's daughter, Janet Scott Burwell, took place when he had a rather elderly lady passenger. Scotty used to close his eyes occasionally and place his head near the window to listen to the motor and determine how well it was running. When the woman saw him do this she waited a minute or two and then hit him over the head with her handbag. "No pilot is going to go to sleep while I am up in the air with him!" she declared. Scotty then explained what he had been doing.

In his earlier flying years, in 1932 and 1933, he entered various races along the Atlantic coast from Boston to Miami and collected several blue ribbons in these competitions.

Before his Adirondack years, Scotty flew from Utica Airport in Marcy, where he also gave flying lessons. One of his students was John Piersma, whose summer camp on Fourth Lake is never without a seaplane on the shore when he is in residence. Those were the days when Scotty's salesman and technical adviser, Red Panella, gave a special signal when sales exceeded twenty-five dollars. He let Scotty know of this happy state of affairs by lighting up a cigar!

Amelia Earhart, eastbound with her English-design Arvo Avian aircraft, stayed over at the Marcy Airport for three days when Mohawk Valley snowstorms were too wild and frequent for safe flying. She was made most welcome by the Marcy airmen and finally went on her way in the open cockpit biplane, complete with an escort and a pair of wool socks furnished by Scotty. She sent a note of thanks but said she was keeping the socks, since it was the first time on the whole trip that her feet had been warm. All the rest of his life Scotty treasured a picture taken of himself with the famous aviatrix.

In the eyes of the young people growing up in the 30's and later in the Adirondacks, Scotty was their hero, greatly respected as a pilot. It was felt that if anyone could land a plane on some of those Adirondack lakes, he could, but if he wouldn't, then it wasn't safe or feasible. A long-time resident remembers him as having a reputation for never taking chances, but, "in his quiet way, he also had a great sense of humor and there were sometimes screaming females who got a joyride!"

Betty Nelson Spencer recalls Scotty also as a musician, who played bass fiddle with a small combo at school dances and was an accomplished organist. She reminisces:

> Because he lived in Inlet and had to pass through Eagle Bay he would often graciously pick us up on his "gigs" at school. On more than one occasion as we were making our way down the highway, when a number with a good bass part came on his car radio, he would stop on the road and pluck out the accompaniment on his bass fiddle, which he carried with its neck across the back of the front seat and the rest of the fiddle in the back seat. He was a wonderful gentleman.

His daughter, Mrs. William Burwell, who was persuaded by the author to share some of her memories, also likes to think of Scotty as a musician as well as an expert pilot, a man helpful to his neighbors, a truly gentle and caring person. She gives this personal peek at the shared joys of father and daughter:

> As a child, after Mom put me to bed I often climbed out to sit by the window when I heard Dad taxiing his plane up the inlet. I loved to watch the lights as the plane came closer and

Keeping warm in winter flights on Fourth Lake 1930. Credit Dorothy Scott.

Scotty prepared for flying in open cockpit plane at Eagle Bay base; ticket building in background, 1938. Credit Dorothy Scott.

Harold Scott's WACO seaplane YKC-S Edo floats. Eagle Bay 4th Lake Sept. 1944. Credit Merrill Phoenix.

Utica Airport, March 28, 1929, L. to R: Scotty, unidentified pilot, Amelia Earhart, Hughie Jones, Mechanic. Credit Dorothy Scott.

Scotty, daughter Janet, wife Dorothy, 1938. Credit Dorothy Scott.

Dedication of airplane base at Eagle Bay, circa 1942. Credit Dorothy Scott.

Mrs. Eleanor Roosevelt at dedication of Eagle Bay Dock; for security reason did not appear in photo. Credit Dorothy Scott.

Scotty and Stubby Weedmark, who served 1940–47 as ticket salesman for the seaplane business. Credit Bill Weedmark.

Scotty retired from flying 1947; operated Scott's Inn and Gift Shop with wife Dorothy. Credit Dorothy Scott.

listen to the motor until he shut it off to coast into shore, where he docked the plane under the Fifth Lake bridge. When he had only one or two people going for a plane ride, and if the passengers had no objections, he would take me along as his "co-pilot."

We shared a common love for music. One day during a long plane ride I told my Dad that I could hear beautiful music over the roar of the engines. He laughed and said he heard it all the time. It truly sounded to both of us like a beautiful symphony being played only for us.

Our wonderful times when we shared music included listening to him as he played in the local band (a special treat for me). Then in later years he played the piano or organ at Scott's Inn. (After retiring from seaplaning, my father operated Scott's Inn from 1944 to 1968 and also built the Inlet Gift Center, operating it with Mother until his death.)

Other very special times leaving cherished memories came after I was married and had my three children, Kim, Mark and Scott Burwell, his grandchildren, of whom he was so proud. He enjoyed playing favorite songs just for them. He nicknamed them his three little Indians.

As a charter member of the *Quiet Birdmen of America*, he kept his brass membership card always with him. In later years he often sat polishing it with loving care. He was proud to have been an original member of this fraternal flying organization because aviation was such an important part of his life in the Adirondacks, which he loved so well.

Harold Scott died February 23, 1976. The family had engraved on his monument the first stanza of the *Quiet Birdman's Prayer:*

> Brother Q.B., valiant friend,
> Go in the grace of God.
> Go where the ships come down to park
> When day is done and night falls dark
> And landing gears etch deep their mark
> Upon eternal sod.

Albert (Red) Panella

Albert (Red) Panella could well be called the Lindbergh of the Eagle Bay and Central New York regions. Flying was his all consuming interest and he often said that there were just two loves in his life — his wife and his airplane.

A Utica native, he pioneered aviation in several ways. He was a licensed commercial pilot with single and multi-engine ratings for both land and sea routes. He was proud of his low license number — 5832. He also was a certified airplane mechanic with airframe and powerplants.

Red's love of flying and ability as an expert instructor were put to good use during World War II, when he was responsible for training more than six hundred pilots for the Army and Navy under the Civilian Pilot Training Program. Holder of a New York State teacher's certificate for aviation, he served in the program of which Hamilton College in Clinton was coordinator.

In the early 1930's he became associated with Dante O. Tranquille, chief photographer for the Utica newspapers. Through Red's service as a pilot, Tranquille made aerial photographs of the city. He also took pictures of many pioneer aviators who visited the Utica area.

Panella was a busy flier. Besides performing in air shows, he barnstormed on water, flying right up to the hotel docks on the lake or to the camps to pick up passengers in his Waco biplane equipped with floats. He also carried parachutists, transported hunters, participated in search and rescue missions and was active in the fish-planting program in the lakes.

At his Utica Aviation School at the old Utica Airport in Marcy he became acquainted with some of the most distinguished aviators of the day: Amelia Earhart, who was in the area to fly an autogiro on goodwill tours for the Beechnut Packing Company of Canajoharie, and some years later disappeared on a flight over the Pacific; Wiley Post, who with Will Rogers, was killed when their plane crashed in Alaska while they were on a round-the-world trip; Jimmie Doolittle, who visited the area on a goodwill tour for an oil company, and Douglas (Wrongway) Corrigan, who flew from Brooklyn, to Dublin, Ireland, while reportedly thinking he was flying west.

In later years Red had a private airport at Woodgate, known on Federal Aviation Administration maps as Panella's Stolport. He was a charter member of *Quiet Birdmen,* an international fraternal flying organization.

The esteem in which he was held was shown at a testimonial dinner in May, 1966, at Barneveld, attended by more than two hundred aviators, most of whom he had instructed. This was the first such gathering of pilots in the area in forty years.

Tributes were paid by aviation leaders throughout the country. A sampling:

> I sincerely believe that you and people like you have made aviation the tremendous success it is today. I often think of the impression you left upon me regarding the outlook on life that you had. You were never bitter or felt the world owed you a living, nor were you jealous of your fellow men. This is one of

"Red" Panella WACO C50 Piseco, 1932. Credit Bill Abrams.

"Red" Panella. Photo by D. Tranquille.

"Red" Panella, pilot and instructor. Credit Helen Jane Panella.

the finest traits a human being could be endowed with. — George J. Harlow, Federal Aviation Agency, Oklahoma City.

The days of wood, fabric and propeller aircraft were the best part of the aviation age and you helped to pioneer it . . . a great guy and a great pilot. — Johnnie Seal, Cornell Aeronautical Laboratory, Buffalo.

I have many warm memories of my early days in aviation under your skilled tutelage . . . I particularly remember hanging in the open cockpit upside down while you flew paying sightseers alongside in the comfort of the luxurious cabin. — Robert E. Peach, president of Mohawk Airlines, Utica.

Some of my happiest days of flying were with you . . . Remember when we used to go barnstorming together? I really learned to slide-slip from you. Also remember the time Amelia Earhart was there before the hangar was done, and we all sat around in the canvased-in area with two blowtorches blowing on some bricks to keep warm? — Jack Grady, owner, Thrifty Wash, Hemet, California.

The old photograph depicting a somewhat classic landing (plane landed upside down) by one of your former students graphically bears out this testimonial of character we submit on your behalf . . . Who but the legendary Red Panella could view such a mess, then turn to his chief instructor and remark, "Next time this guy goes up to solo, you go with him!" — Jack and Dottie Rowe, Marcy Flying Service.

Among others giving tributes were Joe Hunter, American Management Association; Howard E. Partlow, president of the Partlow Corporation, New Hartford; George Van Epp, New York City, Civil Aeronautics Board administrator for thirteen states; Stuart Davies, New Hartford, who in 1919 flew the first air mail out of Utica, and Sy Bitner, chief pilot for American Airlines, who phoned his congratulatory message from Los Angeles.

Helen Jane Clohecy Panella, whom Red married in 1941, has an amusing recollection of their first meeting. It was in the spring of 1931, when she had just returned from Florida to begin work in the insurance agency of County Judge Frank E. Tiffany at Inlet. Her account:

> In those days my Florida tan was some contrast from the pale winter residents, when not too many people were traveling back and forth to the South. With my long, dark hair and sun-tanned skin, you could never tell that I was of Scotch-Irish Yankee, German and Dutch ancestry (really all-American).
>
> Red loved to tell the story of how he first saw me . . . He was

standing on an Inlet corner talking to his aviator friend, Scotty, when I walked by on my way to work. Red asked Scotty 'Who is that?' and Scotty said, 'Some Indian who just came to work for Judge Tiffany.' Right then and there, Red said, 'I don't care if she is an Indian. I am going to marry her.' And Scotty told him, 'You're crazy!'

Exactly ten years later, on March 6, 1941, Helen Jane and Red were married in Our Lady of Lourdes Church, Utica.

Mrs. Panella also recalls an incident in mid-winter in the 1930's, when Red flew up on skis to Inlet to see her. The temperature dropped to 50 below zero that night, and the next morning he had to drain the stiff oil and heat it on the Wood Hotel kitchen stove to start the engine for takeoff.

Besides his aviation enterprise, Red, along with his brother, operated the Utica-to-Inlet Bus Line in the 30's. He named the bus "The Lady of the Lakes."

His most famous passenger was a man in fisherman's attire whom he picked up along the road near McKeever. Red noted that the man was smoking an unusual, curved pipe and looked familiar. Red kept glancing at the man through the rear view mirror, trying to place him.

Finally, the passenger, observing Red trying to identify him, said, "Yes, I am Charles G. Dawes." Then vice-president of the United States, he had been on a fishing trip all alone, with no Secret Service men along.

Red died April 18, 1974, in Utica and was buried in Riverview Cemetery, Old Forge, in the heart of the Adirondack Lakes region he had flown over and loved so much.

The bronze marker on his grave bears this inscription:

> Life is eternal and love is immortal.
> Death is only a horizon, and a horizon is
> nothing, save the limit of our sight.

Bud and Chuck Windhausen

The Windhausen brothers, Matthew (Bud) and Charles (Chuck), were Eagle Bay fliers for more than twenty years. The record of their part in the Adirondack aviation story is told mainly in pictures. Photos in the collection of Merrill Phoenix indicate that their first flights in the area took place about 1946 and pictures by Bill Weedmark show dates from 1948 through the 50's.

The Windhausens took over the Eagle Bay seaplaning after Harold Scott retired in 1945, and in 1946 Phoenix flew their 285 H.P. cabin Waco most of the season. The brothers had purchased

The Windhausens began operating from Eagle Bay with the WACO on Edo floats NC 2588 with 285 H.P. engine. Phoenix flew it for most of the season 1946. At steamboat landing — Blue Mt. Lake. Credit Merrill Phoenix.

1946 Windhausens WACO seaplane NC 2258 Edo floats. The 285 H.P. Jacobs powerplant gets a routine check-over. Credit Merrill Phoenix.

1949 the NC2258 WACO at Windhausens' base in Eagle Bay. Alice Windhausen on the left, Stewie Nelson holding the wing, Chuck Bird on top and Bud is stepping onto the dock. Credit Bill Weedmark.

June 1949 Windhausen's Seaplane base at Eagle Bay. In the photo the WACO NC2258 with Chuck standing on the dock. The photo was from the Bell Helicopter "Bugbeater" which was used for black fly spraying. Credit Bill Weedmark.

Feb. 5, 1949 about mid January of that year Chuck brought the NC14077 to Eagle Bay to try winter flying. Operated depending on the winter sports enthusiasts. About Feb. 16 the airplane was badly damaged in a landing accident on Honnedaga Lake in an attempt to fly out a badly injured caretaker. This ended winter operations. The airplane was rebuilt only to be destroyed in an accident in Old Forge Pond on Oct. 31 of that year. Chuck is shown here preheating the engine prior to starting. Credit Bill Weedmark.

July 6, 1950 Bird and Bud Windhausen (L to R) tying lumber on the N2258 WACO for an aerial delivery to Chain Lakes for a hunting & fishing lodge. Additional lumber was carried in the cabin. Credit Bill Weedmark.

Chuck and Bud Windhausen with a 195 during a black fly spraying operation April 1960. Credit Bill Weedmark.

May 1952 Windhausens' base at Eagle Bay. The cars are those of fishing parties who were flown into some of the more remote lakes. Credit Bill Weedmark.

Nov. 11, 1950 during the big wind storm of that year, the airplanes (WACOs) were beached at Eagle Bay and the floats filled with water to prevent damage to the aircraft. Shown here are Stewie Nelson and Chuck Windhausen using a bilge pump after the storm (which lasted 3 days) to get the aircraft back in operation. Credit Bill Weedmark.

Feb. 25, 1958 Chuck Windhausen, Bus Bird, Gerald Kenwell and Sue Puffer load bails of alfalfa on the wings of a Stearman for flight into the Moose River plains where they were scattered by ground crews operating from a tractor in an attempt to feed deer in the area during a severe winter. Credit Bill Weedmark.

their seaplane base property from Leon Schopfer. It was part of the Eagle Bay Hotel property, later Eagle Bay Villas.

Stewart Nelson, who did some work for the Windhausen brothers, recalls that Bud came to Eagle Bay in 1946 with his first plane. After Phoenix flew the plane in the 1946 season, Chuck took over in the period before Bud became a permanent resident of Eagle Bay. Both brothers had homes on the old Eagle Bay Hotel grounds.

Bud, who started his flying career at the age of 12, called his Eagle Bay operation the Adirondack Airlines. He served in the Army Air Corps in World War II as a chief test pilot for the Transport Command and was awarded the Air Medal in Wilmington, Delaware.

The record of the brothers' Eagle Bay operation is sketchy as Chuck died several years ago and Bud died November 24, 1980, after a flight from Syracuse to Portland, Maine. He had been preparing some information for this book.

During the brothers' flying years, seaplanes became more and more sophisticated and safer. They dismantled their base sometime before the sale of the Windhausen home to James and Mary Evans in 1975. Norton Bird had bought the Windhausen Cessna 185 in 1966.

Norton Bird and Son

Norton (Buster) Bird's flying career began in 1947, and he has operated a seaplane service since that year. The operation has remained essentially the same as that of his predecessors, Harold (Scotty) Scott, Merrill Phoenix, Bud and Chuck Windhausen, Albert Brussel and Harold K. Van Auken.

Bird flies charter flights, scenic tours from the area hotels, fishing and camping trips to remote areas, fish planting, ambulance service, Olympic area tours and airline connections. He also handles cargo and conducts photographic flights.

Until 1970, his company was called Bird's Adirondack Flights. That year his son, Donald, joined him in the business and a corporation was formed. The new name, Bird's Seaplane Service, Inc., was adopted. Along with their other services, the Birds fly for New York State on forest fire patrol and search and rescue under contract.

Allen Wilcox of the Mohawk attests to Norton Bird's exceptional skill as a pilot, noting that he flew sightseeing and passenger trips from the hotel dock many times in the 50's. Wilcox recalls this incident:

> I flew with Bus Bird out of Beaver Lake one winter day when there was a snow squall at the top of Moose River Moun-

Wm. B. Abrams' airplane — *Travel-Air* — Abrams' Beach, Oct. 12, 1930. Credit Herb Helms.

Helms and Sons Travel-Air Service and their new plane — two like this. Compare with other planes shown. Credit Herb Helms.

tain. It was only by the grace of God that we got home because you couldn't see six feet ahead of you. No other pilot I have known could possibly have gotten us safely through that weather, and could have landed like a feather on Sixth Lake.

Norton and Donald Bird fly a Cessna 185, a Cessna 180 and a Super Cub.

Other Adirondack Pilots

HERB HELMS — Although he seldom has flown from Fourth Lake, Herb Helms, pilot and seaplane operator, is well known in the Eagle Bay area. His operation of well over three decades is based at Long Lake. He is the owner of Helms Aero Service with seaplanes and ski planes, offering charter flights, hunting, fishing and scenic flights. He occasionally flew in and out of Eagle Bay at the time of the Windhausens and Merrill Phoenix.

GEORGE HAND — He flew the Fulton Chain for Curtis-Wright a month in the summer of 1929. His service was terminated when his plane was destroyed by fire.

JACK MORTON — He was the first pilot with Central Adirondack Aviation Corporation, having come to Eagle Bay from New York City in 1929. On arrival he already had to his credit 4,500 certified flying hours. He began flying in 1917.

STUART DAVIES — He was a World War I pilot from Utica. In 1919 he flew the first air mail from Utica to Old Forge. His plane took off from the first Utica airport, located off Culver Avenue near the present site of Mohawk Valley Community College. He was groundman in 1929–30 before becoming CAAC pilot.

RAY HYLAN — He operated the Utica Aviation School at the old Utica Airport in Marcy as a partner of Red Panella.

CHARLIE SMITH — He flew a Waco Straight-Wing. Based at Lake Pleasant, he did some commercial flying. He often would tie up overnight at June's Camp on Third Lake.

HOLLAND (DUTCH) REDFIELD — A former resident of Syracuse, flew an F2 Waco, 220 horsepower Continental, with an official rating of UBF-2. About 1936 he ran a successful seaplane service at Eagle Bay and for some seasons afterwards at Alexandria Bay. He later became a flight check instructor for Pan American Airways.

BOB JUNE — In 1932–33, June, who had a camp on Third Lake, worked with Brussel's Stinson and saved the bows on the Fairchild floats from damage many times by working from the stern of the floats as canoe paddle rudder man. Water rudders for seaplane floats were just being designed at the time and the Stinson had none. June worked with Dutch Redfield for a few seasons at

Eagle Bay and Alexandria Bay. In World War II he did some classified flying for the Air Corps in the Middle East and later flew for Pan American Airways and the Arabian-American Oil Company. He capped his career with a position with the Federal Aviation Agency in Washington.

JOHNNIE DONOHUE — An Adirondack flier from Brooklyn, Donohue qualified for all the required licenses and became an airport pilot.

CHAPTER XI

Organizations, Churches, and Schools – Integrate Communities

Organizations — Eagle Bay Volunteer Hose Company

The aftermath of a devastating fire on Cedar Island in 1934, and one or two earlier serious fires in Eagle Bay, warned Eagle Bay businessmen that they needed much more fire protection than they could get from neighboring fire companies. Perhaps the older men had been waiting for the younger ones to bolster the effort it took to organize a fire department. At long last the two groups got together, and on November 15, 1948, the Eagle Bay Volunteer Hose Company was formed and incorporated. The jurisdiction of the company was designated as "The Hamlet of Eagle Bay, Town of Webb, Herkimer County, State of New York, and all that part of The Town of Webb within three miles of the Hamlet of Eagle Bay." They purchased what had been a garage built for Dan Doran, and later owned by Lauterbach. The Hose Company has since operated from this garage building to which they have added needed improvements.

A constitution was written naming officers to be selected, their duties, setting meeting times, regulations as to contracting debts for the compamy. Membership consisted of active, associate, and honorary groups. A board of directors of six members was to conduct the corporation affairs between meetings.

On April 4, 1969, Charles P. Hansen, treasurer of Eagle Bay Voluteeer Hose Company, mailed the notice of a special meeting of the board of directors. The notice of this special meeting had been written by Frank Teich, president, to notify the directors that a meeting would be held at the Fire House at Eagle Bay the 8th day of April 1969, for the purpose of considering a proposition.

Allen Wilcox presented the resolution to construct an addition to the fire house to provide space for its equipment and for new restrooms at an estimated cost of $10,000. It would be necessary to borrow the sum of $7,500. The resolution included that the money be borrowed from Oneida National Bank and Trust Company in

Utica and to give as security a first mortgage on the premises now owned by the corporation situated on the south side of Route 28 in Eagle Bay. The resolution was seconded by Alfred Nelson, and signed by secretary, Richard H. Lum.

The above was put into an application and presented to the Honorable Edmund A. McCarthy, county judge, State of New York with the instrument of mortgage and was approved by Judge McCarthy, April 28, 1969.

The meeting was held with the following directors and officers present: Board members — Frank Teich, Allen Wilcox, Alfred Nelson, S. B. Youmans, Charles P. Hansen. President, Frank Teich; vice-president, Harold Youmans; secretary, Richard Lum; treasurer, Charles P. Hansen; chief, James Squires; asst. chief, Robert Hansen (all residing in Eagle Bay).

The equipment in the Eagle Bay Volunteer Hose Co. building is up-to-date and adequate. All vehicles are radio equipped. The company also owns two Pacific Marine portable pumps, and one floating portable pump.

The firemen spent in excess of $3,000 of treasury funds during 1978-1979 on building improvements — mostly for winterization projects and building maintenance.

The Ladies Community Club of Eagle Bay Becomes the Ladies Auxiliary of the Eagle Bay Volunteer Hose Comapny

The ladies of the Eagle Bay community have long been a social and civic minded group. They organized bridge clubs, held picnics, gave birthday parties, and generally were responsible for Eagle Bay being a place where one could "belong" and enjoy life.

One of the organizations was The Ladies Community Club of Eagle Bay. The first fall meeting of this club in 1955 was held at the home of Mary Evans with the following present: Ginger Ball, Hilda Guzzardo, Mary Evans, Betty Harwood, Jane Kopp, Frieda Nelson and Marguerite Windhausen. As their first project they planned a Christmas party to be held at the Eagle Bay Fire Hall.

On March 8, 1956, a meeting featuring a spaghetti supper served by Gloria Newton was held. The purpose and future of the club was discussed. Joining the members mentioned above were; Gloria Newton, Marg Hansen, Louise Youmans, Gert Merlau, Sadie Hinman, Mae Atkinson and Sue Wilkins.

In a secret ballot it was decided that the organization would become the Ladies Auxiliary of the Eagle Bay Volunteer Hose Company. Officers were elected for an annual term with Jane Kopp, president; Marguerite Hansen, vice-president; Mary Evans, secretary and Frieda Nelson, treasurer.

Besides the women listed previously many have joined and worked for this organization. Among them are; Jane Breakey, Violet Dittl, Rose DeFusto, Helen Hartnett Johnson, Alice Kimmel, Ruth Lefevre, Mary Mulchy, Marie Ortner, Kay Parker Longley, Evelyn Pole, Lillian Payne, Mary Roach, Ruth Roach, Emma Southard, Alyce Windhausen, Al Wood, Barbara Wood, Regina Youcum, Helen Brittingham, Frances Von Holle, Jewel Montgomery, Noreen Hiscox, Winnie McCarley, Theresa Winslow, Dorothy Smith, Helen Michaels, Viola Lefevre, Dot Spafford, Marguerite Fuller, Elaine Payne, Clara O'Brien, Martha Barkauskas, Margaret Hall, Betty Dean, Eleanor Hansen, Nancy Sehring, and many more in recent years.

Over the years this organization, besides supporting the Eagle Bay Volunteer Hose Company, has performed many community projects. The ladies have organized and served at Halloween and Valentine parties for the children, Christmas parties for the community's families, and social gatherings with other women's groups in the Inlet, Big Moose and Old Forge area.

To earn money for equipment and various needs of the Volunteer Hose Company and to contribute to other community organizations, such as the Town of Webb School scholarship fund, the women have had spaghetti suppers, annual St. Patrick's Day dances, numerous bake sales, bazaars and raffles, many items being handmade by members.

Churches

Church has been a vital part of the life of permanent residents of Eagle Bay. Since the population of the hamlet is small, no attempt has been made to build churches. Many Eagle Bay summer residents attend beautiful Big Moose Chapel. Inlet has three churches, and there is St. Peter's by the Lake between Eagle Bay and Old Forge. Below are pictures of the churches most often attended by both summer and permanent residents.

Schools

The Eagle Bay children have attended Old Forge public schools since Highway 28 was paved in 1926. Before that time the children were taken by sleigh or carriage, depending on the weather, to the little Minnowbrook School, pictured with the churches. Minnowbrook School was located near the driveway where the Roberts (former Burnap property) family lives. When the school closed, the students either went on to Old Forge, moved away, or never finished. Some of the students attending Minnowbrook from the Eagle Bay area were; Harold Youmans, Ernest Liddle, Jessie Lid-

Big Moose Chapel interior. Credit Kiefer postcard.

Big Moose Community Chapel. Built of natural stone from nearby Dart's Mountain. Designed by local summer residents, Earl Covey chief architect.

Raquette Lake Chapel.

Church of the Lakes, Inlet, N.Y.

Inlet Community Church, perhaps the newest church in the area.

St. Anthony' Church.

Nicholls Memorial Church.

The Minnowbrook School located at the entrance to the Burnap Property — built by Leon Burnap's father. Eagle Bay children attended school here from about 1915 until 1926. Credit Edith Tuttle Morcy. Identified left to right: Back row, Anita Burnap, Marion Burnap, Teacher Miss Bergholz. Center, Don Burnap, Ken Burnap. Sitting, Fern Tuttle, Edith Tuttle.

dle, Helen Liddle, Elizabeth Liddle, Virginia Sperry, Anne Sperry, Harold Brush, Alwyn Grindland, Ella Wells, Charles Wells, Harry Wells and Ruth Wells.

Addendum

In the past building was big business in the Eagle Bay area and some fine men did the building. Over one hundred years have passed since Fred Hess with his axe, his hammer and his nails came into the area. It is almost a hundred years since he built the beautiful log structure which stands on Dollar Island in its original outward state. Other log structures still standing were built in the early days. Still the builders come, and still they build. Yet for the first time in many years a real log house has been erected in the area.

The Paynes from Inlet have been builders for at least four generations. They continue to build, and Theodore Payne II is building a real log house for himself and his wife, Patty. He is not using the Fred Hess block end construction, but is grooving the ends of the logs together in a beautiful fashion. Strong men make good builders, but they also make other important contributions. This addendum is to show how building of houses and the building of men is continuing in the Eagle Bay area.

Below are the pictures of some of Eagle Bay's young sons who just may follow in their father's footsteps, as builders or as businessmen in a joint effort to guarantee the future of God's Country in this unusually beautiful area.

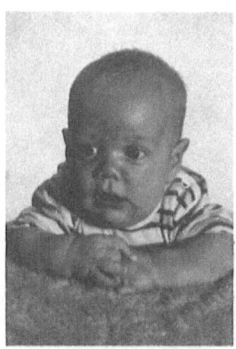

L. to R. John Warren Wright III, holding Richard Avery Wright. Their parents, Kathy and John Wright, owners of one of the best eating places in the area, Eckerson's.

Joseph Earl Hansen, son of James & Cynthia Hansen. James, head of the meat department in Tim's Foodland.

Kenneth Neil Thibado, 4th generation of Thibados in Eagle Bay area, all have been builders. Son of Thomas & Deborah Ritz Thibado.

L. to R. Jesse Ryan Payne & Theodore Payne III whose father is Theodore Payne II & mother is Patty Ball Payne. It is their father who is building the log home.

Being built, 1981 in Eagle Bay, on the road back of Tim's Foodland is this lovely log home. Builder: Theodore Payne II.

Appendix

A Summary of Some Important Deeds

The following is an interpretation of the documents herein described and only where indicated by quotation marks is any material contained herein taken specifically from said document or documents.

All of the documents described below have been duly recorded in the County of Herkimer, State of New York, and The Central New York Abstract and Title Company, upon examination of the records of conveyances of the Herkimer County Clerk's Office, by Deed, etc., certifies that the following documents were found:

No. 1 Deed — Dated May 11, 1891 from Ravand K. Hawley as President of the Adirondack Timber and Mineral Company to William Seward Webb — Recorded June 4, 1891. Hawley conveyed to Webb with other lands, "In Brown's Tract, Township number eight (8) the whole of this Township, Excepting the two following described parcels, to wit: —"

1. Beginning on North shore of 3rd Lake to east shore of 4th Lake containing approximately 250 acres of land.

2. Beginning at the head of 1st Lake on "middle branch of Moose River and near the South East corner of Township number eight (8) Browns Tract," to a point on 2nd Lake containing approximately 160 acres of land and water "leaving in this Township after said two Exceptions, thirty two thousand six hundred and fifty (32,650) acres."

Subject to the following:

1. Reservation of right of way in a deed from The Adirondack Railway Company to Robert H. Cromley dated June 1, 1899.

2. Certain agreement between the Adirondack Railway Company and Janet L. Durant dated December 9, 1886.

3. Contract between William H. Durant & wife and Adirondack Railway Company dated June 7, 1889 conveying to the company sufficient land for road bed, etc.

4. Contract between William W. Durant & wife and The Chateaugay Railroad Company dated June 7, 1889 conveying to the company sufficient land for road bed, etc.

5. Contract between Robert W. Cromley and the Adirondack Railway Company dated June 7, 1889 conveying to the company sufficient land for road bed etc.

6. Contract between Robert W. Cromley and The Chateaugay Railroad Company dated June 7, 1889 conveying sufficient land for road bed, etc.

No. 2 Warranty Deed — dated February 19, 1894 from William Seward Webb and Eliza Osgood, his wife, of the City, County and State of New York to Joseph Porter of the City and County of New Haven, Conn. — Recorded October 25, 1894. Webb conveyed to Porter a 10 acre tract of land adjoining on the north Lots 138, 139, 140, 141 of the 4th Lake allotment together with right-of-way for teams, etc. over Lots 141, 140, 139, 138 excepting that the selection of the location for the right of way will do as little damage as may be to any present or future camp site or Camp sites on said lots 141, 140, 139, 138.

No. 3 Warranty Deed — dated October 10, 1895 from William Seward Webb, et al. to Dwight B. Sperry of Old Forge, Town of Wilmurt, Herkimer Co., N.Y. — recorded July 7, 1897. Webb conveyed "All that certain piece or parcel of land situate in Township eight, John Brown's Tract in the towns of Wilmurt and Morehouse, Counties of Herkimer & Hamilton and State of New York being (with other lots) Local No. 137 upon Fourth Lake," with the standard fire conditions and that Sperry shall within 2 years from October 10, 1895 erect a hotel or be divested of all title to said property.

No. 5 Warranty Deed — dated July 1, 1897 from Dwight Sperry to The Eagle Bay Hotel Company of the same place — recorded July 7, 1897. Sperry conveyed property described in No. 3 above to The Eagle Bay Hotel Company subject to the same terms and conditions as contained therein.

No. 6 Quit Claim Deed — dated January 5, 1903 from Eagle Bay Hotel Company to William J. Thistlethwaite, et al. Eagle Bay Hotel Company conveyed to Thistlewaite ¼ of acre being portion or portions of Lots 137 and 138.

No. 7 Deed — dated May 5, 1899 from William Seward Webb to Raquette Lake Railway Company — recorded July 10, 1899. Webb granted to Raquette Lake Railway Company right-of-way to build and operate street surface railroad over highway upon his lands in Township 8, Brown's Tract and "I do also hereby grant and convey to the said Raquette Lake Railway Company, a right-of-way for this railroad twenty-five (25) feet wide on each side of the center line thereof, as the same is now located across and upon said Township

Eight (8) together with the right to take such additional land as may be necessary for cuts and fills, with all my right, title and interest therein."

No. 8 Warranty Deed — dated December 10, 1902 from William Seward Webb et al to William J Thistlethwaite of Little Falls, N.Y. — recorded Janury 7, 1903. Webb conveyed to Thistlethwaite all those certain parcels situated in Township 8, John Browns Tract, being (with other lots) Nos. 138, 139, 140, 141, 142, 143, 144 upon the standard fire and forestry conditions.

No. 9 Quit-Claim Deed — dated January 5, 1903 from William J. Thistlethwaite et al to Eagle Bay Hotel Company, etc. recorded September 19, 1904. Thistlethwaite conveyed to Eagle Bay Hotel Company 5 acres of portion or portions of lots 137 and 138.

No. 10 Warranty Deed — dated March 29, 1904 from William J. Thistlethwaite et al to James Thistlethwaite — recorded April 10, 1914. William Thistlethwaite conveyed to James Thistlethwaite all that certain parcel of land situated in Township 8, John Brown's Tract, being (with other lots) Lots No. 139, 140, 141, 142, 143, 144 and No. 137 and 138 with the same exceptions as contained in No. 8 above. And excepting 50 foot wide right of way of The Raquette Lake Railway.

No. 17 Warranty Deed — dated Decmber 29, 1906 from William J. Thistlethwaite to William G. Barrett of Town of Bedford and William A. Guinand of Town of New Castle — recorded July 12, 1907. Thistlethwaite conveyed to Barrett & Guinand all that certain parcel of land situated in Township 8, John Brown's Tract, containing 5 acres and reserving a right of way for a highway or road 25 feet wide.

No. 18 Right-of-Way Deed — dated December 22, 1909 from William G. Barrett et al to Howard C. Weller — recorded December 27, 1909. Barrett granted a right-of-way in and to premises held by Weller in Thistlethwaite allotment of Eagle Point in Township 8 of John Brown's Tract.

No. 19 Warrent Deed — dated June 1, 1907 from William J. Thistlethwaite to William Preston — recorded July 5, 1907. Thistlethwaite conveyed to Preston all that certain parcel of land situated in Township 8, John Brown's Tract, containing $7^{3}/_{10}$ acres and Lots 15 and 16 of the Thistlethwaite allotment of Eagle Point.

No. 20 Mortgage dated June 1, 1907 from William Preston to William J. Thistlethwaite — recorded September 25, 1907. This covers the premises described in No. 19.

No. 25 Warranty Deed — dated January 5, 1909 from William J. Thistlethwaite to Howard C. Weller — recorded October 13, 1909. Thistlethwaite conveyed to Weller all that certain parcel of land situated in Township 8, John Brown's Tract, containing 12.45 acres of land.

No. 34 Warranty Deed dated February 26, 1915 from William G. Barrett et al to Arthur A. Weller — recorded March 13, 1915. The premises described in No. 17 above.

No. 35 Quit Claim Deed — dated July 6, 1915 from Citizens Trust Company of Utica in individual capacity and as trustee for Howard Weller to Howard Weller — recorded July 6, 1915. Citizens conveyed all that certain parcel of land in Township 8, John Brown's Tract, consisting of 12.45 acres being the same premises described in deed from William Thistlethwaite to Howard Weller recorded October 13, 1909, except Lot 66. Citizens conveyed all that certain parcel of land in Township 8, John Brown Tract, containing $7^{3}/_{10}$ acres except a deed to Arthur Weller recorded July 18, 1912. Also conveyed were Lots 15 and 16 of the Thistlethwaite allotment of Eagle Point.

No. 36 Quit-Claim Deed — dated July 15, 1915 from Arthur A. Weller et al to Howard C. Weller — recorded July 27, 1915. The Premises described in No. 34 above.

Wharf and Dock Rights to Durant from Sperry

"A deed from Dwight B. Sperry to W. West Durant, gave the right to build and maintain a private wharf, a dock and store house in a suitable and convenient place at Lots No. 134, 135, 136, & 137 on Fourth Lake, and the necessary approaches thereto for his and their use and purposes in running a yacht or boat with steam power or otherwise to and from said dock or wharf on the Fulton Chain of lakes together with a right of way to and from said boat house and dock and the highway running across said lots to Raquette Lake with teams, wagons, vehicles, loads or otherwise for his and their benefit and advantage and his agents and representatives.;" Recorded Sept 21, 1896, Book 160 of Deeds page 96.

On the letterhead of Snyder, Cristman & Snyder and dated September 10th, 1929.

"Mr. Howard C. Weller, Mr. John P. Petersen,
Eagle Bay, N.Y.

Gentlemen —

I am in receipt of Mr. Weller's letter of the 9th instant.

I have just received from the Clerk's Office, two copies of abstract of title, which I herewith enclose you. The two searches were $15.00.

As regards the enclosed abstracts would say, that a very small portion of the Eagle Bay Allotment of Dr. Webb, Lot 137 if I remember the number correctly, is included in what was the original Eagle Bay Hotel property, conveyed by Dr. Webb to Dwight B. Sperry. The Eagle Bay Hotel Company subsequently conveyed this portion of Lot 137 to William J. Thistlethwaite, No. 4 on enclosed abstract; so that from Thistlethwaite I acquired the title to that part of Lot 14 that was in the original Lot 137 of Dr. Webb's allotment.

The maps on file in the Herkimer County Clerk's Office make this very plain. Quite likely you are familiar with and will recall the details.

As regards the Sperry agreement with William West Durant, No. 2 on the enclosed abstract, giving Durant the right to use a dock would say that this, on its fact, does not and can not apply to Lot 137, now Lot 14, for the reason that the language of the deed locates the wharf or dock on the Fulton Chain as follows —

> 'To and from said dock or wharf on the Fulton Chain of Lakes together with a right-of-way to and from said boat house and dock *and the highway* running across said lots.'

This is a very clear cut description of the present boat house and dock of the Eagle Bay Hotel, which was the one originally used by Durant.

There never was any road or way running from the Highway to any boat house or dock on lot 14. There never was any dock to begin with on lot 14; but there was and always has been, ever since Dr. Webb's sale to Mr. Sperry, a road running from the highway to the present dock of the Eagle Bay Hotel.

I have gone into this matter somewhat at length so you may have the facts to place before Mr. Lisle, who you state is to act for the parties who are purchasing from you.

Very truly yours,
s/ Charles E. Snyder"

THE ADIRONDACK EAGLE

Thursday, September 11, 1929

Who Is Who in Eagle Bay Park

In order that everyone may know the make-up of the Eagle Bay Park summer community and its contiguous territory of Eagle Point, we publish here the names of camp and lot owners in the Weller Development.

From New York City and vicinity: Samuel S. Peck, retired lawyer; M. J. Anspach, realtor; Mrs. Dora J. Guinand; Pierre J. Guinand, journalist; Mrs. John J. Tucker; O. C. Bennet, sales manager; Mrs. Kathryn Bennet, teacher; Miss Mildred Rich, teacher; John Black, insurance, O. W. Olsen, former manufacturer; Miss Gertrude Littlejohn, teacher; Mrs. A. M. Goode, secretary; James Dederick, manufacturer; A. Augustas Low, owner of Old Forge Electric Corp.; Dan Doran, garage-proprietor; Frank Teich, garage-proprietor; Reinhold Teich, restaurant-proprietor; Dr. G. Pitt Beers, minister; Mrs. Agnes McLaughlin, retired merchant; Miss Loretta Fitzgerald, teacher; Dr. Frances C. Vogt, physician; Miss Jane Fitzgerald, teacher.

From Rochester and vicinity: Mrs. Henry Remington Howard, widow of prominent attorney; Mrs. Anna Rattike, widow of manufacturer; Hon. H. F. Remington, counsel of the law firm of Harris, Beach, Folger, Remington, Bacon and Keating; Prof. R. A. Searing, secretary N.Y. State Teacher's Assn.; Chas. Edward Main, employee Eastman Kodak Co.; Robert Wohlrab, teacher; J. Howard Hudson, chemist; Leroy B. Dodge, employee Eastman Kodak Co.; Miss Mabel Stark; B. C. Bennett, mechanic; Theo. W. Fuller, with Marks & Fuller; E. Sturman, merchant; Robert Searing, with General Adjustment Bureau; Mrs. Hattie Smith, Stanley Stever, electrical engineer.

From Syracuse: F. W. Huntley, contractor; A. A. Avon, contractor; E. M. Reid, bond dealer; I. Kallet, contractor; Miss Ida Davis; Mrs. Kenneth Gilbert; Justus F. O'Hara; retired merchant; Dr. J. Bienenfeld, minister; L. Manson, retired; S. B. Klein, insurance; M. Gais, retired manufacturer.

From Utica and vicinity: Byron J. Jones, merchant; Geo. W. Burton, owner of the Burton Stove Stores; Dr. Edwin M. Griffith, physician; Thos. E. Howlan, with Utica Gas & Electric Co.; Jack Kemp, entertainer; G. W. H. Dieffenbacher, with Highway Dept.; Guy Finney, Hardware dealer; Mrs. Lorena Edwards, operator; J. J. Domser, vice-pres. Black River Telephone Co.; Fred Petersen, builder; Mrs. Angie Furlong; Leroy Moore, mill supt.

Appendix 269

From Herkimer: Robert Earl, bank president; Margaret E. Kehoe, insurance; L. E. Lanning, auto dealer; C. E. Alborn, clerk; C. E. Snyder, lawyer.

From Little Falls: Theo. Fallis, cigar manufacturer; Daniel Sheehy; Edw. A. Coyne, retired manufacturer.

From various places: C. E. Haines, manufacturer, Gainesville, Fla.; C. H. Moyer, retired theatre operator, St. Petersburg, Fla.; II. C. Whitford, motion pictures, Wolcott, N.Y.; E. E. Buckminister, cannery operator, Wolcott, N.Y.; Mrs. Helen King, saleswoman, Albany; Evan R. Jones, merchant, Carthage, N.Y.; J. J. Gudmundsen, administrator, N.Y. College of Agriculture, Cornell University, Ithaca, N.Y.; Arthur Patterson, retired farmer, Lowville, N.Y.; Willaim Carkhuff, inventor, Norwich, N.Y.; Lewis Mulchy, mechanic, Old Forge; Jack Gennett, salesman, Charlotte, N.C.; M. A. Barnes, retired journalist, Elmira, N.Y.; Walter Elmer, salesman, Greenfield, Mass.; Louis Butler, mechanic, Springfield, Mass.; Pat McCarthy, caretaker, Gabriels, N.Y.; H. F. Bowman, contractor, Fourth Lake; L. E. Beach, contractor and guide, Old Forge, Otis Wakefield, retired farmer, Lowville, N.Y.; L. P. Smith, hardware dealer, Fulton, N.Y.; M. J. Cervo, N.Y.C.R.R. agent, Saranac Inn, N.Y.; Mrs. Geo. Crowe, Detroit, Mich.; Geo. B. Ginther, tax collector, Thendara, N.Y.; Mrs. Geo. Burdick, hotel proprietor, Big Moose, N.Y.; W. L. Armstrong, garage proprietor, Big Moose, N.Y.; W. L. Armstrong, garage proprietor, Old Forge, N.Y.; E. A. Cameron, former hotel proprietor, Inlet, N.Y.; Paul Schaltegger, contractor, Kinderhook, N.Y.

Residing at Eagle Bay are the following: J. P. Petersen, contractor; J. Ivan Brush, guide; John T. Gorman, street and water supt.; Alfred Nelson, contractor; J. E. MacLaren, with State Highway Dept.; O. M. Liddle, contractor; E. U. Smith, postmaster and merchant; S. B. Youmans, plumber and electrician; Howard C. Weller, engineer and surveyor.

Bibliography

Books

Aber, Ted, and King, Stella, *History of Hamilton County*. Great Wilderness Books, 1965. Lake Pleasant, New York.

Beetle, David H., *Up Old Forge Way*. Rochester, New York: Lewis Heindl & Son, 1948. Utica Observer Dispatch.

Donaldson, Alfred L., *A History of the Adirondacks* Vol I. Harrison, New York: Harbor Hill Books, 1977.

Donaldson, Alfred L., *A History of the Adirondacks* Vol. II. Harrison, New York: Harbor Hill Books, 1977.

Grady, Joseph F., *The Adirondacks Fulton Chain – Big Moose Region.* Old Forge, New York: North Country Books, (c) 1933, 2nd Ed. 1966.

Graham, John Jr., *The Adirondack Park A Political History.* New York: Alfred A. Knopf, 1978.

Harter, Henry A., *Fairy Tale Railroad.* Sylvan Beach, New York: North Country Books, 1979.

Hochschild, Harold K., *Life and Leisure in the Adirondack Backwoods,* Blue Mountain Lake, New York: Adirondack Museum, 1962.

Reed, Frank A., *Lumberjack Sky Pilot.* Old Forge, New York: North Country Books, 1965.

Second Annual Report of the Commissions of Fisheries, Game and Forests, Wynkoop Hallenbeck, Crawford Co., New York and Albany, 1897.

Wallace, E. R., *Wallace's Guide to the Adirondacks.* New York: The American News Company; Syracuse, New York: Waverly Publishing Company, 1875.

Wessels, William L., *Adirondack Profiles.* Lake George, New York: Adirondack Resorts Press, Inc., 1961.

White, William Chapman, *Adirondack Country,* New York: Duell, Sloan & Pearce; Boston: Little Brown & Company, 1954.

Acknowledgments

Berns, Cornelia
Blue Mountain Museum (Marcia Smith)
Burwell, Janet Scott
Burak, Carol
Burnet, Nellie

Chapell, Ike
Campagna, Mary

Delmarsh, Arch III

Evans, Mary and James

Foulds, William (Mrs.)
Frendt, Mrs. H. T.
Fuller, Ted (Mrs.)

Gardner, G. B. and Laurine
Goodwin, Cleon (Mrs.)
Grasso, Gladys

Harter, Henry
Helms, Bill
Historical Society, Town of Webb
Hinman from West Virginia
Mrs. Hans Holl
Holly, Donna

Kiefer, Charles
Knox, John

Ladies Auxiliary
Lamphear, Frank (Mrs.)
Le Fevre, Viola
Lennon, William

Mineker, Mrs. Paul (Donna)

Nelson, Adolph and Caroline Longstaff

Acknowledgments

Ottaway, Neal and Alberta
Park Association (John Vaccaro)
Perry, Alfred
Pope, Andy
Purcell, "Red"
Roach, Beryl, Mary and Ruth
Scott, Mrs. Harold

von Oetingen, Anneliese
Volunteer Hose (Andy Pope)
Weedmark Studios
Westfall, Freda
Youmans, Eddie
Youmans, Harold and Louise
Zurl, Blanche

Maps

From the County Clerk's Office, Herkimer County, a complete collection of maps of the Eagle Bay, Fourth Lake area are owned by the author and have been consulted.

Documents

Collection of legal papers from William Cusak covering Eagle Bay Land Transactions.

New York Geological Survey — Cultural Education Center, Albany, Yngvar W. Isachsen (Principal Geologist).

The Adirondack Eagle — 1925–1930 from Jon Breakey of Eagle Bay.

Collection of press news items from: *Utica Observer Dispatch, Utica Daily Press, Rome Sentinel, Syracuse Herald Journal* — contributed by Marion Holmes and Margaret Hart.

Tape Interviews

Valuable information was gained from tape recordings furnished by the following: Bud Kopp, Helen Liddle, Madeleine Clark, Mary Evans, Shirley Mearns, Frieda Nelson, Dr. George Longstaff, Bert Gardner, Donald Burnap, Norton Bird and Yock Youmans.

The County Courthouses

To a researcher, a county clerk's office is a source of unlimited information. A very special thanks to Francis A. Nichols of Central New York Abstract Company for his invaluable help in tracing ownership from Brown to Webb in Township 8. Mary Campagna and her staff in the Herkimer County Clerk's office were always cordial and helpful in copying deeds and maps which were needful for research.

The Hamilton County Clerk's staff gave the same cordial and valuable help.

This story of *God's Country*, Eagle Bay Area could not have been written without the help of some longtime area residents who responded to the author's call for help.

Mr. Roy Higby, a nephew of Dwight Sperry, gave the author his memories of his uncle's connection with the Eagle Bay Hotel.

Dr. George H. Longstaff grew up in the area, and was the founder of the prestigious summer camps for girls and boys. His parents owned and operated the Camp Mohawk for almost half a century. He gave generously of his time in both written and taped information.

Allen Wilcox, for half a century in the area hotel business, was a most valuable source of information on almost any topic. He was especially knowledgeable regarding hotel life in the area. A special thanks to Allen for generously sharing his fine library of Adirondack books.

Other lifelong residents of Eagle Bay who gave interviews, tape recordings, and written accounts of the area as they knew it, even from childhood, were Helen Liddle, Shirley Mearns, Ruth Nelson Brussel and Betty Nelson Spencer. Helen Liddle's remarkable grasp of the total Eagle Bay story was a most valuable source of reference. Shirley Mearns contributed early pictures, and records of community life. Betty Nelson Spencer drew liberally from her girlhood memories, and did valuable interviewing of older summer residents now living in Rochester. Betty, Ruth Nelson Brussel, and Stewart Nelson, shared their fond memories of their father.

Without the inspiration and help from Merrill Phoenix, one of Fourth Lake's most prestigious fliers, the chapter on Adirondack Aviation would not have been possible. Especially helpful in this portion was William Weedmark, John Knox and Herb Helms, as was Helen Jane Panella, and Mr. and Mrs. Al Brussel. To Janet Scott Burwell for her untiring help on her father's biography and work in aviation, many thanks.

The author is indebted to Mr. Craig Gilborn and his library staff for access to the Charles Snyder papers.

Marion Holmes was always available to the author in checking the historical accuracy of early developments, and proofreading the first few chapters of the manuscript for historical authenticity.

Marietta Schultz Kelley helped in the organization of the content. She also was a great help in arranging contacts for the author. This was especially true in contacting reliable sources of information on the aviators.

The author is grateful to Mr. and Mrs. Robert Igoe for their understanding and help in making the publication of GOD'S

COUNTRY possible. The assistance of Miss Margaret Hart was invaluable. She took time from her busy schedule to do the kind of copyreading that only one with her skills can do. She gave the author confidence to carry forward.

Then there were the first ones who gave information from their years of residence in the Park in the early days. They were a wellspring of inspiration. Very special tribute is paid to Frieda Nelson, Yock Youman, Bud Kopp, Donald Burnap, Bert Gardner, his dear wife, Laurine, and Norton Bird. Their recorded interviews were turned to again and again for information.

There are so many others who helped, some with just a word or two, others, as was the case of William Cusack, with the answers to real estate questions. To them all, and any whom I have missed, I am deeply grateful.

After the research was completed, the whole story had to be written and typed. For help in this field special thanks go to Jane and Dick Knight of Old Forge, and Deborah Thibado of Eagle Bay. They never refused a call for help and finished the task in record time. A special thanks to James Evans and his staff at Burkhard-Evans for all the help they so generously gave to the author. Sallye Gossman literally took over the aviators and the Indians. She put aside her own project of writing a novel to help the author get the research on individual fliers and on the Indians organized.

To Bill Wing, Tax Map Technician of the Hamilton County Tax Records, I am deeply indebted for his generous work in providing many important records including the records of Dr. Gaylord, and the Anderson records.

To Vijay Nair, Adirondack Museum, Blue Mountain Lake, librarian, for his help in research.

The Boonville Herald, June 19, 1974, Boonville, N.Y. (for the Adirondack Aviation Corporation Story — Al Brussel and Van Auken — Their Stinson).

INDEX

ADIRONDACK EAGLE 8/8/25 ARTICLE (Hotel Guest List) 47
ALEXANDER, Christ 87, 90; Jo 78, 90; John 90.
ANDERSON, Frank 8, 151; Maude E. 151.
ARMSTRONG, W. L. (Army) 131.
ARNOLD, Otis 90, 102.
ATWOOD, Harry 232
AVERY, Ken 210

BAINES, Margaret 126
BALL, Virginia 118
BARKAUSKAS, Charles 218; Martha 218, 261
BARRETT, Maude W. 41, 42; William G. 41, 42
BARRY, John J. (Mr. & Mrs.) 217; T. A. 33
BEAUCHAMP, Leon 46, 218; Mrs. Leon 218
BECKER, Fred 73, 208; Mrs. Fred 73, 77, 91, 208; George 78
BECKINGHAM, Gertrude 124
BERG, Otto 138, 139
BERNS, Cornelia 210
BIRD, Donald 250, 252; Norton (Buster) 222, 223, 250, 252
BIRNIE, M. J. 95
BLAIR, Elmer 57, 62
BLAKEMAN, George 202; Janet Fuller 202
BLASLAND, Warren V. 100; Warren V., Jr. 100
BREAKY, Jane 218, 261; John 218; Jon 218
BRICKLE, Edward 167, 168; Donald J. 168; Doris 167, 168
BRITTINGHAM, Helen 211, 261
BROWNELL, Audrey 167
BRUSH, Andrew 174; Elizabeth M. 92; Ivan 205; Melvin A. 92, 93
BRUSSEL, Mrs. 220; Albert 189; E. Albert (Al) 219, 220, 221, 222, 250; Ruth Nelson 189; William 189
BUCHANAN, Etta J. 168; Thomas 168
BUETNER, Carrie 218
BULL, Milo 33, 82, 92, 102; Mrs. Milo (Millie Wood) 91, 102
BURAK, Carol 216; Norman 216
BURKE, F. Kenneth 102; Louis 102
BURKHARD, Howard 106, 107, 164
BURNAP, Don 18, 106

BURRELL, D. H. 62, 63
BURTON, George 217; Pearl 119, 217
BURWELL, Janet Scott 234, 235

CAPRON, James C. 160, 164
CARKHOFF, Slim (William) 205
CARLSON, Gerda 101; Victor 101
CARR, F. (Dr.) 91
CARROL, Frank 174
CASE, Donald 167, 168; Madeline 167
CASTELLO, J. Martinez 174
CERVO, James 107, Mrs. 107
CHAPELL, Ike 46, 203, 204; Marion 203
CHENEY, Jim 233
CHILDS, Amy 159
CHOPER, Wayne (Dr.) 119, 188
CLARK, Harry 8, 149, 151, 152; Madeleine 149, 151, 152
COATS, Pearl Burton 217
COHEN, Moses 139
COLE, Fred (Dr.) 233
COOK, A. 46; Tom 182
CORRIGAN, Douglas 241
CORTS, Ralph 44, 46
COSWELL, James 52
COUGHLIN, Rev. Thomas 73
COUSINO, Brad 210
CRAWFORD, John 57
CREIGHTON, Lawrence (Mrs.) 168
CROWE, Mrs. 166
CROWLEY, Mr. 158
CUNNINGHAM, E. 53
CUSACK, Bill 44, 46, 167, 195; Shirley 195; Virginia Pellor Ball 134, 195

DALLARD, George (Captain) 150
DARDENNE, Peggy Fuller 202; Philip 202
DART, Bill 73, 77
DAVIES, Stuart 243, 252
DAWES, Charles G. 244
DEAGMAN, Gordon 101; Ruth 101
DEAN, Betty 108, 118, 261; Roger 46, 107, 108, 118
DEDERICK, James 195, 198; Kate 195; Ralph 195, 198
DeFUSTO, Rose 261
DELMARSH, Arch 18, 60, 62, 138; Arch, Jr. 60; Arch II 56, 60, 61; Arch III 61; Arch IV 61; Chris 61; Eri 18, 138, 139; Shirley 61; Terry 61
DeMEZA, Harry 124
DEW, Donald (Mrs.) (Sarah) 123

DePREZ, Dave 46
DICKOW, Anna 87; Fred 87; Kurt 87
DILLON, John 46
DITTL, Alfred 82; Fred 82; Violet 82, 261
DIX, Governor 20
DOGGETT, Edward 134
DOMSER, Paul (Mr. & Mrs.) 126
DONOHUE, Johnnie 253
DORAN, Betty, 123; Dan 123, 124, 131, 255; Eileen 123; Jack 123; Mike 123
DRAKE, Michael 182; Steven A. 182
DUNAY, Bill 223
DUNN, Ann Westfall 77; Murray 217

EARHART, Amelia 235, 241
EARL, Robert 168
EASTMAN, George 199
ECKERSON, David 126; Ernest 126; Lois 126
EDWARDS, Amy Murray 152; E. W. 126, 152, 153; Harold 158; John 152; Joseph 158; J. J. 157, 158; J. J., Jr. 158, 159; Oliver 158; Oliver, Jr. 159; Oliver Murray 152, 153, 157, 158, 159; Ray 87; Sally 87; Talmadge 152
EVANS, Albert 100; Carl 130; Doris Shorey 130; James 53, 54, 250; Mary 52, 53, 54, 250 xi

FALLIS, Mary Dussalt 216; Theodore M. 216; Theodore P. 216; Theodore R. 216
FARRELL, Suzanne 139, 140, 141
FENTON, Betty Simmons 159, 160; Merle 160
FLECIANO, Charles 134
FOGARTY, Chris 125; John (Pat) 125
FOLEY, Mildred 160, 168
FREDETTE, Dominic 133
FREELY, Ethel 104; Gordon 104
FREEMAN, J. R. (Mrs.) 78
FRENDT, Harold (Dr.) 165; Mrs. Harold 165
FULLER, Marguerite 202, 261; Theodore (Ted) 46, 199; William 199

GAIS, Mark (Mr. & Mrs.) 217
GARBUTT, Jay 211; Shirley 211
GARDNER, Bert 18, 30, 31
GAYLORD, Edward S. (Dr.) 33, 148, 149, 150; Harriet 148
GERSNER, Dr. 21
GITELMAN, Judge Jacob 202; Mrs. Jacob 202

Index 275

GLADWIN, Donald 107
GOODWIN, Cleon 166, 167, 168; Mrs. Cleon 119; 166, 167, 168
GORMAN, Johnny 46, 198
GRADY, Jack 243; Joseph 2, 5, 13, 33, 90, 173
GRANT, Dwight 16, 101
GRAY, Charles 189; Paula Nelson 189
GRIEBNO, Carl [sic] 46
GUDMUNSEN, John 46, 218
GUINAND, Dora J. 42; William 42
GUZZARDO, Frank 118; Hilda 77, 118; Joseph (Joe) 77, 118

HALL, Frank 123; Louis 182; Margaret 261
HAMEL, William 217
HAND, George 219, 252
HANSEN, Carl 130, 131, 205; Charles 133, 255; Eleanor 133, 261; Norman 133; Robert 133; Ronald 133
HANNAH, Norman 102
HART, H. 33; L. G. (Mr. & Mrs.) 85
HARTER, Henry 29, 30, 124; Robert J. 134
HARWOOD, Betty 135; Ted 135
HATTER, Doris Simmons (Mrs. Fred) 159, 160
HELMS, Herb 234, 252
HESS, Fred 8, 34, 56, 137, 148
HIGBY, Roy 51
HINMAN, Ernie 223; Louis 218; Sadie 218
HISCOX, Noreen 261
HITCHCOCK, Tim 118, 119
HOAGLAND, Claude 82
HOCHSCHILD, Mr. 21
HOLL, Anna 164; Hans 164
HOLLIDAY, Mrs. 33
HOLLY, Donna 140
HOWARD, Jack 221; Remington 100; Remington (Mrs.) 100, 169
HOWDEN, Richard 46
HOWLAND, Thomas E. 123; Thomas E. (Mrs.) 123
HUBER, Ferdinand 90; Helen 90
HUDD, Amos 205
HUDSON, Donald 95; Harold (Mr. & Mrs.) 95; Robert 95
HUNTLEY, Frank W. 100
HYLAN, Ray 252

JACKSON-PERKINS 168, 169
JOHNSON, Helen Hartnett 261; Oscar 109

JONES "By" (Mr. & Mrs.) 217; Shirley 107; Warren 107
JUDSON, Christine 123; Patricia Higby 123; William (Bill) 123
JUNE, Bob 252

KANE, John 203; Rose 90, 91; Tom 90, 91
KATSANIS, Jody 210
KELLEY, Marietta Schultz 72, 208; Paul, Jr. 217
KELLOG, Lina Lou 218
KIMMEL, Alice (Mrs. Harry) 119, 261; Harry 125, 131, 133
KINNEY, Jack 166
KIRKLAND, Jim 46
KLEEMAN, Fritz 180
KNIGHT, Marion 168
KOFMEIHL, Charles 167, 168; Marian 167
KOLB, Herb 46
KOPP, Bud 53, 125; Jane 125

LAUTERBACH, Eugene H. 124, 255; Katherine 124
LAWLESS, Mr. 123
LAWSON, Don 18
LEDGER, Eleanor 101; Terry 101
LEE, Alice E. (Wagner) 82, 105; Arthur E. 82; Delia M. 82; Frank 82
LEESON, Beverly Ann (Mrs. Lyle) 140
LeFEVRE, Elton 218; Ruth 218, 261; Viola 116, 218, 261
LENNON, William 44, 46
LEWIS, Dick 123; Mary Beth 123
LIDDLE, Elizabeth 187; Ernest 187, 261; Helen 131, 187; Jessie 103, 187, 261; Orr 41, 107, 182, 187
LINDSEY, Ed 123; Rosamond 100; Thelma 123
LITTLEJOHN, Mrs. 216
LONGLEY, Kay Parker 261
LONGSTAFF, Caroline M. 64, 66; George (Dr.) 67, 139, 140, 173, 174, 178, 180; Herbert (Dr.) 57, 66, 173; H. H. (Mrs.) 33, 64, 173

McCARLEY, Richard 78; Winifred 78, 261
McCURDY, William 104
McDONALD, Edward J. 100
McDUGAL, Mr. 95
McKEE, Clark 46, 94, 95, 160; Clark (Mrs.) 94, 160
McLAUGHLIN, Hazel, 134

McLEAN, Chester 221
McLOUGHLIN, D. C. 95

MADIGAN, Aprile A. 182; June 182; Roger 182
MAMOONE, Joseph Jr. 108
MANTOR, Ed 203; Marje 203
MARCHANT, Lillian 195; Richard 195
MARKS, Henry 116, 117, 199
MARTINI, Paula 135; Steven 135
MEARNS, Shirley Marchant 198
MEEKER, Harriet 16, 100, 101; Jonathan 8, 13, 16, 100, 101, 151
MEIGS, Ferris 178
MEJIA, Paul 139, 140, 141
MERLAU, Gertrude Puffer 107, 124, 134
MEURER, Emil 73
MICHAELS, Helen 261
MILLER, Mrs. 218; Fred 218; Russell 166
MINEKER, Donna Ficker 140, 211, 212; Paul 140, 211
MONTGOMERY, Jewel 261
MONNEY, G. L. 33
MOORE, Mr. 131; Clarence 52
MORGAN, J. P. (J. Pierpont) 19, 82; Jerry 123
MOSS, Jean 168
MORTON, Jack 219, 220, 252
MOYNEHAN, Dennis 47; Patrick 47
MULCHY, Lewis 218; Mary 218, 261
MURRAY, Daniel 152; Oliver 152

NELSON, Alfred 53, 107, 130, 167, 188, 189, 203, 204; Frieda Pfahl 46, 107, 189; Kim 189; Mary Ann Lum 189; Pauline 202; Stuart 172, 189, 211, 250
NEWTON, Gloria 134; Spencer 117, 134
NILES, James H. 57
NOLAN, Jack 46
NORRIS, Claude 232
NUNN, Martin 217

O'LEARY, Elizabeth 52
OLSON, Ole 208
ORTNER, Carl 217; Marie 217, 261
OTTAWAY, James 169; Jeanne 169; Marian 169; Neal 100, 137, 169, 172
OWENS, Earl 117

PALMER, David 93; Helen Whiley 94; Katherine 93, 94; Lu 135; Robert 93;

Rev. Stephen 93, 94; Stephen, Jr. 93, 94
PANELLA, Albert (Red) 220, 240, 241, 243, 244; Helen Jane Clohecy 243, 244; Phil 131
PARKER, Charles 44, 94; Sidney 46, 217; Sidney (Mrs.) 217
PARSONS, Ben 13, 194; Ira 13; Riley 12, 13
PARTLOW, Howard E. 243
PAYNE, Dick, Sr. 52; Dick, Jr. 52; Elaine 261; Joe 134; Lawrence 167; Lillian 261
PEACH, Robert E. 243
PEARSE, James 77; Margaret 77
PECK, Judge Samuel 202; Samuel (Mrs.) 202
PEGLOW, Leo 46
PERRY, Al 46; Jack 107
PETERSEN, Fred 166, 188, 195, 216; John 13, 41, 52, 103, 119, 124, 130, 131, 166, 169, 188, 195, 202, 216
PETERSON, Ida (Mrs.) 16, 101
PHOENIX, Merrill 202, 223, 244, 250, 252
PIEPER, Gayle (Mrs.) 119
PIERSMA, John 169, 172, 235
POLE, Evelyn 124, 261; Nick 124
POPE, Barbara 46
PORTER, Joseph 33, 138, 148
POWERS, Fred 90
PRESTON, Alfred 41; William 41, 50
PUFFER, Clifford 133
PULLING, William 9, 217; William (Mrs.) 217
PYLMAN, Clarence 218

REED (Mr. & Mrs.) 217; Elaine 217; Kathy 217
REDDINGTON, J. O. C. (Mrs.) 33
REDFIELD, Holland (Dutch) 252
REID, Allison 210
REITTINGER, Mr. 46
REMINGTON, Francis K. 94; Harvey T. 41
RETON, Josephine 159
RETTIG, Dick 46
RIDER, Jane 175, 180; Robert 175, 180
ROACH, Beryl 104, 107, 134, 167; Mary 104, 261; Patricia 104; Robert 104; Ruth 104, 107, 261
ROBAK, Frank 90
ROWE, Dottie 243; Jack 243
RYAN, Jim 123

SCHMEER, Connie 104; Richard 104
SCHOELZ, Oswald 78; Sylvia 78
SCHOPFER, Leon E. 52, 53, 125, 250; John 53
SCHULTZ, David 167
SCHUMACHER, Frank 46
SCOTT, Andrew 232; Dorothy McIntyre 232; Harold (Scotty) 223, 232, 233, 234, 235, 240, 250; Mary 232
SEAL, Johnnie 243
SEARING, Alvina 46, 194, 195, 211; Richard 195; Robert (Bob) 46, 194, 195, 211
SEEBER, Theodore 12, 13
SEHRING, Nancy 261
SELIHOFF, Alexis 174
SHEEHY, Daniel 46
SHEPPARD, Jack 13
SHISHKIN, Nicholas 174
SIMMONS, Aline 159, 160; Col. E. A. 84, 158, 159, 164; Ida (Mrs.) 159, 160
SIMPSON, Helen 124
SIMS, Joanne 77; Richard 77
SLAGEL, John 216; Mary 216
SLATER, David 157; Kenneth 166
SLITER, "Skeet" 220
SMIRNOVA, Helmy 175
SMITH, Al (Smitty) 169; Allen 46, 203; Alice 166; Charlie 252; Dorothy 203, 261; Edith Irene 149, 150, 151; Ernest U. (E. U.) 41, 103, 104, 135, 199; Henry 202; Louise 158; Mabel Wescott 202; Patricia 157; Perry 202; Ray 166
SNYDER, Alonzo 208; Charles 12, 20, 178, 194; Eva 178; George S. 66
SOUTHARD, Arthur 92, 101, 119; Emma 92, 101, 119, 261
SPAFFORD, Dot 261
SPAULDING, Roger B. 63
SPEACH, Beverly 102; Richard 102
SPENCER, Betty Nelson 95, 103, 109, 118, 119, 189, 202, 205, 234; Raymond 189
SPERRY, Anne xi; Benjamin 9, 167; Clarence 51; Dwight 50, 51, 52, 105; Franklin 9; Ida 9; Louie 9; Mabel 167; Vera 134; Virginia xi
SPRING, Raymond 102; Sophie 102
SQUIRES, James xi
STEPHENSON, Cleo 166; Julia 166
STEVER, Stanley (Stan) 46, 94, 203
STRONG, Helen Lay 119
STURMAN, Leon 202
SULLIVAN, Amos 218; Dorothy 218;

William 46
SUNDAY, Billy 158
SYMONDS, Charles S. 168

TANNER, Bob 126; Jan 126
TARTAGLIA, Mr. 217
TEICH, Catherine 108; Frank 108, 109, 116, 208, 255; Reinhold 108
TERWILLIGER, Eugene 133
THIBADO, Hattie Payne 204; Henry 204
THISTLETHWAITE, Anna 42; Gwendolyn 168; W. J. (William) 33, 34, 41, 42, 50, 166
THOMAS, Carol A. 168; Kenneth 166
THOMPSON, J. George 47; Scott 130
TIFFANY, Judge Frank E. 243, 244; Judge Lansing 119; Mary 119
TRANQUILLE, Dante O. 241
TRAVERSY, Mary Anne 42; William 42
TUCK, John 203
TURNER, Al 119; Carroll 91; Edwin W. 91, 92; Ina Brush 91, 119; Isaac 91; James Larence 100; Thekla A. 91

VACCARO, John 46
VanARNUM, Evie (Mr. & Mrs.) 157
VanAUKEN, Harold 219, 221, 250; Lucille 221, 222
VanBUREN, George 232
VANDERLINDE, Hazel 218
Van EPP, George 243
Von OETTINGEN, Anneliese 208, 210
VICKS, Mr. 46
VonHOLLE, Frances 140, 261
VOGT, Evelyn 150; Frank C. (Dr.) 131, 149, 150; Jean 150

WAKELY, John 187
WALKER, Grace D. 33
WALLACE, E. R. 8, 11; R. G. (Dr.) 9, 33; William T. 46
WARD, C. G. 217; Phoebe 6; Samuel 6
WEBB, Eliza Osgood 47, 64, 92, 151; William Seward 12, 16, 19, 33, 47, 64, 92, 100, 137, 148, 149, 151, 166, 178

WEEDMARK, Bill 244
WEISS, Mrs. William (Louise) 78
WESTFALL, Connie 77; Freda Becker 77, 102, 208; Leo 77
WHIPPLE, O. W. 173
WHITBECK, Joseph 126; Lloyd 126; Mandy 126; Merle 126; Russell 126
WHITE, Hazel 134; William Chapman 11
WHITTAKER, Ben 46
WIESTER, Rebecca (Dr.) 210
WIKANDER, Gertrude 46, 216
WILCOX, Allen 65, 67, 73, 130, 208, 223, 232, 233, 250, 255; Cecelia O. 102; Charles 116, 117; Margaret 67, 208
WILKINS, James A. 166; Sue xi
WINDHAUSEN, Alyce 261; Charles (Chuck) 244, 250; Matthew (Bud) 244, 250
WING, William 63
WINSLOW, Theresa 261
WOLF, Irma 166; Otto 166
WOOD, Alonzo 16, 90, 102, 130, 131, 137, 261; Alonzo (Mrs.) 91; Barbara 131, 261; Bonnie 131; David 47; Ernest 131; Philo 137; Prentice J. 124, 130; Prentice J. (Mrs.) 124; Tammy 131
WRIGHT, John 126, 203; Kathy 126, 203

YONKEY, Fred 103
YOUCUM, Regina 261
YOUMANS, Edward 106, 194; Louise 133, 134; Yock (Harold) 44, 133, 134, 194, 261; Burt (Seth Burton) 44, 105, 106, 107, 133, 134, 189, 194; Burt (Mrs.) 194
YOUST, A. J. 203

ZIELENSKI, Eleanor 166
ZINNOCH, John 174, 175
ZURL, Blanche Pellor 218
ZYMOSKI, Daniel 101; Eileen 101

Note: Jane Knight spent many hours locating, listing and organizing the names for this index. Because of limited space, the reader will find no places listed, and some names deleted.

Clara V. and Herbert (Irish) O'Brien

Clara V. O'Brien is a retired teacher of history and English. She earned her B.S. degree from Southwest Texas State University and masters and doctoral study at Syracuse University. The last twenty years of her teaching career were in New York State — much of it in Rome, N. Y.

From early childhood she has been fascinated with history in most any form. Her first magazine article was published when she was a high school senior and since then she has had several historical articles published. 1972 saw the publication of her first book, DEEP ROOTS AND STRONG BRANCHES, a highly successful genealogy of her family which achieved national recognition as an authentic and thorough piece of research.

Mrs. O'Brien first came to Eagle Bay in 1937 and since then the beauty, history and folklore of the area have absorbed most of her leisure time. GOD'S COUNTRY is the result of that interest and untiring research.

Mrs. O'Brien has a son and daughter by her first husband who died when the children were very young. Her third husband, Herbert Sheldon O'Brien, has his M.A. from Purdue where he was captain of the football team. From his election in 1914 to this day he has been president of Purdue's class of 1915.

www.ingramcontent.com/pod-product-compliance
Lightning Source LLC
Chambersburg PA
CBHW030308080526
44584CB00012B/488